A WALK ALONG
THE WALL

A WALK ALONG THE WALL

Hunter Davies

Weidenfeld and Nicolson   London

Contents

Illustrations

The author and publishers are grateful to the photographers and copyright holders for permission to reproduce the pictures.

Diagrams

The illustrations in the book were drawn by Jane Susa Evans.

Acknowledgements

I am grateful to Professor Eric Birley for his encouragement and most of all for agreeing to read through the finished manuscript, to Lord Wardington for access to his library of Northumberland books, to the Earl of Lonsdale for information on the Lowther family, to Lord Henley and to Tommy Bates for hospitality, to everyone else who gave me help along the way, from the Tyneside dockers to the Solway fishermen, and to Tony Godwin.

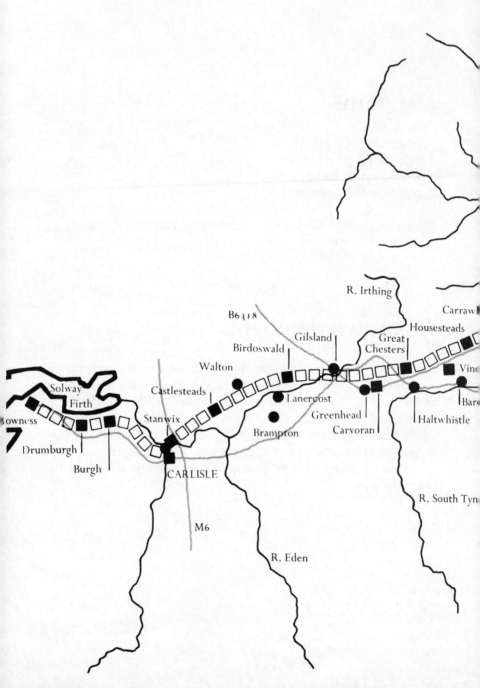

HADRIAN'S WALL

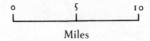

Miles

0　　　5　　　10

R. Irthing

Carraw

B6318

Gilsland

Housesteads

Great
Chesters

Birdoswald

Walton

Vind

Solway
Firth

Castlesteads

Lanercost

Bar

Greenhead

Bowness

Stanwix

Haltwhistle

Drumburgh

Brampton

Carvoran

Burgh

CARLISLE

R. South Tyn

M6

R. Eden

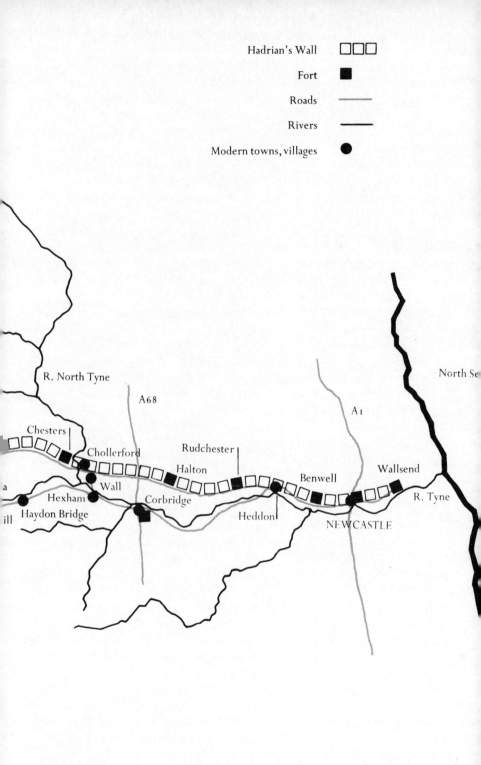

Hadrian's Wall ☐☐☐

Fort ■

Roads ———

Rivers ———

Modern towns, villages ●

R. North Tyne

A68

North Se

A1

Chesters

Chollerford

Rudchester

Wallsend

Halton

Benwell

Wall

Corbridge

Heddon

R. Tyne

Hexham

NEWCASTLE

Haydon Bridge

ill

a

Introduction to the 1984 Edition

It is ten years since this book was first published, a mere blink of an eye in archaeological time, so small a span as to be scarcely worth noticing when you think that the Romans were here on these shores for 350 years and that the Wall they left has been standing for over 1,760 years. What possible difference can a paltry ten years make? Why bother to write a new introduction after only a decade?

Good questions. The first answer is public demand. This book has been frequently reprinted since its first publication in 1974. I only wish that all of the books which I have written since then had done as well.

It was the first walking book I ever wrote, and it set me upon a slightly new path, one I am still following, with great pleasure and enthusiam, though I still have to find a topic quite as perfect for me. I like doing walking books in which I have several stories to tell, in the past and in the present, two lines of thought from which I can diverge, go off at tangents as the mood takes me, then come back on the straight and narrow and push forward with the main topic, the main narrative. The follow-up book to this one, *A Walk Around the Lakes*, did even better, but all the time I had to create my own route round the Lakes. With this book, thanks to old Hadrian, everything was laid out for me, in every sense.

The public demand for this book has been very gratifying. I still get letters every week about it, and not all of them are pointing out errors. It did seem to strike a chord and I find wherever I go that there are so many people who feel the same sort of enthusiasm for the Wall, its story and its countryside, that I still do. I feel I can boast about this continuing public demand, and the healthy sales, because I personally have gained no financial advantage from it. Some people might have noticed in the 1974 edition and in this one the copyright line 'The Vindolanda Trust'. I did not draw attention to this at the time, though several cynics thought it might be some bank account in Switzerland. What happened was that while researching the book, back in 1973, and becoming rather fed up with the lack of help from various government officials, mainly the London ones at the Department of the Environment, and disappointed by the old-fashioned presentation at several of the museums and sites along the way, I suddenly chanced upon Vindolanda. This was, and is, a private archaeological enterprise. It amazed me. I was so excited by what they were doing, especially their work with and for children and students, that I decided, in a moment of wild generosity, to give all the proceeds to them. So I worked during that year for nothing. They are a charity and need all the help they can get.

It is nice to know that their work has expanded enormously in the last decade and that their museum is now the biggest on the Wall, greater even than Housesteads or the two city museums in Newcastle and in Carlisle. Everyone who has bought the book, in the past and in the present, has helped a good cause. Thanks.

The second and main reason for doing a new edition is not of course simply the public demand, because after all the publisher could have gone on churning out the same old edition for ever, but that important changes have taken place in the last ten years. It was felt they should be recorded in some way and a few warnings given.

The original text has been reprinted word for word, from chapter one to twenty. To start tampering with the body of the text would have been pointless. Whole episodes on people now dead would have had to be dumped or put in the past tense. It is this new introduction, and the revised appendices which are different.

I could of course have walked the Wall in its entirety once

again, but that would have produced a new book. Perhaps in the future I will do that, in another ten years or so, but that does not necessarily mean that the old book would then become worthless. It was interesting that in 1973 I had in my hand, for many miles of my walk, a book on the Wall published in 1802 by a 76-year-old Birmingham shopkeeper, William Hutton. I found it fascinating to look with so-called modern eyes at what he had seen and felt. I like to think that in the future I will not actually need to do my book properly again because someone else will, carrying mine in their knapsack. In my wilder fantasies I see this book being rewalked and rewritten in 2074. The Wall will certainly still be there, even if we won't.

'Your book cannot be updated,' Robin Birley of Vindolanda kindly wrote to me, when the idea of a new edition was first mooted. 'It is a priceless picture of an area ten years ago – not a long time, but light years away from the reality of today. Most of the people you met would have different tales to tell. The greatest difference lies in the philosophy of the area. In 1973 it was perhaps a quaint and rather backward part of England. Today it is a bitter and depressed province.'

I fear that Robin Birley is slightly exaggerating, getting right perhaps the mood of the nation as a whole, in these troubled economic times, rather than just the mood of his native province. On my visits to Newcastle and Northumbria over the last ten years I have witnessed two incredible and positive achievements which I would certainly investigate and write about today, should I be doing this book again.

Firstly, there is the new Metro railway system on Tyneside. (You will in chapter one notice my scathing comments on the local suburban lines of 1973.) Then there is the Kielder Dam project, now completed, at a cost of several millions. I would certainly devote a chapter to Kielder, and no visitor today should miss seeing the massive lake, and all the leisure activities which have been created.

Robin Birley is of course ten years older and since 1973 he has become a local politician, currently leader of the Northumbria County Council. Naturally, he now knows at first hand the problems of funding and running vital local services, not to mention the less vital but nonetheless worthy problems of preserving our heritage. Archaeology, alas, is just one area having a hard time and it cannot expect much, when things like health and education are suffering much more serious cuts.

These then are just two of the new developments but there are many things in the original book which have altered. The main point to bear in mind when reading the chapters now (or perhaps *after* you have read the book), is that many of the people interviewed or mentioned by name have moved away, or retired. What they said or did was correct at the time, as they went through and checked what they were quoted as saying, but many are no longer there. Dorothy Charlesworth, the Government Inspector of Ancient Monuments, is dead, and so are several other people I met along the way. Robert Hogg, formerly at Tullie House Museum in Carlisle, has retired, as has Charles Anderson, the foreman in charge of the Wall's workmen.

Many places have also experienced rather drastic changes. I had such fun in chapter six when I joined the revellers at a medieval banquet in Langley Castle, but all that fun is now finished. The castle is empty and closed, and the last news I heard was that it was going to be converted into flats. That strange little museum near Banks, the LYC museum, run by the enterprising Chinaman, managed to survive for quite a few years and achieved some national attention from magazines and television, but that too has recently closed.

Socially and politically, the changes have been quite startling for such a short stretch of time. In the very first chapter there is a mention of the shipyard workers at Swan Hunter being on an 'average' wage of £34. On paper, if not in reality, wages have rocketed since then. I did make it clear, in 1973, that times were hard in shipbuilding, but if I were writing it again today I would probably have to keep talking about those 'formerly great Tyneside industries' of coal and shipping.

Cumberland does not now exist as a county and as for the local goverment changes round Tyne and Wear, my head aches even at the thought of trying to bring those up to date. It would be a pretty useless exercise. Even as I write, they are about to alter their names once again as the government starts doing away with metropolitan councils. So when you come across references to local borough councils or urban district councils, don't try too hard to look them up in the local telephone directories. Probably the same sort of people are running them, even looking after the same sort of boundaries, but modern politicians have this obsession for changing external names and appearances, hoping to persuade us that they have effected some marvellous internal surgery. Fat chance.

Physically, as you walk along the route of the Wall today, there have been alterations in the urban areas. There has been rebuilding near Wallsend, and Newcastle now has seven major bridges across the Tyne, not five as I said in 1973. Meanwhile, out in the country, the great gaping hole in the earth at Cawfields (chapter eleven), where work was just beginning, has now been turned into a huge and rather magnificent picnic site.

Archaeologically, there has been some major work done on sites in South Shields, Wallsend, Newcastle and in Carlisle, but the results are still being published. A new breed of thrusting young archaeologists has come along, doing quick excavations whenever there are major road or building works in progress, aided by labour from the Manpower Services Commission, having a look at any likely holes before they are filled in for ever. Some of the older archaeologists say that most of the reports produced by these younger people are unreadable. In other words, nothing has changed; personalities are still clashing.

There have been many specialist papers and publications in the last ten years, of interest mainly to experts, and I have tried to list a few of them at the end, but I suppose the most interesting finds in the last ten years, as far as the amateur enthusiast is concerned, have been at Vindolanda where the earliest known Roman ink-writing tablets have been found and at Carlisle where evidence of pre-Hadrianic military occupation has been discovered.

For those simply walking the Wall, perhaps first-time visitors with no real archaeological knowledge, there have been some welcome improvements. As ever, the Walk itself is still growing, as new chunks are uncovered and cleaned up. There is talk at the moment of rebuilding a five-hundred-yard stretch at Wall-town Quarry. The Wall, as I kept saying in the original book, is still a living Wall.

The new Information Centre in the car park at Housesteads is magnificent and a great help to all Wall visitors. The Department of the Environment must also be praised for their fine new museum at Corbridge and also for the new toilet block at Chesters. There is also a new Roman Army Museum at Carvoran.

The future of Rudchesters fort could be rather exciting. In the original book, chapter three, I could find nothing to see on the site, except a rather barren-looking farm. Since then, the farm has become derelict, and it looked for a while as if building developers would be allowed to take over the site and it would be lost for ever, but now Northumbria County Council has stepped in to save it.

While there is indeed some gloom and doom amongst some residents about the state of their part of the country, it has to be said nonetheless that for visitors going to look at or walk along Hadrian's Wall, it has been a decade of improvement. There have been notable gains which make the Wall even more worth visiting.

When this book first came out, there were some people, in a few local papers, who said that this book, and the television film which I did at the same time, could only ruin things. All the publicity, such as it was, and all my enthusiasm, which is of course boundless, would result in hordes of people rushing all over the Wall.

Emotionally I am on the side of the tourist, and reject the implied elitism of those who wish to keep out the rubbernecks. Hadrian's Wall, like the Lake District, or the London parks, belong to us. They are all *our* treasures. The unthinking, even those just sheltering from the rain, might well be converted and help to preserve them for future generations.

Naturally many clumsy feet can cause damage. For a while, it did look as if the Wall might be in danger, especially on the stretch near Housesteads. The National Trust was very worried, and so was the Department of the Environment and the

Countryside Commission; eventually a committee of investigation was set up which produced the Dart Report.

But then a strange thing happened. Just after my book came out, the crowds at Housesteads did begin to soar – and I am not saying there was a connection – and in the mid–1970s it had reached a peak of 175,000 a year. Today, however, this figure has dropped to 110,000. I am unable to offer any factual explanations. Perhaps people have less money to spend on day trips to the Wall, thanks to unemployment and the price of petrol. Perhaps they prefer to stay at home with their videos and home computers. Your guess is as good as mine.

But this drop in visitors does present a final reason for bringing out a new edition of *A Walk Along the Wall*. The Wall has even more to offer than it did ten years ago. There are now fewer people and more amenities. That is good news which should be passed on. Accommodation has also improved in the last ten years with a greater choice of hotels and restaurants, as you will see in the appendix.

The Wall can easily cope with more visitors, although as always, you should not walk on top, unless told otherwise, and please do not try to chip off any bits as souvenirs. I hope this new edition will spur people into going to Hadrian's Wall. Even more than ever, it is a living, breathing, expanding, improving, moving, even breathtaking Wall. Go now, before the next wave of visitors . . .

Hunter Davies
London NW5   February 1984

Preface

Hadrian's Wall is the most important surviving memorial to the military power of the Roman Empire. It stretches seventy-three miles across the neck of England, from Wallsend on Tyne to Bowness on Solway. There is approximately ten miles of it to be seen today, plus many forts and milecastles. As a chunk of history, it's unique. I was brought up at one end of the Wall and educated at the other, even to the extent of taking a course in Roman Britain archaeology. I have to admit that I always found the subject incredibly boring.

From school at Carlisle we were taken on uplifting trips to look at the forts which turned out to be a load of old stones without a centurion in sight or a chance to get wet in a real Roman bath. At Durham, I was looking for an easy way of getting a degree. At no time did it dawn on me that studying Roman Britain was more than a matter of studying dry as dust inscriptions. I'd never looked for the people beneath. Slowly, with age, I've come to appreciate that it was a living Wall, then as well as now, as this book will try to show.

I've had to relearn the basic facts, the ones I'd picked up parrot fashion all those years ago, and I've tried to be up to date with the latest archaeological thinking and discoveries. One of my aims has been to give the general reader a grasp of what life was like in human terms along this stretch of northern Britain under the Romans. I've also been as interested in how the archaeologists go about their work as in what they've dug up.

In walking the Wall, taking a whole year over it, wandering off at tangents as the mood took me, my other major aim has been to capture life on the Wall today. On the north-eastern coast where the Wall began there is tragic unemployment, as the traditional coal and shipping industries decrease. In the middle are some of the largest estates in the country where life today is in many ways almost feudal. At the western end, on the Solway coast, life has always tended to pass them by, in good times and in bad, while they've gone on with their strange, isolated life. As a view of Britain today, it would be harder to find a more varied cross-section.

The archaeological and present-day life is in each case seen through the people involved. There are the professional archaeologists, hoping for the find which will justify a lifetime's searching; private enterprise excavators, upsetting the locals but managing to find things unseen for almost two thousand years; and Government masons, going up and down the Wall, repairing and unearthing, revealing more and more of the Wall every year.

Many of the bigger landlords wish the Wall would go away and leave them in peace with their pheasants. Some of the smaller tenant farmers wish the tourists would go away and stop walking past their parlour windows. But the tourists are here to stay, arriving in their hundreds and thousands from all over the world, to tramp round forts like Housesteads or try newer, rowdier attractions like medieval banquets.

Tyneside, where the walk begins, is but a crowded triangle in the corner of a very large county. The British public tends to associate the *whole* of Northumberland with shipping and coal, Tyneside's best known industries, thereby missing one of England's last unspoilt areas. The Wall soon leaves Newcastle and strides into the beautiful Border hills of Northumberland and Cumberland. As a walk, it's not far, but there can be few walks anywhere so rich in history, scenery and people.

I
Wallsend:
Beginning at the End

I got off the Inter City train at Newcastle and made my way along the platforms for the local train to Wallsend, four miles the other side of Newcastle. The journey up from London had been highly civilised, quick and comfortable and terribly clean. I'd had breakfast on the train, British Rail's nicest surprise for every modern traveller in these Isles.

Newcastle's Central Station looked large and splendid, though not quite as clean as on that day in 1850 when Queen Victoria opened it and the whole world wondered at its two miles of platform and its eighty yards of portico. It is still a fine station, which is only fitting. Newcastle was the home town of George Stephenson. It was from this corner of the North East of England that the world's railways were born.

The local train was filthy. I sat at the front behind the driver's cabin and watched as he carefully arranged his *Daily Mirror* to protect himself from the grime before he sat down and unlocked his controls. Every local station on the way out of Newcastle looked abandoned. I was amazed each time when the train dragged itself to a halt, convinced that the broken glass on the platforms, the graffiti on every wall, the rusted wrought iron arches and the general air of an industrial wasteland meant that the natives had long since fled, leaving their settlements to the ravages of time and hooligans.

The North East, in Government terms, is now a depressed area. It's hard to see it in Newcastle, a big bustling city, a provincial capital still able to put on a show. But once away from the centre, industrial Tyneside looks empty, mean and deprived. Even the people appear at first sight to be somehow left-over, as if the youngest and fittest had moved south, leaving the elderly or the romantic. All the good things in life now seem to be reserved for the main lines, the Inter City set, those with good connections to the south.

The Romans made a point of spreading their good things. The Roman army not only took civilisation with it, in the form of roads and towns, law and order, but carried the Empire's top people to every corner of the known world. It was part of a public figure's advancement to do his national service. And as a deliberate piece of policy, the bright young men were sent out to the provinces. They didn't look upon being sent to Gallia or Germania or even Britannia as being sent to the ends of the earth. Being sent to Britain was in fact geographically the ends of the earth as they knew it – but not metaphorically. It was where a young man could make his name. Many Senators and even Emperors achieved early success while stationed in Britain.

I came out of the station at Wallsend, right into the middle of nowhere, emerging from a bridge into an empty street. It's not known what Hadrian thought of Wallsend when he arrived in these parts around 122 AD, but Wallsend remembers him, hence its name.

Wallsend was where I had to begin, at the end of what was once the northern limit of an empire which stretched three thousand miles across Europe to the Euphrates. Not many people, tourists or academics, start by studying the Wall in Wallsend. Not many people actively choose to study anything in Wallsend.

The Romans had been in England for eighty years before Hadrian arrived on the Tyne, since the conquest by the Emperor Claudius in AD 43. Every schoolboy knows that Julius

Caesar was the first Roman to land in Britain but he was little more than a day tripper. He made a couple of short trips, in 55 and 54 BC, losing a lot of ships through ignorance of the Channel tides, and a lot of soldiers to the British chariots. He took a few slaves, got a few local tribes in the south east to pay taxes, then he called it a day and returned to Rome where he had much more important things to worry him, such as civil war. All the same, his invasion of Britain had caused a sensation back in Rome. Twenty days of public holiday were proclaimed. The conquest of Gaul had called for only a fifteen day holiday.

Over the subsequent decades, once the contact with the Roman Empire had been made, merchants from Europe started trading along the south-eastern coast of England and the local tribal kings began to acquire certain Roman styles and habits, such as wine and coinage and fine pottery. But once away from the coast, Celtic tribal life continued untouched.

After the conquest proper in AD 43, the Romans pushed west and north through England. The Welsh put up a hard struggle and so did the Brigantes, the largest English tribe who inhabited the area of the Pennines. Agricola, Governor of Britain from 78 AD to 84 AD, subdued the Brigantes and set up a line of forts and roads from Carlisle across to Corbridge. He then pushed north into what is now Scotland, and defeated the Caledones, though the tribes of Scotland were never properly subdued or Romanised.

Hadrian became Emperor in 117 AD and determined on a policy of consolidation, working out which acquisitions were too expensive to hold and getting rid of them. He toured the Empire personally, seeing for himself what should be done. He obviously enjoyed exploring new places ('curiositatum omnium explorator'), and it's recorded that on a campaign he lived the life of the soldiers in his legions, often marching twenty miles a day fully armed and bare headed.

Hadrian arrived on the Tyne in mid-122 AD, no doubt with his head bare in honour of summer. He was fresh from reorganising the frontiers in Germany where he'd strengthened the forts around Frankfurt. The boundary lines of the Roman

3

Empire were often simply tracks and streams, or perhaps now and again earthen walls or wooden fences. Armed with his experience of sorting out the European frontiers, Hadrian arrived to put Britain in order. The stone Wall which resulted bears his name to this day.

Whether he arrived on the Tyne, spied out the land as he rode quickly across to Carlisle and then told the soldiers to start building, is a problem which the historians and archaeologists are still trying to sort out. The building of the Wall was a gigantic and complicated task. One theory is that he gave orders for a Wall to be started *before* he actually arrived, basing the plan on information received. The building of the Wall was supervised by Hadrian's new Governor of Britain, Aulus Platorius Nepos. There were numerous changes of plan during the building of the Wall. The arrival of the Emperor to see how work was progressing, and not liking some of the things being done, would account for some of the more major changes.

The trouble is the lack of evidence. There are just no contemporary accounts of how and why the Wall was built. Archaeologists have had to build up the story from the fortifications which remain, from pottery, coins, altars, inscriptions and other scraps. All those acres and acres of books which have been written about Hadrian's Wall over the centuries are little more than intelligent conjecture. Therein lies the endless fascination.

Agricola got a tame historian to write down the details of his campaigns as Governor of Britain – his son-in-law, Tacitus. Tacitus did the interviewing later, safe in Rome, and didn't venture to Britain himself. But Hadrian never got round to his British memoirs in any form. The only historical reference to the fact that Hadrian came to Britain and built the Wall occurs a hundred and fifty years later. This was by Spartianus who was doing a Life of Hadrian.

'Having restored the army's morale, he crossed to Britain where he set many things to rights and built a wall eighty miles long to separate the Romans from the barbarians.'

These few harmless words have been stood on their ends and

reinterpreted continuously over the centuries. One of the most enduring arguments about the Wall concerns what it was actually meant to do: was it offensive or defensive? Spartianus cleverly doesn't commit himself. 'Separating' is giving nothing away.

But it is definitely known that Hadrian came to Britain, from literary and epigraphic evidence. While he was in Britain, the poet Florus poked fun at him:

> Ego nolo Caesar esse
> Ambulare per Britannos

Roughly translated that comes to:

> Caesar I'd not like to be
> Touring Britain doesn't suit me.

Generations of Roman soldiers had arrived and settled in Britain by this time and generations of Roman generals had passed through on their way to higher things, but in literary circles, Britain was a bit of a joke, a Roman Siberia. Later in the same poem, Florus says 'I can't stand those Scythian winters.' In other words, the weather was hellish.

I felt decidedly cold too as I walked down Station Road towards the Swan Hunter shipyards, though as Wallsend weather goes, it was a grand September day. I was clutching the town's official guide book in my hand. In the first paragraph it said that Hadrian built the Wall 'to keep out the marauding Picts and Scots'. I got out my pencil and wrote 'Surely not!' in the margin, the way they do in London Library books. The Picts, as I'd recently discovered, were not known as such until 297 and as for the Scots, they were still living in Ireland when Hadrian arrived on the Tyne and didn't start settling in Scotland until the fifth century. Pedantry is very catching.

On the town map I could see a Hadrian Hospital, a Hadrian Road, a street called Roman Wall and a new shopping centre called, very grandly, The Forum. The town's coat of arms proudly boasts its Roman origins with the motto 'Situ Exoritur Segeduni', risen about the site of Segedunum, which was what the Romans called Wallsend. It must make rather a mouthful when blazoned on the town's football shirts. The main motif is a Roman eagle perched on the battlements of a wall. The background is jet black, symbolising the part which coal mining has played in the growth of Wallsend. Wallsend is very much a nineteenth-century industrial town.

The Romans probably started the coal industry. They were known to have used open-cast coal (though they did dig mines), carrying off the easy surface stuff which they used to heat their baths and run their central heating systems. Coal mines proper began in Wallsend in 1781 and were at their height in the middle of the nineteenth century. Bringing coals to New-castle, one of the best-known phrases from the height of the British Empire, is now sadly a fact rather than a typically British understatement. Coal mining ceased in Wallsend in April 1969 with the closing of the Rising Sun Colliery.

Shipbuilding, the Tyne's other major industry, began about the same time – the first dockyard in Wallsend was constructed in 1759. Wallsend achieved world-wide fame in 1894 with Sir Charles Parsons's development of the turbine engine. The Turbinia, built in Wallsend, was the world's first turbine driven ship. (There was a great campaign in the 1960s to preserve the Turbinia, backed by engineers round the world, and it is now in the Newcastle Museum of Science and Engineering.)

Perhaps even better known to the general public was the *Mauretania* which was built by Swan Hunter at their Wallsend yard in 1906. It won back the Atlantic Blue Riband from Germany and held it for twenty-two years. It was in clearing this slipway in 1903 that Swan Hunter dug up a section of the Roman Wall, the only bit of the Roman Wall between Wallsend and Newcastle which exists today. Swan Hunter's yard was going to be my first port of call.

Though things are bad in the British ship building trade generally today, the Swan Hunter group seems to be doing well. They're the largest ship builders and repairers in Europe and employ 33,000 workers in yards throughout the world, all run from their headquarters in Wallsend. In Wallsend itself they employ 12,000. That week the local paper was full of Sir

John Hunter, the chairman of the firm, receiving the Freedom of Wallsend. 'Without shipbuilding,' said the Mayor at the official ceremony, 'there would be no Wallsend worth speaking of.'

Alas, there wasn't much sign of life. I'd arrived in the middle of a strike. Five yards were out. The boilermakers were wanting an increase of £4 a week on their average wage of £34.

Nobody was blaming the workers for striking – every executive was bustling around working very hard at labour relations. I soon found the bogeymen when I picked up a copy of the latest *Swan Hunter News*. There was a front page Comment headlined 'Japanese Menace'. The initials at the end were J. H., standing for Sir John Hunter. He made it clear how unfair he thought it was that the Japanese could produce their ships so cheaply, thanks to massive backing from the Japanese government.

I went to see George Murray, editor of *Swan Hunter News*, who had said he would show me around the yard and its treasures.

'Let's have a drink first,' he said. 'The Roman remains will keep for later.' He guided me straight back into the town, saying he was glad of an excuse to get out of the office. The phone was ringing nonstop with the press wanting the latest on the strike.

From his name, I thought he would be of Border origin but he turned out to be a Lancashire man who'd only been in the North East three years. He hadn't had good reports of the natives, but had been more than pleasantly surprised by what he'd found, especially the Newcastle Brown ale. 'I can't drink that Manchester muck now.'

We went to a pub called the Penny Wet. I expected it to be empty, being early in the day and a Wednesday, but it was standing room only.

'Where's all the poverty then,' he said, waving his hand around. 'Everyone is always on about us being a depressed area, but there's no sign of it here.'

I said perhaps the drinkers were all ship workers on strike but he said no, it was like that every week. Business was always good in the pubs. As we squeezed into a corner I sensed several people staring at me. 'That's a bonny suit,' said a bloke with two pints, one in each hand. His mates all nodded, coming over, not being facetious, asking who I was, have a drink, what was I doing in Wallsend.

George said he liked the Geordie's openness, his straight-forward interest in everything and everyone. He admitted some newcomers didn't like it, considering the Geordies bloody nosey, but he was all for it.

Back at the yard we went down towards the river to look at the spot where they dug up the piece of the Roman Wall in 1903. They've preserved a few yards of the original stones, setting them out in a new piece of wall. In the centre is a gold plaque recording the discovery. Judging by a photograph I saw later, taken in 1903 when the discovery was made, they've moved the stones from where they were found (to make room for the slipways) keeping only a few as a memento. The rest were given to the council and are now preserved in the public park. The 1903 photograph indicated that the Wall was partly buttressed, to protect it from the tide. The Wall ran directly from the Tyne two hundred yards or so up to the south-eastern corner of the fort at Segedunum. The fort had been carefully situated above an angle of the river, giving a perfect view down the river both ways so that any raiding party could easily be seen trying to slip over or up the Tyne.

It didn't take long to look at the few stones and I can't say my heart exactly leapt. I'd been led to believe, by the archae-ological books, that the Wall's facing stones are so special and so different that you would recognise them anywhere. They just looked grey bits of stone to me, symmetrically shaped, but not much different from any of the other grey stone walls around the town.

I asked if I could see Sir John Hunter, as the natural inheritor of the end of the Wall. We went up in the lift to the director's corridor but he wasn't in.

Bidding farewell to Swan Hunter and all who sail with them, I turned my back on the yards and walked back along Station

Road to the centre of Wallsend to search for the Roman fort of Segedunum.

The fort's first garrison was the Second Cohort of Nervians and later on, in the third and fourth centuries, inscriptions have shown that the Fourth Cohort of Lingones took over. Neither was a Roman legionary force (the legions were stationed further south) but were strictly auxiliary forces. They were conscripted from the provinces – in this case both Cohorts came originally from Gaul. They were about five hundred strong and in the case of the Lingones included some cavalry.

Today, there's not a scrap of the Fort left and I wouldn't advise anyone to try and look for it either. Wallsend Corporation has the limits of the fort marked out in white-washed cobble stones, which is very kind of them, but they're hard to find. I was almost knocked over several times as I stooped in gutters, attempting to see which cobbles were less filthy than the others. I tried for a long time to find Roman Wall Street but failed. The whole area seemed to be in the process of being knocked down. There was rubble everywhere and it looked as if a bomb had fallen.

This eastern end of the Wall never had a chance to survive, what with the Saxon invaders knocking down everything Roman in sight and carrying off the best bits for their own use. (The Saxon buildings in Jarrow were built of Roman stones from the Wall and its forts.) But it was the nineteenth-century industrial boom, with its factories and mines and back to back houses, that really finished off any Roman relics. All the same, as late as 1850 there are local records of bits of the Wall and fort foundations being clearly visible. Collingwood Bruce in his first edition of his *Handbook to the Roman Wall*, published in 1863, talked to someone who as a boy remembered running down to the river to swim and passing bits of the Wall on the way.

The last chance to have saved anything of Roman Wallsend occurred in 1887. In that year the whole of the fort site, still open land, was up for sale for only £680. A local committee tried to get the town to buy it, or anyone else who might preserve it, but they failed. Instead, a builder bought the lot and threw up the rows of terrace houses, the ones which now appeared to be coming down. No one seemed to know what was going up in their place, presumably high-rise flats, but excavation now would be expensive and probably pointless. Several finds have been made over the years in Wallsend and no doubt a few more things might turn up. The best was an inscribed altar stone set up by the Fourth Cohort of the Lingones, found in 1892 and now in the Museum of Antiquities in Newcastle. (That's how it is known which troops were stationed there.) There's also been a few coins, but nothing special. The last finds were in 1903 (the Swan Hunter stones) and in 1912 when a Roman well was found during the excavations to build Simpson's Hotel.

I went along to Simpson's hotel to see if the well was still there, thinking I might have tea, perhaps stay the night if it looked nice. When I got there I thought at first it was the Workhouse, or perhaps a prison. On the rather forbidding outside wall I read a plaque saying that just twenty yards away stood the Eastern Gateway of the Roman camp of Segedunum. I went inside, passed huddles of inanimate elderly men who were standing, staring into space, as if frozen in some long forgotten experience. It would be unfair to call Simpson's Hotel a doss house. It all looked clean, if very spartan, but I could see at once why I'd been unable to find it in the *Good Food Guide*, or even the AA handbook. Their speciality is single men of uncertain age, such as pensioners, migrant workers and people on social security. I enquired the charges which turned out to be exceedingly modest, just £3 a week. I decided not to stay the night. My London suit had stood out in the pub. It might have caused a riot in Simpson's Hotel.

An efficient looking young lady behind the counter, surrounded by panel upon panel of heavy looking keys (the hotel has 330 rooms) said she'd never heard of any Roman well. I thanked her and left, coming out again to be hit in the face by a blast of Scythian sea mist. I'd earlier admired some carefully chosen euphemisms in the town's guide book. 'Wallsend is conveniently situated for the bracing North Sea Coast.'

Along Carville Road I stared in the window of a boarded-up Shelter shop, wondering if Shelter (the campaign for the homeless) had perhaps failed to find either homes or people in this area of Wallsend. It all seemed deserted. Next door was a fish shop advertising 'Dressed Fresh Whiting, 3p. each' which I thought was a good bargain, but there was no sign of any customers.

There was a little display of relics at the front of the town's library – a very handsome modern building I must add, opened in 1966 and a pleasant change from the bomb sites. An assistant librarian was very apologetic about the paucity of Wallsend's Roman relics – a few coins, bits of pots and antler horns which were said to have been used by the Romans as instruments.

Before I set off along the Shields Road in the direction of Newcastle, I had a last walk round the cobblestones. At the end of Hunter Street I came across a tablet on a piece of overgrown ground which marks the south-east wall of the fort. It was chipped and faded, surrounded at the bottom with weeds and rubbish, and it was with some difficulty I read the rather plaintive plea: 'The inhabitants of Wallsend are requested to co-operate for the protection of this interesting memorial of antiquity from which their town derives its name.'

2
Newcastle:
Down in the Suburbs

Hadrian's first plan was a wall ten feet wide from Newcastle to the Solway, to be built of stone for two-thirds of the way then turf when stone became scarce on the Cumberland plain. It was to be fifteen feet high with a six foot parapet on top. Altogether, a Wall over twenty feet high.

On the north side there was to be a deep V-shaped ditch, the standard Roman military ditch which they put in front of most barricades and fort walls. Every mile there was to be a mile-castle, big enough to house around thirty-two soldiers, with two watch tower turrets between every pair of milecastles. The Wall garrison would live in the milecastles and patrol up and down, keeping a look out from the turrets. The main bulk of the troops in the area would continue to live as before in the forts a few miles to the south, the ones built by Agricola along the Stanegate route.

This first plan was put into action by the Governor Nepos, who brought up the three legions stationed in Britain to do the building. They were the Second Augusta from Caerleton in South Wales, the Twentieth Valeria Victrix from Chester and the Sixth Victrix from York. The Sixth was newly arrived and replaced the Ninth, a legion whose subsequent movements are still not clear. Inscriptions found on the Wall show that all three were involved. They signed their names when they'd finished a good stretch.

A legion contained experts in every field, from clerks to stone masons and heavily armed infantry soldiers. They did all the craftsmen's jobs, no doubt assisted by the auxiliary soldiers, the ones who were to be left to patrol the Wall when the work was finished and the legions had gone back to headquarters. There must have been thousands of native labourers, local or imported, and thousands of ox carts to do the digging and hewing, fetching and carrying. It has been estimated that the Wall when finished contained twenty-five million facing stones – that's counting the turf section which was later converted to stone. The quarrying and shaping of twenty-five million stones must have been as difficult as building the Wall itself. The stones were uniform in shape – about six inches by ten at the front, twenty inches deep, tapering slightly at the back where they were imbedded into the central core of the Wall – and tooled on the front in a uniform pattern. The core of the Wall was rubble set in puddled clay or mortar. Archaeologists have identified the stone quarries where the stones came from, and the lime quarries and lime kilns where they made their mortar. Charcoal was used for burning the lime (specks of charcoal dust have been identified in the lime mortar) then it was ground into a powder and mixed dry with sand and gravel. Only when the mixture was about to be poured into the Wall foundations was water added. On the west side, over in Cumberland, where there is no limestone, the mortar is of an inferior quality.

The legions split into separate work parties, some doing the ditch, some the milecastles, some the turrets and some the Wall itself. Excavations have indicated that the work parties doing the foundations of the Wall went ahead first, then the mile-castles and turrets were built, then the work parties came back and completed the Wall to its full height.

During the building of this first plan of the Wall, there were several modifications. They'd got about twenty-seven miles west, working their way from Newcastle, when it was decided to narrow the width of the Wall, changing from a ten foot wide wall to one eight feet wide. There's a section where this

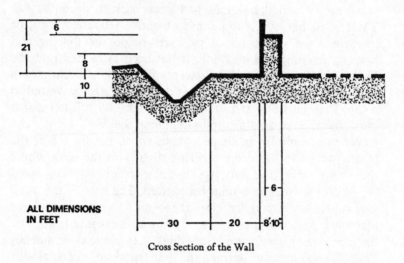

Cross Section of the Wall

Narrow Wall is built on the old Broad Wall foundations – showing how far ahead the foundation party had got when the order came to narrow the width. It's these changes in width and its effect on milecastle and turrets, all easily seen on the Wall today, which has enabled archaeologists to deduce the order of the works. At the same time as the change in width, the Wall was extended from Newcastle to Wallsend, building it in the new narrow measure. Wallsend, therefore, despite its present civic pride and Latin motto, was an afterthought.

The thinking behind this first plan would suggest that things were pretty peaceful around the Wall area; or expected to be so. The Wall was a patrolling boundary line which didn't need a lot of men to run it. *Why* on earth they should have planned a patrolling Wall on such a colossal scale in the first place is another matter. Perhaps because it was the furthest flung frontier Hadrian wanted something extra special, a warning

The Vallum

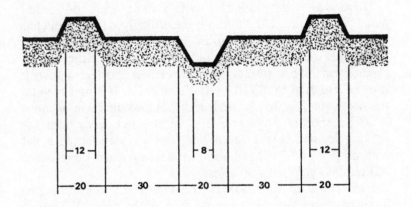

and at the same time a celebration of the Empire's military power.

Then we come to the second plan, as it's always called, which clearly represents a major change in tactics. No less than sixteen forts were built on to the Wall itself, permanent military towns each about twenty times the size of a milecastle. Almost overnight, the Wall became a heavily fortified barrier with a *fighting* and not simply a patrolling garrison. In man power, the troops on the Wall increased from around three thousand to fifteen thousand. There is one obvious reason for this sudden change – the Wall was in danger. Either the Caledones to the north or the Brigantes whose territory the Wall crossed were becoming restless. There might have been a disaster, a legion perhaps overthrown, something grave enough to warrant a major change, a change which must have involved the Emperor personally. Hadrian is known to have visited

15

Britain but once, which is why some experts think he came at this stage, making the big decision to move up the forts from the Stanegate.

It was also decided to build a road, the Military Way, behind the Wall. With the huge increase in manpower and equipment, a proper road was deemed necessary to link the forts. The Wall itself, whether ten or eight feet wide, was only for walking along.

There was a third addition which came with the second plan – the Vallum. The Vallum is exceedingly puzzling and has been argued about for centuries. It was a large flat-bottomed ditch with the earth piled up in two mounds on either side, a gigantic earthwork system which stretched 120 feet across. It ran the length of the Wall – on its *south* side. If it had been on the north side, facing the barbarians, one would have assumed it to be another protective line. It couldn't have been for fighting in, not on the south side, and anyway it had a flat bottom. Nor could it have been a road, not when there was a Military Way. What was it for?

Bede confused the issue in the first place when thirteen hundred years ago, he wrongly gave it the name Vallum, a name which stuck for ever. Vallum in Latin means wall.

For a long time, the accepted theory was that Vallum was the civil frontier – manned by civilian officials while the Wall was run by the military. Adaptations of this idea have described it as a sort of customs barrier. Later it was agreed by everyone that it was definitely a military line, marking the end of the military zone. The Military manned it, keeping out any trespassers or thieves.

There's a relatively new theory (put forward by C. E. Stevens) that it was to keep people *in*, a prototype Berlin Wall, stopping any native British tribesmen who'd been pressganged into serving on the Wall from escaping south to their homes. Another attractive theory suggests it was a way of keeping the garrison's cattle and horses safe. The space between the Wall and the Vallum was where the soldiers did their farming – a nice idea till you realise that the Vallum, like the Wall, crossed many miles of completely unfarmable land. Perhaps in walking

the Vallum and the Wall some other theories, daft or otherwise, might suggest themselves. Suffice to say at this stage that
the current thinking is that the Vallum was the military
demarcation line.

Hadrian's Wall, then, was a complicated and massive structure, a fortified line made up of many elements – a ditch, the
Wall itself, milecastles, turrets, forts, a Military Way and a
Vallum. In the first place it must have been intended as a
political barrier. When the heavy brigade moved up, it became
a definite military establishment, though exactly why and
when has still to be explained. In all, it took around ten years
to complete.

Even on the map, it can be seen what miracles the Roman
engineers managed, keeping the line straight, despite the crags,
rocks, hills and rivers. They built three major bridges to carry
the Wall and the Military Way. The most magnificent bridge of
the whole complex was at Newcastle. It didn't carry the
Wall – as the Wall kept to the north bank of the Tyne – but it
carried the road and was a vital part of the Wall fortifications.
It was from here that the engineers began.

Approaching Newcastle I could see many bridges. Newcastle
is a city of bridges, five major ones in all, which sounds
romantic until you see the bridges. Apart from the spectacular
single-arched Tyne bridge, they're the usual drab and dirty
industrial antennae. But at least they break up the sky line,
giving contrasting space and height. Newcastle is lucky to have
the river, unlike other northern industrial towns such as
Sheffield, Leeds and Bradford.

Hadrian's bridge, Pons Aelius, was on the site of what is now
the Swing Bridge. It was eighteen feet wide, rested on timber
arches and was seven hundred feet long. Collingwood Bruce
records that in 1872, when they were working on the Swing
Bridge, he observed wooden piles and other evidence of the
original Roman framework being dug out of the Tyne. In 1875
Roman coins were found beneath the bridge. Like today, people
dropped coins from bridges as a good luck sign. Later, when the
river was being dredged, two altars were found to Oceanus and
Neptune, put up by the Sixth Legion as part of a shrine to

protect them against the tide and floods. There is no sign of the Roman bridge today. It was last seen in 1248. I had a quick look in the dirty waters but could see no coins or altars or even likely looking bits of wood. It was all plastic debris. It's hard to realise that just a couple of hundred years ago the Tyne at Newcastle was noted for its salmon.

The fort at Newcastle was also called Pons Aelius, but its exact situation is not known. It's thought to have covered the area of the present Castle. It's a building well worth visiting though it's little more than a Castle Keep, the remains of a Norman Castle. William the Conqueror's son had a castle built on the site of a Saxon fortification. The Saxons called it Monkchester but the Normans changed the name to Newcastle, after their new castle.

It was an important fortification during medieval times. Charles I was a prisoner in the keep. Gradually it was over-shadowed by other buildings as Newcastle became an important port, especially in the nineteenth century when Newcastle suffered every joy of the industrial revolution. Today it's been ruined by the railway and looks like a ship-wreck, a stranded bit of masonry, fallen off the back of some passing century.

The Cathedral is also thought to be on the site of the fort and it too is of Norman origin. It has a famous crown shaped spire, known as a Scottish Crown spire, similar to the one at St Giles in Edinburgh and the same as St Dunstan's in London. (Sir Christopher Wren pinched the idea when he was designing St Dunstan's, which is how it came to be the same.) Its status as a cathedral is fairly recent, dating from 1882 when the diocese were altered. It's not even the oldest church in Newcastle – both St Andrew's and St John's are older.

Most of Newcastle's famous sons attained their fame in the nineteenth century. There was Admiral Lord Collingwood right at the beginning of the century who led the fleet at Trafalgar in 1805 and took over from Nelson on his death. There was George Stephenson who built his first locomotive in 1814 to haul coal from the mines and went on to be the engineer of the world's first public railway from Stockton to Darlington in 1825.

His son Robert was also an engineer. He became known for his railway bridges like the High Level one in Newcastle or the one across the Menai straits. The nineteenth century produced Newcastle's only prime minister, Grey of the 1832 Reform Bill.

It was the railway business which ruined the last of the Roman remains in Newcastle – there are none at all left today – and destroyed all but a few chunks of the medieval town walls. All the same, Newcastle was fortunate in having two excellent town planners in the mid-nineteenth century, Richard Grainger and John Dobson, who built many handsome, classical streets, terraces and arcades. 'Newcastle can claim to be the only major city in England with a planned centre,' wrote Sir Nikolaus Pevsner in his 1957 book on Northumberland buildings, raving about the work of Grainger and Dobson and how they'd created curved Regency style streets on an existing medieval network. Their best work has been disappearing fast since the 1960s when a panic of concrete town planning has thrown up monster skyscrapers, carved out new throughways and a giant civic centre building.

From the fort at Newcastle, Hadrian's Wall headed west where the station and the Royal Station Hotel now stand. I'd booked a room at the hotel. I asked the girl on the reception desk where the Royal came from. Newcastle has had its share of royal connections over the years, from Hadrian, Charles I (locked in the keep), Queen Victoria (opening the station) and a whole host of royals who opened the many bridges. She said she didn't know which royal it was. I asked if she'd heard that the Roman Wall ran under the hotel, but she didn't know anything about that either. If I wanted dinner, I could choose the dining room or the Viking Restaurant. I asked what the difference was and she said the Viking was more informal. 'The waitresses are younger,' she added, so that settled it. It was like a plastic Valhalla with plastic shields and plastic horns all over the walls and the young waitresses done up like Brunhilda. The menu was in Danish, with English subtitles, and was very pleasant. I had egg and chips.

Newcastle has always had a strong Scandinavian connection.

The Tyne has been an important North Sea landing place since Roman times. (The Romans actually used South Shields as their supply base for the garrisons on the Wall.) There are many Scandinavian firms in the City, mainly in shipping. Newcastle's proud new Civic Centre was opened by a foreign royal this time, King Olaf of Norway.

In the morning I thought I'd go to the castle and look at the Black Gate Museum which, according to all the history books I'd been reading, contained Roman treasures belonging to the Society of Antiquaries of Newcastle upon Tyne. I rang up first to check the opening times, and a very helpful lady gave me all the details and even the curator's home phone number. It was a Wallsend number and I thought no, not back to Wallsend. I said I'd just have a look at the Roman relics, perhaps see the curator another day. 'Roman remains? We're a bagpipe museum.' Six months ago, apparently, they'd become the home of the world's biggest collection of bagpipes, so she boasted. Over one hundred in all. I asked where they'd all come from and she said a man had died and left them in his will. 'People are always coming here looking for the Roman stuff They get really furious when they find it's been moved. We're in a one-way street and they have a lot of trouble leaving their cars. Personally I'm bored by the Wall. I had enough of it on boring bus trips from school.'

All their Roman relics had been moved to the Museum of Antiquities in the University, which is the main centre for exhibiting Roman Wall antiquities. Most of the treasures found over the years on or around the Wall end up in this museum, particularly those found on the eastern side. Tullie House, over in Carlisle, is the centre for western finds. The Newcastle museum has the advantage of being in the academic centre for Wall Studies – there is no University in Carlisle. The Department of Archaeology at Newcastle University, along with the similar department fifteen miles down the A1 at Durham University, are the fountains of wisdom and research on Hadrian's Wall. All universities have, of course, a Roman Britain department of some sort, but they tend to specialise in that bit of Roman Britain nearest to them. The late Sir Ian

Richmond (he died in 1965) was Professor of Roman Archaeology at Newcastle and then Oxford and in his lifetime he was
looked upon as the world's leading Hadrian's Wall man. Today,
the greatest living expert is Professor Eric Birley who has just
retired from Durham.

One of the leading active Wall experts is John Gillam, Reader
in Archaeology at Newcastle. I rang the university, thinking I'd
be able to talk to him or one of their experts into showing me
round the Museum. No luck. They'd all swanned off to
Rumania for three weeks on a Roman Frontiers Conference. I
did speak to Professor Harrison, in charge of the Department of
Classics (which includes archaeology), who was kind but
couldn't help. Roman Britain wasn't his subject. Instead he said
that a young postgraduate called Roger Miket, the department's
archaeological technician, would take me round, not that there
was much to take me round as the museum itself was only half
open and things were quite chaotic due to rebuilding. Bagpipes
would have been a lot easier.

The museum seemed to be all packing cases and empty
rooms and walls. I wanted to see the forty-seven foot long scale
model of the complete Wall, made in plaster of Paris some
years ago, complete with forts and milecastles. All the reference books describe it. It was in pieces in an upstairs room.
When the work was finished, in a month or two, it would be
splendidly mounted once more.

But I did see a lot of their inscriptions and sculptural
monuments, all beautifully displayed and preserved, and best of
all, their reproduction of Mithras Temple. The Royal Shakespeare Company couldn't have done it better. It's a full-size
recreation with altars, statues of the worshippers and priests in
their robes. The lights are dimmed, there's a bit of moody
music, and on comes a commentary describing the service and
what the worship of Mithras meant to the Roman soldier. The
week before, so Mr Miket said, they'd had a visitor who'd come
all the way from Texas, just to see their Mithras temple.

The museum at Newcastle is not to be missed by anyone
interested in the Wall, though I can't decide whether it's best
to see it first or last. Until you've been out in the wilds and seen

the fortifications in their natural setting, it's hard to appreciate the inscriptions, tools, pottery and other relics. Perhaps see it first *and* last.

Roger Miket has done a lot of excavating himself. He's particularly proud of some work he did on Turret 33 B along with another student. (Milecastles run 1 to 80 across the Wall, a numbering which was devised by R. G. Collingwood some years ago and now followed by all. Turrets take their number from the milecastle to the east, and are in order A and B.) The sites of the turrets are known but few have been excavated, which is fortunate for students doing PhDs on Roman Britain in the years ahead. Original research is almost impossible to find in most subjects these days, but with the Wall, there's eighty miles to dig up, spadeful by spadeful.

At Turret 33 B, which is near Sewingshields, Roger unearthed an inscription by the Sixth Legion – yet in structure the turret was of a type built by the Twentieth Legion. This is where the fun begins. 'We were left with five or six alternatives. Was the Sixth just doing repair work on the turret or were they blocking it up? Was it a complete rebuild after an invasion and if so, when did it happen? You can rarely prove anything, just conjecture.'

So what they do is record the findings. Perhaps later when more evidence comes to light, other attributions might be affected. Maybe in twenty years the small piece of inscription found at 33 B might turn out to be vital when someone is trying to prove a new theory.

In Roman days, inscriptions were one of the major means of communication. They were the chiselled announcements done in stone, as captions to a piece of sculpture, a heading to an ornament, telling who did it and why. In many ways, inscriptions were the mass media. Some were huge, covering the front of a building, others were just one word on a stone. Today they represent the chief source of our knowledge of the Romano-British world, military and social. The inscribed stones in the Newcastle Museum are really 'a library of unique historical documents,' which is how R. G. Collingwood described them.

They're a bit hard for the layman to translate as the masons, having to knock out the same old phrases every day, often used abbreviations. D.M., for example, at the top of a stone stands for *Dis Manibus*, to the Gods of the Shadows, which shows it's a tombstone. I.O.M. is for a religious inscription dedicated to Jupiter, Best and Greatest (*Iovi Optimo Maximo*). When the legions were commemorating some triumphs or good bit of work or even just a safe arrival, they always signed it with their own initials, which were as familiar in those days as, say, RAF today. The Sixth Victorious Legion always signed itself LEG. VI. VIC. P.F., showing a bit of class, but the Second Augusta limited itself to LEG. II. AUG. C. written backwards indicates a centurion or his century.

Experts can often date inscriptions by the style of lettering as much as the contents. Not all the inscriptions were by soldiers but often by more humble folk and some of these are not exactly works of art, having the odd letter missed off the end of a line and stuck at the beginning of the next line. One of the tombstones at Newcastle is to a surgeon, another to a slave from his collegium, his craft guild as it would have been called in medieval days. There's a touching memorial which came from the fort of Carvoran on the Wall from a centurion to 'his blessed wife who lived thirty-three years without blemish.'

A lot of the inscriptions in the museum have the letters picked out and painted in red. Careful analysis of Roman stone lettering has shown that many had originally been painted. Inscriptions could be colour supplements, not just black and white newspapers.

Archaeologists now have many scientific aids to help them, which is one of the reasons why research in the Wall has been so rapid in the last thirty years. Wood, for example, which was always thought to be useless as a means of dating, can now furnish many clues. If Collingwood Bruce had kept some of the wood he saw coming out of the excavations for the Tyne Bridge they would have been very valuable. He *knew* they must be Roman, because of coins and other evidence and because of the site of the bridge, but he couldn't have proved it, not in 1875. Today the science of dendrochronology (dating wood by the tree rings) is much more advanced. More important, there's a new way of analysing wood called the Carbon 14 dating method. Everything organic absorbs carbon elements. When it's dead it loses this carbon at a very slow but measureable pace. The carbon content can therefore be analysed and a date exactly fixed. It's an expensive business so you have to be pretty sure that your piece of wood is what you think it is. The Japanese are about the cheapest at doing wood analysing by the Carbon 14 method, but even so it can cost about £50 for one little piece.

I set off along the Westgate Road from the centre of Newcastle, wondering if on my journey west I'd come across any Roman bits worth examining. Legally, if you find anything it belongs to the owner of the land on which you find it, though in practice the more ordinary objects, like fragments of pottery, are just pocketed. Before a proper archaeological dig begins the leader usually gets the farmer or the land owner to agree that anything of historical value will go to the museum in Newcastle or in Carlisle. If it's gold or silver, and many silver Roman coins and a few gold ones have been found, then it may count as treasure trove. If it does, the local coroner has to decide its future as technically it belongs to the Crown. What usually happens is that it goes to the British Museum while the finder gets a suitable monetary reward.

The first fort after Newcastle is in the city suburbs at Benwell, only two miles away, which means that today it's still in Newcastle. No one knows why it's so near. Forts were not built at a standard distance, like the milecastles, but as a rule they occur every five miles. Perhaps the Newcastle fort was primarily to protect the bridge while the Benwell fort was a base for guarding from the North.

Every city has a Benwell, one massive sprawl of pre-war semi-detached houses, prim and proper but now a bit left behind by the lusher, all mod con desirable detacheds that you get in the outer suburbs. The ambition of every good solid working man in the 1930s was to live in Benwell. I had a friend at Durham who came from Benwell. His Dad was an electrician at Thomson House in Newcastle.

Benwell fort covered 5.6 acres and in the second century had a cavalry garrison. Its Roman name was Condercum, meaning place with an outlook, which it must have had in those days, being on a level hill-top guarding the gap formed by the Denton Burn. I started by walking down Condercum Road asking people in the street how they pronounced Condercum. Written down it looked a bit obscene. They pronounced it as it looks, in three equally stressed syllables, but nobody knew its origin. Nobody was aware that there had been a fort in Benwell, though they all knew about the Wall. Many houses in the area have suffered from cracked ceilings ever since they were built, the blame being put on the Vallum which hadn't been properly filled in. The subsidence is supposed to be still going on. (Do insurance companies cover themselves against this – Acts of God and the Emperor Hadrian?) I saw a lady coming out of one house in Condercum Road who said she was Mrs Bowden, wife of the chimney sweep, and she said yes, she definitely had cracks in her ceiling. Everyone in the road did. And at the top end, so she said, they got water seeping through the road when it rained badly. 'Our cracks are very bad.' She recommended Anaglypta. 'It's very good. Everybody puts it over their ceilings round here. Anything else you want to know, pet?'

Benwell fort, like all forts, had an active vicus (village) life which went on outside the fort walls, though it's only in the last ten years that it's been realised how active and how rich this life was. Up to now, nobody had bothered to excavate much in the way of vicus life, not when they've had a fort or a milecastle or turret to get stuck into.

The outline of Benwell fort was established in the 1920s and 30s, before the semis were built, though nothing is left today. However, there are a couple of remains just outside the fort which are worth seeing, if only for their present-day incongruity.

In Broomridge Avenue there's the remains of the temple of Antenociticus, beautifully restored and cared for today by the Department of the Environment. It's really just a rectangle of foundations, sixteen feet by ten, with an apse at one end and a few remains of pillars. (The altars and the head of the young god which were found here are now in the Newcastle Museum of Antiquities.) Nonetheless, there's something quaintly attractive about it. It's stuck in a space between two semis at the end of the Avenue (next to number 48) and you could easily go right past it, thinking it was another garden, with a few strange ruins instead of gnomes. It has an ordinary low suburban fence, which a baby could crawl through, and a notice stating proudly 'Admission Free'. Nobody was in at 48 – you have to go down their front path to get into the temple – but the lady on the other side said she took a keen interest in the temple and was always chasing boys for climbing the walls or pushing over the pillars. She'd even caught some kids chalking on the temple the other day. Worst of all, there were some people from the next street, whose names she well knew, who persisted in bringing their dogs to the temple to do their business.

The other Roman remain in Benwell is even more interesting, at least to an archaeologist – the Vallum gateway. When it was discovered in 1935 by Professor Eric Birley it proved to be a vital piece of evidence about the nature and purpose of the Vallum. It is the only Vallum gateway to be seen today along the line of the Wall.

For many centuries the Vallum was thought to have been Hadrian's only contribution to the Wall fortifications – the Wall itself being attributed to a later Emperor, Severus. (Severus did major rebuilding on the Wall at the beginning of the third century, rebuilding it in parts from scratch, which was where the confusion arose.)

Birley's work in 1935 showed the direct relationship between the Vallum and the Wall and led to the theory that the Vallum was the boundary line which kept the civilian population away from the military area. No one knew until then that the Vallum had such gateways.

The foundations and remains of the Vallum gateway at Benwell are in a railed-off garden and are quite spectacular. Through the railings I could see quite clearly where the double doors had been and the road across the Vallum. I have to take the experts' word for it that the gateway was not a military one, on the style found at forts, but a non-defensive gateway, suitable for checking carts and people going through the

Vallum. All the same, I couldn't help wondering why the Romans wanted such an enormous and continuous customs barrier? Why couldn't the Wall itself, which had enough forts and milecastles with their own gateways, act as customs posts? Professor Birley had now retired from Durham and lives in a cottage in Hexham. I made a note to knock on his door when I reached that area and ask him to explain further.

In the meantime, I knocked on the door of number 65 Denhill Park, a house opposite the Vallum gateway. It was opened by a very jolly lady called Mrs Chiston, a widow for thirty-one years, who gets the princely sum of £7.50 a quarter for keeping the keys to the Vallum gardens. 'When I get it, that is. There's been a fault in the computer this year. My money hasn't come through yet from the Ministry.'

Mrs Chiston's main problem is stopping the kids playing football on the Vallum. Like the temple a couple of streets away, it's bang in the middle of the semis, but it has a lot more grass, all beautifully manicured by Department of Environment workmen. 'The kids get fly now and come and ask for the key, saying they want to go and look for the Warriors. They're always asking me if I can remember the Warriors. I'm not that old! I tell them ten minutes, then I'll cut their stocking tops off if there's any nonsense.'

She's done the job for nine years and enjoys it very much. She used to worry about it during the war, when nobody was in charge and the railings were taken away for the war effort. Now she delights in giving visitors the keys, showing them round if necessary and if she likes the look of them, inviting them into her house for a cup of tea. She has endless correspondence with American ladies whom she's taken in out of the rain and given genuine home-made English teas, all out of her own pocket. 'I don't invite people in if I don't like the look of them. I can't manage coach loads, of course. In the summer the coaches arrive three at a time. You should see the crowds, going through that gate in their hundreds. I had Alan Ladd here a few years ago. He had his own cine camera and took a lot of film of the Vallum. I didn't know it was him at first, till a neighbour told me, then I recognised him immediately.

27

'People are very good on the whole. I've had no trouble with vandals. I wouldn't let them in if I thought they'd cause trouble. "Just use your own discretion," that's what Mr Anderson told me when I took over the job.'

Mr Charles Anderson is the foreman in charge of the thirty masons and labourers, employed by the government, who go up and down the length of the Wall, patching and preserving. He was someone else I hoped to meet on my travels.

Continuing through the Newcastle suburbs I came to Denton, where, wonder of wonders, you can see a bit of the actual Wall, in its original position, the first bit which is visible on the east. I'd been well prepared for this delight. The 1964 Ordnance Survey map of Hadrian's Wall (two inches to the mile price 60p. from HMSO) announces proudly in black lettering: 'First extant fragment from the East'. It turned out, not surprisingly, to be a disappointment, just a few yards of dirty stone covered in broken glass and litter, surrounded by a broken down fence.

It's on the left side of the main west road, not far past Two Ball Lonnen, in that bit of Denton called Denton Burn. Perhaps I saw it on a bad day. Mr Anderson and his gang were no doubt due to tidy it up. The thunder of the lorries on the main road and the smell of fumes and the general grime and dirt of the road and pavement didn't help. However, there are two more bits of the Wall just a few hundred yards further along the road, both nicer, neater, longer and more interesting. The second includes a real treasure, turret 7 B, the first turret visible today. I climbed into it and up the steps. Even though the Wall is only five courses above ground, there's a feeling of height. I could look straight through the pernickety front room window panes of the semi-detached house opposite in Turret Road. When Birley, once again, excavated this turret in 1929 it was surrounded by fields. The view in those days was decidedly rural.

I was particularly pleased because I'd misread the map. I'd been so used since leaving Wallsend to referring to the map and seeing in red letters MC 3 or MC 5 or whatever, knowing that even if I found the exact spot, which is almost impossible, there would be nothing at all to see. Once the lettering changes from red to black, that means you *can* see something. Black signifies 'extant or identifiable'.

I was now feeling uplifted, after the grime of Newcastle, and in good fettle for the road ahead, even though I knew that for many miles yet it was going to be lorry-ridden. At least I would be out of Newcastle. And most of all, the *real* Wall country would be stretching ahead to the west, the parts beloved by learned archaeologists and simple walkers for centuries, the parts where you can always see something, unlike Wallsend and Newcastle, the parts where your imagination can roam and you can believe the Wall was real and not just a few bits of red ink on a map or dry inscriptions in a museum.

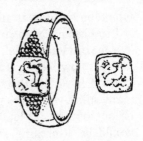

3
The Military Road:
Following the Historians

There's nothing unique about walking the Wall, nor in recording one's impressions, It's all been done before. The second-
hand bookshops of Newcastle, as I'd found, are stuffed with
little monograms by nice Victorian ladies who published their
own tour at their own expense, complete with their own nice
Victorian drawings and sketches. They're a joy to read, at least
I found them so, and for historians they do give a record of what
the Wall was like in years gone by. There are even books
written about the History of the History of the Wall, about the
experts and the laymen who've dug amongst its ruins over the
centuries. It's certainly thrown up some stout characters.

Bede, the one and only Venerable, is the earliest known
author (AD 731) to give the Wall's dimensions. From his monas-
tery at Jarrow, which was built with stones taken from the
Roman fort at South Shields, he could look across to the fields
of Wallsend and see the Wall as it went down into the Tyne.
He described it as being 'eight feet wide and twelve high on a
straight line from east to west, as is clear to beholders to this
day.' His dimensions are thought to have been correct, but he
was responsible for those two errors which continued for
centuries – calling the earthwork the Vallum (the Romans must

surely have called it the Fosse) and suggesting that the Vallum and the Wall were built in different periods.

William Camden, the great Elizabethan antiquary, wrote the first important account of the Wall in 1599 when he included it in his *Britannia*. He had been headmaster of Westminster and wrote his massive book in Latin. It was later translated into English. He covered the realm in person and explored the Wall on foot, noting the milecastles and turrets and forts. 'I have seen the tract of it over the high pitches and steep descents of the hills, wonderfully rising and falling.'

Like Bede, Camden said the Vallum and the Wall were separate constructions, giving Severus the credit for building the Vallum first. At Carlisle he wrote, 'The Pictes wall, which was late superimposed on the vallum of Severus, is to be seen at the village of Stanwic.'

Camden explored Cumberland and the coast thoroughly, but he was a bit scared about the middle section. He'd risen from being a headmaster, though he couldn't have done much head-mastering with all that topographical exploring, and been made Clarenceux King of Arms and was probably rather conscious of his new position. 'I could not with safety take the full survey for the rank robbers thereabouts.'

It was after Camden that we get the series of local English gentlemen, especially reverend gentlemen, who began to take a serious interest in the antiquities of their homeland. Perhaps the most notable was the Rev. John Horsley whose *Britannia Romania* was published in 1732. Horsley was a Presbyterian minister who ran a private school at Morpeth. With his book he established himself as the first scholar of Hadrian's Wall. Almost two hundred years later it was still a standard work.

In 1802 there appeared what had already become my favourite reading on the Wall. William Hutton, a seventy-eight-year-old Birmingham shopkeeper, set off from Birmingham on foot and did the whole length of the Wall twice, from the Solway to Wallsend and back to Birmingham, a length in all of six hundred miles. When you consider that today's elderly gentlemen are supposed to be far fitter and longer-lived than they were a hundred and seventy years ago, it was a remarkable achievement. He called his book proudly, 'The History of the Roman Wall which crosses the Island of Britain from the German Ocean to the Irish Sea, Describing its Antient State and its Appearance in the year 1801'.

He was fully aware of the absurd nature of his enterprise but he obviously loved every minute of it, castigating every vandal he met and going off at absurd tangents to describe people and incidents during his journey. He picked his outfit for the journey with care; a black suit, a bag, an umbrella and an inkhorn. The black suit caused him everywhere to be viewed with suspicion, either as a clergyman, a spy or as a tax man. At times it was so hot that he actually unbuttoned his waistcoat. He used only one pair of socks for the six hundred miles and didn't hole them either.

It took him thirty-five days 'and a loss by perspiration of one stone of animal weight and an expenditure of forty guineas.' He was far from modest about his achievement. 'Perhaps I am the first man that ever walked the whole length of this Wall and probably the last that will ever attempt it.' The first boast might possibly have been right. The second decidedly wasn't.

I had a copy of his book with me, borrowed from the local library, though I was nervous of it falling into the hands of any rank robbers I might meet hereabouts. After all, I was now entering the wild Wall countryside. I'd enquired at several Newcastle antiquarian bookshops about getting a copy of Hutton's book and had sent postcards to various other rare book people, but with no luck. I was determined to buy a copy, if it wasn't too expensive. I'd already encountered the funny ways of antiquarian book people. Many of them don't have shops but back rooms which they won't open up if they don't know you or don't like the look of you. 'Yes, I have a copy,' one had told me, 'but it's not for sale.' I pointed out that on his notepaper he described himself as an antiquarian book*seller*, but it made no difference. As a folly, Hutton's book is prettily written and nicely decorated; as an archaeological record it's still studied today; and as a piece of social observation, it's one of the few contemporaneous accounts of life in Northumberland and Cumberland in 1801. I saw Hutton as my model and planned to quote from him and perhaps bring his observations about the local men and mores up to date.

It wasn't long after Hutton, in 1839, that the Rev John Hodgson, the incumbent of Jarrow, devoted the last volume of his *History of Northumberland* to the Wall. On examining the recent inscriptions he proved that the Wall and Vallum were contemporary. (The Vallum, he considered, was the rearward line of defence.) This theory was given wider publicity with the first edition of J. Collingwood Bruce's *Handbook to the Roman Wall*, when it was published in 1863. He was the leading expert on the Wall throughout his lifetime. The pilgrimages to the Wall, which he began in 1849, are copied to this day every ten years, world wars permitting.

Apart from the Bible and Shakespeare, as they always say on Desert Island Discs, it's hard to think of a book which has been selling for as long as Bruce's *Handbook to the Roman Wall*. Since 1863 it has run through twelve editions – each one bringing everything up to date – and three reprints. Each edition and reprint has run to about 10,000 copies, which means that in all about 150,000 copies have been printed. Today it's still selling steadily – in 1972 they sold 1,200 copies – even though it hasn't been brought up to date since the last edition in 1965.

John Collingwood Bruce was a Northumbrian. After graduating at Glasgow he returned to Newcastle as a school teacher and lived there till he died in 1892 at the age of eighty-seven. He spent a lifetime researching and writing about Roman antiquities. His major work was *The Roman Wall* out of which the Handbook sprang. On its first appearance in 1863 it was called *The Wallet Book of the Roman Wall*, a confusing title but it sold out within a year. The second edition came out in 1884 with Wallet changed to Handbook and it sold out in a matter of weeks.

Andrew Reid of Newcastle was the printer and publisher of the book from the beginning. In fact he owned the copyright. Dr Bruce, apparently, received only a flat fee for his work. So despite those huge sales there are no Collingwood Bruces today receiving royalties. They all belong to the Hindson Print Group, a large Newcastle commercial printing group which bought

Andrew Reid some years ago. It's the only book they own or even publish. They thought at one time of selling off the copyright of the Handbook, perhaps letting a publisher take it over, as it is an anomaly in their present empire, but decided to keep it on for sentimental reasons.

The latest edition contains several of the original illustrations from 1863 – using the same hand-made wood cuts, now of great interest to typographers. The first three editions also had fine copper engravings but they became too worn to be used by the time of the fourth edition in 1895. From that year on, photographs were introduced.

The first edition of the Handbook is now a collector's piece. Hindsons haven't got one as their old premises were destroyed by fire, but they have copies of all the others.

As they own the handbook, it's in their gift to choose the next editor. Sir Ian Richmond was the obvious choice in his day, now it's not so obvious. There are several younger archae-ologists jockeying for position but no apparent heirs to Richmond. 'I'll take soundings when the time comes,' so Henry Davy, the firm's managing director, told me in Newcastle. 'This edition should sell out in a couple of years then I'll ask around amongst the academics. Whatever happens, the new editor will get a flat fee and we'll continue to use Collingwood Bruce's name.'

The two great Wall scholars of recent decades have been Richmond and Birley, but most of their best work was done in the 1930s. In many ways, the thirties saw the height of the Wall discoveries. Though work is still going on all the time, it was in the 1930s that many problems were ironed out, such as the purpose of the Vallum, and major sites finally outlined and excavated.

There have been many other great authorities on the Wall, some of the best and most important being amateurs, to whom we owe a great debt for saving great stretches of the Wall from either neglect or speculators.

Perhaps the greatest non-professional was John Clayton, town clerk of Newcastle in the late nineteenth century. He purchased in turn four of the Wall's forts (Carrawburgh,

Housesteads, Chesterholm and Carvoran) adding them to the one he already owned, Chesters. He bought up many miles of the course of the Wall itself and began an enormously ambitious programme of excavation and restoration. Without him, much of the finest and most beautiful sections of the Wall would have been lost for ever.

In the 1920s and 1930s there was another gifted amateur, F. G. Simpson, who did a lot of excavating, using money from his own pocket. He was a Simpson of Stead and Simpsons, the shoe people. It's thanks to him that Wallsend fort was outlined and the white cobbles put down. He's buried in a churchyard beside the Wall, at Nether Denton.

Where are the gentlemen archaeologists of today? The patrons seem to have disappeared, which is the cry you hear in all the arts. There are so many archaeologists dreaming over their sites, waiting for someone to come along and fork out a few thousand. Just think what the Americans would do with such a virgin piece of history. I'm surprised the University of Texas hasn't bought the whole lot and shipped it out, stone by stone. Wasn't it a Texan in Newcastle who'd flown all the way to look at their Mithras temple . . . ?

With such jolly thoughts I shook off Newcastle and headed for Heddon on the Wall and points west. The traffic was still thundering past me, but it was beginning to thin out. The Wall follows the line of the road, at least vice versa, so there is no avoiding it. There's evidence of the ditch and the Vallum on either side of the road which can repay inspection, if you don't mind the risk of being knocked down.

At Heddon there's a magnificent stretch of the Wall, about a hundred yards long, just on the left of the main road before you come into Heddon village. It's here, thankfully, that the road divides, the left fork (A 69) bending southwards towards Corbridge and Hexham while the B 6318 goes straight on. The locals never refer to it as the B 6318. It's always known as the Military Road. For the next fifteen miles or so, as far as Chollerford, the Military Road follows exactly the route of Hadrian's Wall. I had therefore a road march ahead, before the real Wall country, but it was to be a road wreathed in history.

It's all thanks to Bonny Prince Charlie that Hadrian's Wall came to be obscured by the Military Road for so many miles. In 1745 when the Young Pretender was marching South from Scotland, with the crown of England and the whole country perhaps within his grasp, General Wade and the Royal troops were waiting to intercept them at Newcastle. Charlie never came. Instead he struck out towards the west and entered England at Carlisle. General Wade was unable to get across and save Carlisle because there was no east-west road suitable for his artillery. He did try, but the roads were too bad. (Ironically, the reason why Charlie and his troops had made such excellent speed through the Highlands to Edinburgh, surprising every-one, was because of the excellent Highland roads which Wade himself had built).

After it was all over and Charlie turned back at Derby and was finally beaten at Culloden, the government decided to build a proper military road, just in case the Scots should ever rise again. To save themselves too much work, the builders simply levelled flat the Wall and used up any stones they could see around. It was like being presented with a straight set of foundations as far as the eye could see. As late as the beginning of this century, Roman facing stones could be seen peeping through the surface, but since then bitumen has covered all traces.

There is still today a decided feeling of being on top of a wall. Traces of the Wall can be seen at the side of the road, as if propping it up, for mile after mile. And as for the ditch to the right of the road and the Vallum to the left, they're both there for all to see, as clear as daylight. I could hear myself, despite the roar of the lorries (fewer, but far faster than before) giving little exclamations of delight, much to my own surprise. I would never have thought I was capable of being excited at the sight of a ditch, rushing to clamber into it and stare along it as far as I could see, delighted by the way the fences separating the fields have to dip down in a V to go across, exactly the same V which the Romans dug out. The thrill of the views almost made up for the throbbing traffic.

About a mile along the Military Road after leaving Heddon I

came to the next fort, Rudchester, or Vindovala as the Romans called it. It doesn't actually matter what you call it today. There's nothing there to see. It's the fourth fort along the Wall, almost seven miles from Benwell, and it covered about four and a half acres. The site today covers the cross roads, the first one after Heddon. The road right points to Ponteland, six miles away. The fort was mostly on the left of the road which was the way I turned, as I could see nothing to the right. I headed for a farm house which had the rather battered sign outside, Rudchester. It's not a very attractive farm, rather grim and grey. The farmer's wife, Mrs Stobo, said I could wander round the fields if I liked, but there was nothing to see. Twenty years ago there had been some excavations and they'd given her a copy of a book about it afterwards (which must have been the Handbook) but someone had borrowed it and never returned it. I asked about her unusual surname and she said it was Scottish, so she'd been told.

Oh, she added, I might look at that barn over there. There was a bit of lettering on one wall. I raced off and scrambled over an elderly plough and bales of hay and made out some letters on a stone high up on the wall – AVR, RIN, XII, NIS. They seemed to be the middle sections of what had formerly been four much longer lines. I opened my haversack and got out the Handbook, to see if I'd made an amazing discovery, but it was already there, though Bruce said the third line was XIT whereas to me it looked clearly XII but no doubt it was clearer when he first looked at it, back in the 1860s. Unfortunately for once he doesn't give a translation or a guess at the missing words, except to say that DM had probably been at the top, indicating it was a gravestone.

An expert can make a reasonable guess at most Latin inscriptions from just a few clues, as you can see in most good Roman museums where they often complete a huge word from just a few letters. Today, for example, if you saw the remains of a notice with only PU and CON to be seen, most people could recognise it at once.*

* Public Convenience, of course.

In the 1920s excavations revealed the outline of the fort gates, opened up an underground strong room, explored the headquarters building. For some reason all the excavation work was filled in again. It looks from the record books such a rich and relatively easy site to investigate. If I'd had a chisel on me I could have pinched the inscription and carried it off. I bet nobody would have noticed for years.

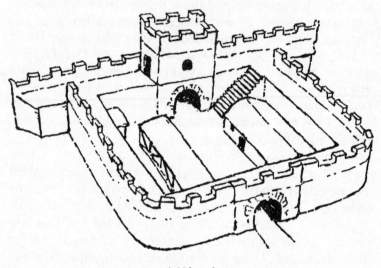

A Milecastle

I came out into the light again and had a look at the rest of the farm buildings, but there were no more inscribed stones. I met Mrs Stobo again who said there was a Roman bath in the wood, straight through the farm yard, if I could fight my way through the nettles. It was completely overgrown, dark and very forbidding. I jumped in the air with fright when I stepped on three geese who'd been nestling in the nettles. Above my head a cloud of rooks were circling, screaming oaths at me for disturbing their trees. I eventually found the bath. It had been hewn out of a solid piece of grey sandstone, about ten feet in length.

In one corner of the bath there's an outlet hole. According to

Bruce, when it was first discovered in 1766 it contained bones and remains of what could have been an iron candlestick holder. It had been some sort of sacrificial bath, used in one of the many temples known to have existed around the fort. The plughole was for blood, not dirty bath water.

On the way back through the farm I thought I'd tell Mrs Stobo that her Roman bath had been a blood bath, but I could see her busy in the cow shed. Outside her kitchen door an aluminium lambing crook had appeared, hanging from a hook, a shining sign of modern farming. Her husband had perhaps come home. I went back to the main road.

On the top of Harlow Hill I came across a gaggle of workmen, all in the uniform and caps of the Newcastle and Gateshead Water Company, rushing around trying to find a stopcock. A lady in a garage was saying she had no idea where it was. They'd have to look. There seemed to be a lot of men for such a little job.

An old Ford drove up with three priests inside who giggled and nudged each other as they watched the consternation of the Water Company men, running round in circles like clockwork toys from Trumpton. It was like the beginning of a French film, all very folksy and whimsical and soft colours, but you know that by half-way, when Chabrol really gets going, there's going to be blood and violence all over the place. I hurried on, keeping up my stride to the top of the hill. On the summit I could see ahead a huge expanse of water, the Whittledean reservoir. No doubt it hadn't been an ordinary domestic stopcock the men had been looking for. Perhaps a vital one which controlled part of the reservoir.

The sun had come out again and I stopped to watch the seagulls on the edge of the reservoir, wading majestically up and down, their chests stuck out as if they were deep sea fishermen, risking their lives, not paddling in two inches of tame reservoired water. Above them some swallows were swirling and diving, rather aimlessly, not deciding yet where or when to go.

I didn't want to rest too long in case I couldn't get started again. My legs were fine, but my back was aching. In my normal London life, I do around two hours walking on Hampstead Heath every day, plus a weekly game of football. Now that at last I was on the open road, I was carrying my stuff with me in a rucksack. (The last time I'd travelled with a rucksack was as a student. In those days I made my wife, a big strapping lass, carry the rucksack except through villages when, for the sake of appearances, I carried it.)

Once over the reservoir, the Wall ditch on the right of the road reappeared again, only being broken at a roadside cottage where it had been filled in to make a front garden. Soon the Vallum on the left could be seen just as clearly. I stopped for a few minutes to chat to an old stone mason who was mending a barn at the side of the road. Earlier that morning two men had asked his permission to take photographs of a field. 'They took hours, just photographing. They didn't howk the earth or anything. I couldn't understand it.' It did look a particularly boring field but perhaps aerial photographs had shown up some ancient settlement.

I hadn't planned to have any lunch, saving myself for a big meal in the evening, but I knew I wouldn't be able to resist a wayside pub. The stone mason had said the Robin Hood was just two miles ahead, so I hurried on. I'd been quite surprised at the lack of pubs or any sort of village since I'd left Heddon.

I arrived breathless at the Robin Hood pub at exactly one minute past three. 'Too late,' said a very unobliging man behind the bar. I couldn't believe one minute would be too late, knowing how country pubs are far from strict about closing time, especially such an isolated one on an empty country road. 'Just half a pint,' I said. 'And a roll. Sorry I'm so late.' There were four other people in the bar, a couple and two lorry drivers, all with full drinks in front of them. 'I said it's too late.'

I looked round, hoping for sympathy. 'I've walked from Newcastle,' I said, pleading. The barman looked grim and the customers averted their eyes. It was the only place in about a ten-mile radius that did refreshments, and here they were closing at the height of the afternoon.

'OK,' I said. 'A glass of water. You can't refuse that, surely, And a roll.'

He made a great show of getting down a clean glass and going to the sink, sighing heavily as he turned on the water tap.

'You might as well have a drink,' he said, stopping and shrugging his shoulders. 'It's just as much trouble. But drink it quick.'

Back on the road, as cars and lorries thundered past me, I realised that not one person had stopped all morning and asked if I'd like a lift. I wouldn't have taken one, of course. Now I thought about it, people had been looking at me with suspicion all morning. Apart from my rucksack, I didn't look like a student hitchhiker or a mature fell walker. I was wearing a black sports jacket and trousers and a black polo neck pullover. What sort of person could I be, walking along a busy country road in the middle of nowhere in the middle of the day? Perhaps that was why the Robin Hood man had been so unhelpful. In towns, it doesn't matter what your business is. People are too busy.

Old William Hutton had the same problems in 1801. He had trouble getting dinner in a Newcastle hotel because seven gentlemen didn't want him at their table, all because of his appearance. 'You deem, gentlemen, to take me for a clergyman,' so he told them. 'But I assure you, I am in a far preferable state for I am a freeman. I have nothing to expect from any man but common civility which I wish to return with interest.'

Apart from that incident the early part of his walk was fairly uneventful. He records that as today, the first bit of the Wall to be seen *in situ* was at Denton. Luckily for him, in those days there was an apple tree growing out of the middle of the Wall. (He has a nice engraving to prove it.) At Rudchester he had about as much luck as I had in seeing anything. 'I have all along inquired for turrets; but I might as well have inquired among the stars.'

Not long after this, Hutton looked for a bed for the night. He doesn't identify the inn, but it might well have been the Robin Hood.

'Soliciting a bed, I was ushered into a parlour where sat three gentlemen. I did not conceive I had a right to intrude, so took my place at the greatest distance. A suspicious silence immediately surrounded their little table. As I never made a secret of myself or the plan I was pursuing, I endeavoured to introduce a communication, for truth makes a wondrous impression upon the mind; when, after a hour or two's chat, one of them remarked "You are the most agreeable companion I have met with; but, I do assure you, when you first entered, I took you for a spy employed by the Government." '

Despite his great success with his chat, he had a bit of a surprise in the morning. 'It does not appear that dishonesty is totally expunged from the Wall; for though my gloves were deposited where they ought to have been safe, yet I found that some person had made free with them.'

Haltonchesters, the next fort on the Wall, is like Rudchester. There's nothing to see, and this time there were not even any farm buildings to explore. It's just after the Military Road makes a series of sharp bends, having to go round some crags and a disused quarry, worked by the Romans in building the Wall. There's a gateway with pillars on the left of the road, exactly on the spot of the fort, and a sign saying 'Bridleway to Halton Castle'. I could see Halton Castle quite clearly across the fields, the home today of Major Blackett. In Hutton's day, as he noted, it was the home of Sir Edward Blackett. In the middle ages, this area was the home of the Carnaby family, now died out, their name being remembered only by London's Carnaby Street.

At the gateway lots of stones had fallen from the field wall, many of them original Wall stones. Inside, the field was like a vast carpet which hadn't been laid very well. Every bump in the underfelt was sticking up. I walked in and out the bumps, thinking of the proud cavalry regiment that had once been stationed there, and wondering why it had never ever been fully excavated. In 1827, while the northern bit across the road was being ploughed, an elaborate bath house was revealed which was examined and recorded, then filled in again. It's of interest because normally the troops' bath house was *outside* the fort. Only the fort commandant had his bath inside his quarters.

I could feel the stones not far beneath my feet as I walked over the hillocks, being careful not to stand on the giant toadstools which grew among the roots of every tree. There were no local worthies around to talk to, unless they were hiding. Previous walkers of old, like Camden in the sixteenth century and the Rev Horsley in the eighteenth, describe meeting people in this exact field who filled them up with stories of Roman 'speaking trumpets' being found on this part of the Wall. This was a commonly held belief for many centuries – and you never know, as no one is exactly sure how the Romans did communicate along the Wall, they may have had speaking trumpets, horns perhaps which they shouted through. However, the confusion was to do with the water pipes and aqueducts which can be seen at every excavated Roman fort. We know they were for water or for central heating, not for shouting along, though it's a pretty thought.

All morning on my walk, I'd been trying to estimate if you could shout and be heard from one turret to the next. As they're only a third of a mile apart and there was no traffic noise in those days, and if the wind was favourable, I'm quite sure you could shout messages along the Wall. Most experts say the Romans used fires or some sort of semaphore. If you had an extra soldier in between each turret, and there's no doubt throughout the occupation the Romans had soldiers to spare (how else did they build that ridiculous Vallum), then shouting messages would be the easiest and quickest way. I estimate you could shout a message, coast to coast along the Wall, in a matter of minutes.

Haltonchester was called Onnum in Latin. We know what the Romans called the forts along the Wall because of several invaluable finds, notably the Notitia, a fifth-century document which records the military establishments in Britain, and the Antonine Itinerary. The Itinerary was like a road map, an AA guide of its day, produced by the Army for its officers in moving troops and sending the Imperial post. It covered the whole of the Empire. For Britain, it gives details of sixteen routes radiating from London with the names of places along the way and mileages between them. The names on these documents have been confirmed by even more surprising finds – souvenirs of the Wall, made by the Romans and sold in souvenir shops outside the Wall forts. The Wall was apparently a great tourist attraction right from the beginning. There's a couple of finely made enamel souvenir cups, both with designs of the Wall and naming the forts in order, which must have been expensive to make and were probably aimed at the officer trade. The best known is the Rudge Cup and is now at Alnwick Castle, the home of the Duke of Northumberland.

Just a few hundred yards after Haltonchester is one of the focal points of the Wall, the Portgate, as it was known in medieval days. This was where the main north to south road built by the Romans, Dere Street, crossed the Wall. Today it's still the spot where the main north–south artery, the A 68 crosses the Military Road. In Roman times, it linked the Wall with the legionary fortress at York and was one of Agricola's main routes to Scotland. Hutton exclaimed when he got to this spot for he could see west to the wild land ahead, with open views to the Cheviots to the north.

It is still surrounded by open land today with magnificent views all around, but I was brought down to earth to find, slap on the crossroads, a brand new set of garage showrooms. Even stranger, it was completely devoted to foreign cars. There was a large sign saying SAAB and another for BMW. In the long, glass windows stood gleaming the latest models. One would expect a main SAAB dealer in Newcastle perhaps, but not here, miles from anywhere. It also advertised ice cream. I went inside and bought one from a Mrs Fawdington, wife of the owner. She didn't think selling SAAB cars in the middle of Northumberland was at all strange. 'We were just an ordinary petrol station till about 1963. My husband used to do a lot of motor racing in Saab cars and when they got popular commercially he decided to start selling them. The farmers round here find them very good for the sort of hard work they have to do. I'm afraid this country lets people down with cars. They're not reliable.'

I was surprised to find that the crossroads itself was now in fact a roundabout. I'd just been reading a book by Birley in which he was saying that if only the council would build a roundabout that would be the time to get in quick and investigate the ruins of the Portgate Gateway. Now it looked too late. Mrs Fawdington said the work had been completed the previous year. 'The Council was willing to let them do some excavating at the same time, but I was told the archaeologists ran out of funds. But the Council's built the roundabout slightly to the side, leaving the Portgate untouched. When they get some funds, the archaeologists can dig it up themselves.'

The only other building on the corner is a large pub, the Errington Arms. It was closed and I didn't fancy further humiliations, so I turned left, leaving the Wall, and headed down the hill towards Corbridge. I was feeling pretty shattered, having done at least fifteen miles, despite all my boasts about being fit. I decided if someone did offer me a lift, I could be persuaded, just for the two miles to my hotel, now that I wasn't actually on the Wall route any more. A car did pull up beside me, a large Renault, very reliable, and a man's head appeared.

'Which is the Military Road?' I pointed back up the hill. He closed his window quickly and drove off, not back towards the Military Road but to Corbridge, where I was obviously heading. He hadn't even bothered to ask if I wanted a lift. I might as well have been a spy, or even a clergyman.

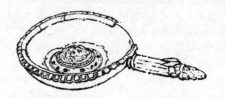

4
Corbridge: An Almost Unwearoutable Experience

Corbridge is an attractive little town with an even more attractive seven-arched stone bridge which spans the Tyne and dates back to 1674. The town itself, perched on a high bank of the river, is full of neat and rather prim grey houses, architecturally very interesting but too prim and too proper, I thought, as I walked down the hill from the Portgate. There seemed a mausoleum quality about the town, despite the huge lorries grinding round the one-way system. Even the antique shops looked grim and cheerless. I came to one called the Centurion which had a wooden model of a centurion's head outside on the pavement, chained securely to the wall. Apart from antique shops, of which there are several, every other shop seemed to be a wool shop, all very refined and genteel.

I met a lot of Americans walking round, terribly impressed, soaking up all the history, but doing it on tiptoe in case they disturbed any of the retired gentry folk. Corbridge has certainly had its share of history. William Wallace burned the town down in 1296. Robert the Bruce did the same in 1312 and so did King David II in 1346. It speaks highly for the quality of the Roman roads – straight down Dere Street from Scotland, first stop Corbridge. Local Northumberland history was equally bloody. Ethelred, King of Northumbria, was slain here in 796.

King John came, but on a peaceful mission. He'd heard about the remains of the Roman fort and had been told stories of buried treasures. His dig, in 1201, is about the first recorded archaeological dig in history. He found nothing 'except stones marked with bronze and iron and lead' which of course he wasn't interested in. There was treasure. His spies were right, but amazingly it wasn't discovered until over seven hundred years later. In 1911, six years after the modern excavation of Corbridge began, a bronze jug was found which contained a hundred and sixty gold coins, the largest horde of Roman gold coins yet found in Britain. (Today they're in the British Museum.)

Corstopitum, the name of the Roman fort at Corbridge, is about half a mile west of the town. I passed a signpost leading to it as I went into the town, but having walked sixteen miles that day, I was leaving such an important chunk of Roman Britain for another day. Instead, I headed for the seventeenth-century Angel Inn, the only Good Food Guide hotel I could find for twenty miles around, a tragic state of affairs and an indictment of the inhabitants. I'd taken the precaution of booking.

The hotel is a long and low terrace, right on the main road and the noise of the lorries through my bedroom window was unbearable. I went downstairs and asked if I could have a bedroom at the back. It was impossible. The hotel, all seven bedrooms, was full. As I stood there, three lots of well dressed, middle aged Americans, almost on their knees, were begging for rooms. All they could be given were the names of local bed and breakfast places, plus a half promise that they *might* be fitted in for dinner, but dinner only. I went back upstairs and discovered the windows were double-glazed, so that was something. It was a nice friendly little hotel, but not exactly full of mod cons. For the best hotel in a very popular town, it must come as quite a surprise to Americans. There was no phone or TV in my room, not that I wanted either, but a notice on the wall boasted: 'All seven bedrooms have electric razor points.' I went down again to ask about the train service from Corbridge, but the reception desk didn't have the timetable. They said ring the station. I couldn't find Corbridge station in the book. I rang

47

Hexham station, but no one answered. I rang Newcastle but all the lines to Newcastle station were engaged. Well, I had a nice evening ahead, that was something.

John Gillam was joining me for dinner, the Reader in Archaeology at Newcastle, the one I'd missed in Newcastle because of his Rumanian jaunt. He lives in Corbridge and has done so ever since he started lecturing in Durham just after the war. Professor Birley told him if he was making the Wall his speciality, then he'd better live there. Now he commutes every day to Newcastle. (From him I discovered that Corbridge station still functions, but it's an unmanned station, which is why there's no phone.)

Gillam was at St Chad's College in Durham before the war, destined for a career in the Church. After war service, like so many, he rethought his career and decided to go back to Durham and teach history. He got a job at Hatfield College, Birley's College, moved to Corbridge and started digging on the Wall. He got his big break, the sort all archaeologists dream about, almost immediately. One Thursday in 1949, a friend who travelled with him on the train said he'd found something interesting at Carrawburgh. He'd pulled back a bit of turf and found a stone with some inscriptions on it. He'd made a sketch of the stone which he passed to Gillam. On Saturday, Gillam went straight out to Carrawburgh. 'By lunchtime four of us had found a Mithras temple, with three perfect Altars still standing in position. I was the first person to read the altars since the fourth century. It's the single most exciting discovery I've ever been involved in.' The altars are now the highlight of the Mithras temple in the Newcastle Museum.

Gillam was only in his second year as a lecturer. He's done lots of good research in the twenty-five years since then but nothing as sensational. He's small and very sociable with a walrus moustache and a shock of greying hair. Like many university lecturers, he has a habit of talking without looking at you, as if disinterested in your reactions, almost half to himself, which makes it hard for a layman to keep up. Almost thirty years of lectures and tutorials, giving out the wisdom to a captive audience, no doubt has this effect on academics. He was very forbearing and repeated things for my benefit.

The Rumanian trip, he said, had been very interesting. There had been a hundred and fifty experts there, fifteen of them from Britain, including Birley who in effect began the whole idea of Roman Frontier Conferences. Back in 1849, Collingwood Bruce had dreamt up the idea of a pilgrimage to the Roman Wall. It was a huge success and they were held irregularly after that until the Second World War. In 1949, the centenary year, Birley resurrected the idea, only this time extending the invitation to overseas Roman experts. To help foreigners to come, Birley used the word 'Congress', which is the OK word when it comes to getting money out of universities or governments. Going on a 'Pilgrimage' isn't the sort of thing easily subsidised. Since then there have been get-togethers every two or three years in different parts of Europe, with every tenth one, as in 1959 and 1969, being held in Britain. So far they've held the congresses in Algeria, Austria, Switzerland, Yugoslavia, Israel and Rumania. The next one is due to be held in Holland, with Lower Germany and then Hungary after that. (They persist in the term Lower Germany, using the Roman division.)

'Rumania was well organised, but it's getting a bit out of hand with a hundred and fifty people. Each of them wants to give a paper, is *determined* to give a paper. Nobody can say they're just going off to Rumania to listen to other people. They've got to be going to speak. They had to have two lecture rooms with papers being read simultaneously. That way you could miss both and just sit and drink Czech beer.'

One of the reasons for the lack of any big archaeological excitements, not just in Gillam's life but for most Wall archaeologists, is that they're living in the shadow of the thirties. When I was in Newcastle, I looked up some pre-war newspapers and the Wall was getting continuous front page treatment as the smart people of the day rushed to look at the latest find or put their names to petitions urging the government to take over the preservation of the excavations. Rudyard Kipling was a great fan of the Wall and was always campaigning about it. (His *Puck of Pook's Hill* takes place on the Wall.) John Buchan was also interested. Stanley Baldwin, George Lansbury and Isaac Foot (father of the present Foots) all spoke about it in the House of Commons. Today, things are much quieter. But you never know. A few big finds could turn the Wall into a Tutenkhamun.

'I spend more time running courses today than excavating, trying to make people realise they're digging up people not things. They get carried away by finding a bit of Samian pottery, especially when they can make it fit with another bit, but it's how it all fits into the total structure of people's lives that matters. If they can't find a bit of pottery, they think, oh, there's nothing to be found. I once excavated a site at Corbridge which had been gone over three times and was said to have provided nothing. I found evidence of six successive buildings on the site. What the others had been looking for were gold rings.

'Since 1945 excavation on the Wall has been chaotic and unplanned. People have done things as the fit took them. It's all been piecemeal. If only we'd all stuck to one unexplored fort and excavated it to death.'

If he had the money, which of course keeps back all excavations, he says he would spend it all on Rudchester, in his opinion the richest unexplored fort. (That was where I looked at the bath in the wood.) I was surprised to hear he'd been digging there the previous Easter, using undergraduate (i.e. free) labour. The farmer's wife never mentioned it.

'It wouldn't be too expensive, as sites go, because it's all fairly open land. I'd estimate to dig two metres deep over an area of 400 by 600 metres. Assuming no inflation over the next two or three years and paying for the labour at the present rates, it would come to £16,000. Several years ago I did a lot of useful work at South Shields for only £3,000.'

John Gillam's speciality is Roman pottery. The south of England, which had a much more flourishing villa life and was nearer the Continent, has generally provided pottery more sophisticated than the northern stuff, but all pottery, whatever the style, can furnish the expert with vital information.

There are two basic types of Roman pottery found in Britain – Samian and Coarse. Samian is the term used to describe the red glazed pottery found throughout the Roman Empire and used by Roman housewives as 'best'. Although it was mass produced in large scale potteries, it was of very high quality. Almost all Samian-ware found in Britain was imported from South and Central Gaul. (A little Samian pottery was known to be made in Britain – a small Samian pottery has been recorded in Aldgate, London.)

The periods when the different types of Samian pottery were in use are known and have been classified and dated. To make it even easier, most Samian potters had their names stamped on their pots. A piece of decoration is often enough for an expert to recognise the work of an individual potter to be able to date it.

Samian-ware comes in many forms: bowls, vases, even inkpots. Samian inkpots are not uncommon, all of them unspillable. I remember at school when unspillable inkpots came in and were said to be a brilliant new idea. I later saw some Samian-ware inkpots in the British Museum – they were exactly the same shape.

Coarse pottery is the term used for Romano-British pottery that's not Samian. It came from many different places, up and down the country. It's a highly complicated field of study – you get people who specialise in just one little bit of it, such as Castor-ware, the Coarse pottery which came from the Northamptonshire potteries. Coarse pottery is harder to identify than Samian. A photograph of a piece of Samian-ware is often enough for an expert to know its date, as long as he can see the decorations. But Coarse pottery often needs to be handled. The feel of Coarse pottery can be as much a clue as its design.

Coarse pottery was everyday ware and therefore was used for everyday objects, such as bowls, dishes, jugs, drinking flagons, beakers, mortaria. (A mortarium was a large, strong bowl, usually with the inside roughened with grit, used for pounding food.) Depending on the type of rim or the steepness of the sides, it can be worked out which period the moratoria come from. A lot of Coarse pottery cheese presses have been discovered – little domestic cheese presses, used by women for making their own cheese, an object you don't find in many kitchens today. The British Museum has children's toys made of Coarse pottery and even a baby's feeding bottle.

For several decades, John Gillam has been using his knowledge of pottery to try to clear up one of the mysteries of the Wall's history. It's recognised in all the standard books that the Wall was overrun four times, the first in AD 197. That's the date that everyone always gives. It all happened when the Governor of the day was away on the Continent engaged in a civil war, trying to be Emperor. When it was all over, the new Emperor, Severus, substantially rebuilt the Wall around 205-208. This was the extensive rebuilding which made historians think for centuries that Severus had actually built the Wall in the first place (until finds on the Wall were conclusively dated and proved to be Hadrianic). Our friend William Hutton always called it Severus's Wall.

For the last thirty years, so John Gillam says, several experts have begun to suspect that the evidence for the 197 date was a bit circumspect, in fact decidedly thin.

'We all agree there was rebuilding in 205. Birley and Richmond found inscriptions of this date at Birdoswald in 1929 – they sent a telegram to Collingwood, telling him of their find. It's from this discovery that the 197 myth started. If there was rebuilding, they had to have an invasion, so they searched around for literary sources, looked at the Civil War of 197 and said that's it! There must have been an invasion when everyone was away, which would explain the repairs. At the time, it was a sensible theory.

'A lot of Birley's pupils have looked for years for somewhere else to put 197 – another date for the invasion presumed to have taken place that year. In 1970, three of us went into print with the theory that there was no 197 invasion – John Mann of Durham and I did an article together and independently Mike Jarrett of Cardiff came out with the same theory. I re-analysed all the evidence that Birley and Richmond had found, plus some new pottery finds, and we said that if they were looking round for a literary date on which to hang an invasion, 207 would be a better one. That of course would muck up the idea of the rebuilding having been in 205. But the main point was that there was no 197 invasion.

'We just got into print, when some brand new evidence came up to prove us all wrong. It's taken me a long time to accept it. I felt a proper Charlie at first, but now I agree with it. It all hangs on some stamped Samian pottery found at Mumrills, a fort on the Antonine Wall in Scotland. The evidence pointed to a final abandonment of the Antonine Wall in 160.

'I'm still definitely against any invasion in 197, but I've had to change my mind about there possibly having been one in 207. I'm now thinking of 180, that's splitting the difference with the 160 theory. In Roman Britain archaeology you're justified in putting dates in a twenty-year bracket. Birley still sticks to his 197 invasion. I think he's wrong.'

I'm not quite sure I understand all the ins and outs of the argument over 197, though John Gillam did take it very slowly. I hope I haven't simplified it too much. But I could see that archaeologists can get pretty heated over their theories. It makes you wonder how many of the facts we've had handed down to us over the centuries are not simply intelligent theories supported by suitable circumstantial evidence.

I set off in bright sunlight early next morning to go to the fort of Corstopitum. In the large open Market Place I had a look first at the sturdy parish church of St Andrew's, the finest Saxon Church in Northumberland, which dates back to AD 786. Inside, between the Baptistry and the rest of the church, they have a complete Roman gateway, a splendid specimen in fine condition. It's presumed that the Saxons brought it from Corstopitum, where it had originally been erected about 150 AD. In the churchyard there's another structure of interest to Roman historians, a Pele Tower built of Roman stones. This was put up about 1300 during the Scottish raids. Cattle were driven into the basement for safety, the middle floors became living quarters and the upper part was fortified to keep out the attackers.

As I came out of the churchyard I noticed some curious

lettering on a shop front across the market square – NWEAR-OUTABLE. My view was partially obscured by a van and I couldn't see all the letters. I moved nearer and realised I'd missed a U at the beginning. Even so, Unwearoutable seemed a funny name for a shop. In very small letters, I saw that the word 'almost' was tucked in front. Underneath was the legend 'shooting stockings'. I went inside and asked the lady what almost unwearoutable shooting stockings were. She said for going shooting in, though you could use them for walking. I said they must either be wearoutable or unwearoutable, not *almost* unwearoutable. 'No, it's true,' she said. 'They're almost unwearoutable. Eric Newby always buys his socks here. We send them all over the world, especially to America. I had a man in the other day who brought back a pair he'd bought twenty-one years ago because he wanted them re-footed. They're made on hand-operated machines by a special technique I can't divulge.'

They make them to measure in almost any colour and they work out around £3.50 a pair. She produced several pairs and they looked very good to me. Anyone in need of almost unwear-outable shooting stockings can write for further details to the Knitting Shop, Market Place, Corbridge.

The fort of Corstopitum, half a mile to the west of the town, is past some council houses and a prep school, just as you enter open country. It is the first excavated fort to be seen. The forts at Wallsend, Newcastle and Benwell are completely built over and the two rural ones at Rudchester and Haltonchester are virtually unexplored. Technically, Corstopitum is not a Wall fort, but no one interested in Hadrian's Wall ever misses it. It was an integral part of the system, lying just under two miles south of the Wall at the point where the Roman roads of Dere Street and Stanegate intersected. Its importance lies in the fact that it became the supply town for most of the central part of the Wall, with factories supplying goods and materials, shops and taverns where the soldiers could relax and a civil community which grew at its height to around forty acres.

The first fort at Corbridge was built by Agricola in AD 79. It guarded the bridge across the Tyne, the vital east–west link road now known as the Stanegate, and acted as a supply base for advances into Scotland. Its garrison was the ala Petriana, a Gaulish unit, later one thousand strong, the only cavalry regiment of its size known in Roman Britain at any time.

Long before Hadrian arrived, Corbridge had its ups and downs. There's evidence that it was burned down around AD 100, perhaps in connection with the disaster which struck the Ninth legion. Later the ala Petriana was moved to Stanwix, outside Carlisle.

Corbridge figured prominently in the first plan for Hadrian's Wall. That was when the Wall was seen as a patrolling system, manned from only milecastles and turrets, with the existing forts a few miles south, such as Corbridge and others on the Stanegate, being the supply stations. When the second plan came into operation and sixteen forts were built onto the Wall itself, Corbridge ceased for a while to have much military importance. The fort's garrison seems to have been evacuated for some time, though the civilian settlement and factories continued to be used.

Different stages in the life of Hadrian's Wall have already been referred to in passing, such as an invasion and rebuilding in or around 197, but the most remarkable event occurred just ten years after the Wall was finished. After all that work, all those millions of man hours and millions of stones, it was decided that they didn't really need it after all. No new broom can ever have swept cleaner than Antoninus Pius.

In AD 138, on the death of Hadrian, he took over as Emperor. He decided to abandon Hadrian's policy of consolidation and to strike forward once again. In Britain, where he appointed a new Governor, Lollius Urbicus, it was decided to expand once more into Scotland. Unlike Hadrian, Antoninus didn't visit the island himself. Perhaps if he had he might have changed his mind, realising that there wasn't much in Scotland to push forward for except glory, and that Hadrian's Wall was perfectly capable of keeping the Caledones out. Perhaps he was determined to go one better than Hadrian. Whatever the reasoning, the Romans invaded Scotland and set up the frontier shop this time between the Forth and Clyde. A Wall was built, this time of turf, and was known as the Antonine Wall in honour of the Emperor. In AD 142 a centurion was given the honour of taking the news back to Rome where there were great celebrations and new coins were struck, declaring the complete subjugation of Britain.

Where did that leave Hadrian's Wall? There's not much evidence to go on, but it's presumed that most of the Wall forts were now held with skeleton staffs. Corstopitum, however, came back into its own again. There are several Antonine inscriptions, telling of structures and new additions, which indicate that Corbridge was used for the military advances into Scotland and as a supply base.

Though half the length of Hadrian's Wall, the Antonine Wall had more forts – nineteen in all – spaced at two-mile intervals as opposed to the average of five for Hadrian's. It secured peace in south Scotland at first, but not for long. The Antonine Wall was first overthrown in AD 155, which meant that Hadrian's Wall was again the main line of defence. The last and final invasion of the Antonine Wall came in 181. It was rebuilt but finally abandoned around 190.

The Antonine Wall was a strange venture, being nowhere as sound in construction or as strategically well planned as Hadrian's. It was continually in trouble and in all lasted little more than fifty years. The Romans continually had to fall back on Hadrian's line.

From 181 onward, Hadrian's Wall became once again the Northern limit of the Empire and remained so for the next two hundred years, till the Romans themselves left the country. It suffered only two invasions during those two hundred years, three if you count the 197 invasion (the one John Gillam thinks didn't exist). It's an impressive record. Almost all the history of Hadrian's Wall is peaceful, which accounts for the size of the civil settlements, especially at Corstopitum.

Corstopitum, through its very richness, is a complicated site. The layer upon layer of archaeological investigations are diffi-cult for the layman to fully appreciate. I hadn't been there for twenty years and I can still remember how deeply I was disappointed by what I'd seen. It was a school trip from Carlisle. To get us in the mood, we'd had lessons beforehand on

Roman baths, temples, turrets and such like and we were all very keen. There is nothing that captures the imagination of schoolboys more than the Roman army. When we got there, all we could see was a pile of old rubble. We'd fondly believed that we'd be able to step *into* the baths and the temples, walk round them and see what they were like. We hadn't realised that all we would see would be foundations.We had to peer down into them desperately using our imaginations.

Twenty years later I was delighted to see so many wonderful foundations, having forlornly looked at the measly few bits of the Wall which are to be found between Corbridge and Wallsend. They were all beautifully preserved, neat, well ordered. With the help of the excellent official guide, written by Professor Eric Birley, I walked round the site. It's best to orient yourself first, using the map, so that you enter along the main road, with the granaries on your left and the temples on the right. It's like a huge Hampton Court maze with stones instead of hedges. You blink when you first see it as there seems to be no pattern, yet it's all so neat and orderly that you know there must be a key somewhere, if you can only stop and work it out.

I walked into the granaries (i.e. over the foundations of the granaries) and examined the huge stone flags on the floors, many of them raised to allow the air to circulate beneath and so keep the corn dry. There seemed to be the remains of fountains everywhere, with aqueducts bringing supplies of water to all parts of the fort. Aqueducts are one thing you don't need an imagination to study. You can see exactly how they worked. When the buildings existed, the aqueducts would be obscured.

On the left is an enormous store house. As Birley says in the guide, 'this is one of the largest and most imposing Roman structures surviving anywhere in Britain.' I know what he means by such words but an innocent might expect to see an actual structure. There is of course none, but the foundation courses of the walls of the store houses are absolutely clear and defined, four large rooms in all, surrounding a central courtyard 165 feet by 150. No one knows the height. What a delight that would be, to actually *see* a Roman military structure at its original height.

I moved on to the temples and the military compounds, to the headquarters and other buildings. At one end of the site there's a raised dais on which is an artist's impression, by Alan Sorrell, of what the fort must have looked like when it was occupied. It's a good painting, very evocative. If they can reproduce a fort on a painting, why can't it be done in real life? I wouldn't have been put off the Romans for twenty years, not if I could actually have *seen* something.

I then went into the site museum, a rather forbidding row of dark browny-green huts, rather like prefabs. They were well cared for, as are the site remains, but somehow impersonal and unattractive, soul-less in the way only a government department can take the soul out of any building or site. Corstopitum, like all the excavated Wall forts and major sites, except one, is in the care of the Department of the Environment. The week I was there a government shuffle brought in a new head of the Department, Geoffrey Rippon taking over from Peter Walker. Mr Rippon is the local MP, being the member for Hexham, the market town only three miles away. The Wall is in his care and protection as a Minister as well as an MP. Perhaps under his protection we would see some changes.

In the guidebook, Professor Birley does say that the museum huts are 'semi-permanent', which means presumably that they were put up as a temporary measure but are now with us for ever. He also says that some of the Corbridge treasures have been moved to the Black Gate Museum in Newcastle, which we know is wrong, unless they found some Roman bagpipes.

However, the contents, almost all of which date from the 1906–1914 excavation of Corbridge, are terrific. They have such a wealth of stones to choose from that I noticed a heap of them behind one of the huts. Inside, some of the things, especially in the South room (on the left as you go in) seemed poorly arranged. There's a whole range of smaller inscribed stones, all of which look interesting, yet none of them labelled. In the Central room and North room are bigger, more important stones, inscriptions and sculptured work, all of which are well displayed. The Corbridge Lion is perhaps the best known – a locally made piece of sculpture from a water tank showing a popular Roman motif, a lion devouring a stag. Considering the sculptor could hardly have seen a lion, it's a pretty good representation. (The Romans took a few lions with them for their large-scale entertainments, such as chariot racing done by full-time professional teams or gladiators fighting lions and leopards, but nothing on this scale ever reached Britain. Gaul was about the nearest place.)

After the Corbridge Lion, the best known Corstopitum find is a pottery mould in the image of the Celtic God Taranis. This shows a knobbly-kneed old man with an even more knobbly walking stick – known locally as Harry Lauder.

There's a fascinating tombstone of Barates, a native of Palmyra in the desert beyond Phoenicia, who died at Corstopitum aged sixty-eight. What's especially interesting is that a tombstone to Barates' wife has been found at South Shields. When you consider the chances of any tombstones surviving and being readable about 1800 years later, then it's a great coincidence that two have survived from the same family. His wife was British and had come originally from Hertfordshire. She was called Regina and had formerly been his slave. She died in South Shields at the age of thirty, leaving poor old Barates very distraught. There's a photograph of his wife's tombstone (the original is at the South Shields museum) above his own tombstone. She sits on a basketwork armchair, her wool in a basket beside her. There's a Latin inscription and one in Palmyrene script which reads 'Regina, freedwoman of Barates, Alas!' Very sad. It's the bare bones of two lives we can only guess at. Barates seems to have been a standard-bearer and had probably served in several parts of the Empire before landing up in the darkest north. How this Asiatic found Northumberland after the desert can only be imagined, but he must have made a good enough job of it to settle down and marry a local girl. The idea of him adding a little bit of his native Palmyrene language is attractive – perhaps there was a large Palmyrene community in South Shields at the time whom he wanted to impress.

This mixture of races and languages is one of the things that shines through the Roman relics on the Wall. Germanic names are mixed with those from Gaul and the Far East, plus Roman and native Celtic. The people were such a mixture, compared with today. Later that week I went into Hexham. It was a Tuesday, market day, and very crowded yet I was struck by the uniformity of clothes and faces and voices. Not a hint of an immigrant. I felt a foreigner myself, because of my voice and clothes, even though I try to pretend I'm a Northerner. I was taken for a Londoner at once.

In the central room of the museum there's a fine collection of tools and instruments, nails, pulley blocks, chisels, saws, soldering irons, drills, trowels and such like, all of them, I swear, not the remotest bit different in design from their modern counterparts. Today's versions are sometimes lighter, using alloys or steel, but as far as looks go, they're identical.

The brooches and beads and other bits of ornamental jewellery are harder to appreciate. They seem to have faded with time, got rougher and more battered, unless the stuff dug up at Corbridge wasn't of the top quality, though judging by the extent of the civil community, there must have been enough merchants' wives who could afford the best and the latest fashions. You see brooches at every Roman museum. For all their cleverness, the Romans knew little about buttons.

I admired a model of a Roman catapult and some oil lamps, again the same shape as today's oil lamps, though made of pottery, and then I came out into the fresh air. It's a rather dusty, grey museum, for all the richness of its contents. There's a feeling, as with the whole site, that nothing has been touched or rethought or moved round for hundreds of years. In fact there's a distinct feeling that *nothing* must be touched. Keep off. We don't want dust or people poking around our precious bits and pieces, thank you very much.

I went to the entrance and bought some books and postcards from the Custodian. There were several cheap models in a plastic material of some of the treasures and I bought some for my kids. I wanted the Corbridge Lion but they hadn't got a copy. I had to be content with two of Harry Lauder. (The kids loved it.) The Custodian, under heavy questioning, said he was called Mr Simpson but wouldn't tell me anything further, not even how business was. He gave a name and number in Carlisle and said I had to have official permission before he could make any statements. I knew he was a Civil Servant but he went on as if he'd signed the official secrets. I shouldn't have said I was working on a book but chatted him up like a normal tripper.

I was leaving when a school bus arrived and out poured about forty ten-year-olds from a Newcastle primary school. I'd been going round the site almost on my own, apart from a party of Danish visitors, as it was so early in the morning. The kids immediately took over, rushing for the museum. One know-all shouted that he knew where there was a Roman catapult but the two lady teachers said hold on, we're going round the site first. They groaned, but turned and raced for the foundations with the teachers yelling at them not to knock anything over.

The teachers gave little bits of lectures, mainly gleaned from bending down and peering quickly at the notice boards on each site, a trick known to all teachers everywhere.

'They're a B stream,' confided one teacher, realising I was watching. 'Their reading's not so hot.'

They then raced for the next site, the granaries. 'That's where the Romans kept their grannies,' said the know-all in a loud voice to his classmates.

They were herded on to the temples where one teacher reminded them of the lesson she'd given about temples and mosaics. 'But there's nothing on the floor, Miss! You said the Romans had mosaics on all their floors.' They were genuinely shocked, staring at the beautifully manicured but absolutely bare grass inside the foundations of the temple walls.

'Now we'll go and look at a very good painting of the fort as it used to be,' said the teacher hurriedly. They all fought to get on the dais, pushing and shoving. It was the thing they obviously liked best about the site, then they rushed at last to the museum huts. It was the know-all's turn to be criticised. The catapult wasn't full size, the way the rest of them had imagined, just a little model. The girls were all taken with the brooches and ornaments, but their interest soon waned.

Altogether, they'd been round everything in about fifteen minutes, despite the teachers stretching it out. Both teachers said they wished there was something for the kids to get involved with, to touch or play with or try to work or get inside. Luckily, they'd had a stop at a sweet shop on the way there, a unanimous demand by every child, where they'd unloaded every last penny. They rushed to sit on the bus and out came the sherbet, lemonades, crisps and chocolates. It was the highlight of their visit. Twenty years ago, I felt much the same.

5
Chesters:
Thoughts from the Bath House

It was a few weeks later that I returned to Corbridge to continue the trail. I got off the train, hoping to find a taxi to take me up to the Wall at Portgate. I wasn't going to count that as cheating. It was now November and the days were getting short. The station had the air of a deserted swimming pool. There wasn't a phone so I set off over the Tyne and through Corbridge, my rucksack feeling remarkably light, as it always does at that stage in a walk.

Going up the hill to the Wall, I thought a Jaguar was going to stop. It slowed down in front and I could read a sticker on the back window which read: 'Whyayeyabugger. Home rule for Geordieland'. He moved off again very quickly, and I was left to trudge alone. I looked for any traces of the chestnuts I'd been kicking a few weeks ago on my way down, but now every tree was bare. Though it was bitterly cold, I felt invigorated, stepping out fast and pulling my hat down and my coat tight. A shower of hailstones hit me and my face tingled with their force. Just as suddenly, they stopped and the sun came out. Typical Northumberland weather.

At the roundabout I turned left at last and said hello Wall, how's the Military Road been treating you. The cars flew past as quickly as ever, each sending a slipstream of showers of mud and rain for about thirty yards. I'd forgotten what a rotten road it is to walk along. Pretty enough scenery on every side to lull you into thinking it's a rural by-way, but there's hardly a minute without a car or a lorry. I kept assuring myself that there wasn't much road left and tried to admire the brilliant stretches of the Vallum on my left and the ditch on my right, both of which are as perfect as anywhere on the Wall. William Hutton positively dribbled at the very sight. 'I surveyed them with surprize, with delight, was fascinated and unable to proceed; forgot I was upon a wild common, a stranger, and the evening approaching. Even hunger and fatigue were lost in the grandure before me . . . lost in astonishment, I was not able to move at all.' In 1801, Mr Hutton didn't have Robson's lorries from Carlisle to contend with or Jaguars with joky insignia.

I looked for a farm house which is supposed to have a centurial stone beside an upstairs window, but I couldn't see it, thanks to the hail lashing into me again. I sheltered in St Oswald's Church in an empty field on the right of the road, just after Hill Head. I expected it to be a ruin, stuck out in the field with no habitation anywhere in sight, but it was a delight, small and very simple and in excellent condition. I wondered where all the worshippers must come from. Hexham was a good four miles away. A notice instructed me to take a leaflet on the history of the church and leave an offering, but there were no leaflets to be seen. I already knew some history of the church, built in 1737 and gothicised in 1887, but one likes to help the writers of obscure leaflets about obscure churches.

Back on the road, I came across a stretch of the Wall on the left of the road, just past Planetrees farm. The survival of this excellent stretch is always credited to our friend William Hutton. He was so inflamed by the sight of a workman taking down ninety-five yards of the Wall in front of his very eyes that he is reputed to have burst into tears. He prints the name of the landowner who had ordered the dastardly deed, Henry Tulip, Esq. (One of the first examples of 'We name the guilty man'.) The said Henry Tulip had already taken down 224 yards of the Wall before Hutton had arrived, all to build a new farmhouse. Hutton commands the workman to go to his master at once. 'Request him to desist or he would wound the whole body of Antiquaries. He is putting an end to the most noble monument of Antiquity in the whole Island and they would feel every stroke.' Thanks to Hutton's entreaties, twenty yards of the Wall are standing to this day.

Slightly further on is Brunton House, a private estate which contains what is considered to be the best turret left on the Wall, turret 26 B, known as the Brunton turret. You have to turn left down the Hexham road to get at it. It's a remarkable relic excavated as long ago as 1876 by Clayton and still the highest chunk of Wall remains to be seen from the east. I counted eleven courses above ground, which makes it about nine feet high, high enough to shelter behind from the hailstones which had started again.

It's around this section that the soldiers received their order to change from the Broad Wall, ten feet wide, to the Narrow Wall, eight feet wide. You can see at Brunton Turret how the Wall runs into the turret at one width and goes out at another. These complications go on for many miles, due to the fact that the work parties had gone on ahead.

Many textbooks still say that the reasons for the change were economic – they wanted the job done quicker and cheaper. It's a reasonable thought, till you recall the structure of the Wall. Narrowing the Wall makes no difference to the number of facing stones required. Only changing the height would have reduced them. The saving is in the internal core, a useful saving but the quarrying and laying of the facing stones was by far the biggest job. A suggestion put forward many years ago by Sir Ian Richmond seems more likely. He noticed that the core so far had been mainly puddled clay – on the narrow sections it becomes a limestone mortar. He thinks the engineers going ahead saw the steep and narrow crags to come, rising and falling very sharply, and decided that a mortar core would be stronger. For this a narrower Wall would suffice. So the change was primarily for strength not cheapness. It also must have been easier to dig narrower foundations on the rocky cliffs ahead.

The Wall now runs straight down to the banks of the North Tyne. I could see my next target beyond some fields across the road, but it's private land and you must go to the Chollerford bridge, then turn left and follow the path beside the old railway. There was nobody around and if there had been they couldn't have seen me in such driving rain, so I hopped over the fence, took a short cut across the fields, climbed over the old railway fence and landed with a squelch on a grey muddy path. In a land rover parked near the river I could see some people drinking tea from a thermos flask, very sensibly keeping out of the rain.

I went down to the river to look at the remains of the Roman Bridge across the North Tyne. The abutment is very clear and well preserved, one of the few remains you can actually climb up on and explore. Two other piers were discovered in the river itself but these days can only be seen if the water is very low. Under the remains of a turret, the hub of a water wheel was found and is now on show at Chesters museum across the river. It's a large circular stone with slots for eight spokes. Water mills were one of the many inventions which the Romans brought to Britain, another example of their cleverness with water. Apart from baths and aqueducts, they drained a large area of the Fenland and built canals, linking the rich farm lands of East Anglia with the legionary headquarters at York. Roman water mills are known only in the military areas, especially along the Wall, all part of the policy of making forts self-sufficient.

In the Handbook it says there's a good example of a phallus carved on the bridge abutment, a well-known Roman good luck symbol, keeping away the evil spirits. It was one of the first things I searched for, but I was having no luck till the occupants of the land rover emerged, now that the rain had slackened. Three middle-aged workmen appeared with rakes and began sweeping the last of the autumn leaves, silently and separately, lost in their own thoughts. They were obviously council workmen. I said excuse me to one of them, where's the phallus. 'Follow me,' he replied, showing no surprise. 'Here's the fellow.' And he was a fine fellow indeed, plump and well formed, with two neat testicles, beautifully carved on a stone facing the river. 'Magnificent workmanship,' he said, beaming.

He swept his arms round, taking in the whole site. 'Measure any of it. Level all the way. Marvellous.' I asked him why so many of the larger stones appeared to be lying around in any old order. 'Jerries,' he said. 'POWs during the war. They were given the job of clearing the river and they just chucked the stones anywhere.'

He'd been with the Department five years, before that he'd worked in a factory. It was the best job he'd had. 'You're lucky to get any work roon here. Have you been to Housesteads? What a lovely fort. I've seen people at Corbridge ask for the Wall then turn away disappointed when they're told there's no Wall. But at Housesteads now, you've got everything, fort, milecastle, turret and miles and miles of lovely Wall.'

I told him I'd admired every bit of the Wall I'd seen so far, except the very first bit at Denton. It had been covered with litter and the fence was broken. 'People are always complaining about that bit, but it's nothing to do with us. Newcastle Corporation are supposed to tend it, but they don't seem to. There's always letters in the local papers about it.'

He's found quite a few bronze coins over the years, plus one silver one which he handed to Miss Dorothy Charlesworth, one of the government's Inspectors of Ancient Monuments. But he hadn't come across any inscriptions. 'I know where there's two more phalluses. I marked one of them myself at Birdoswald. It's on the Wall and we've put a metal arrow at the bottom, pointing up to it.' I thanked him and continued on my way, going a few hundred yards back along the river, across Choller-ford bridge to reach Chesters on the other side.

It's easy to see why Chesters fort is always said to have been the most desirable station on the Wall. It's a natural beauty spot and since Elizabethan days it's been a popular attraction for visitors. I like the simple note found in the diary of a militia officer one Saturday afternoon in June 1761: 'Jack, Bob and Self went to Chesters to view the remains of the Roman Fort and Bridge.' It's nice to think of soldiers through the ages going to look at the work of other soldiers.

We owe Chesters fort and museum to the work of John Clayton, the Newcastle Town Clerk who began his antiquarian work here at Chesters. He inherited the Chesters estate from his father in 1832 and until his death in 1890 devoted himself to the cause of preserving Hadrian's Wall and its fortifications. Clayton uncovered most of Chesters fort as we see it today. For the past seventy years there has been no excavation on the site.

Chesters fort is one of the biggest and most interesting on the Wall – it covered five and three-quarter acres and had a cavalry garrison, one of the four or five cavalry garrisons on the Wall. The Cavalry were on better wages than the infantry and had higher status, which is shown in the general richness of the site, in the size of the commandant's house and in the bath-house beside the river. Professor Birley in his official guidebook to the site says that Chesters is the best example of a cavalry fort to be seen anywhere within the territory of the Roman Empire.

Once again I was disappointed. At Corbridge, for all its faults, you can stand in the middle of the site and look around and get the feeling of a Roman station, imagine its busy streets, its rows of houses and shops and barracks. But the fort at Chesters is simply a field. The Roman remains are somewhere in the middle, hidden behind a few iron fences. As they tend to be sunk into the ground, it's easy to miss some of them. I went from one to another, reading that one enclosure was the West Gate, another the North Gate, and so on. It's hard to see the connection between the isolated bits. If only they could take down the individual fences and mark out the area of the whole fort. Or best of all, excavate a bit more and join the bits together. As the present owner of the field, and the surrounding estate, isn't very interested in Roman antiquities, this isn't likely to happen.

The only decent-sized bit of the fort to look at is the Headquarters building and the Commandant's house. This is well preserved and easy to follow. I found another phallus, which cheered me up, but this wasn't such a fine example. It's near the well in the Headquarters courtyard, carved on a large paving stone. As it's on the ground, not on the side of a wall as at the bridge, it's been worn flat by centuries of sightseers walking over it.

But the two other things to see at Chesters are far from disappointing – the baths and the museum. Of all the Wall structures so far, I enjoyed looking at the Chesters baths most of all. It's rare that a building and its purpose should be so clear, so easy to appreciate. I rushed to look it up in Old Hutton, to see if he burst into tears of joy this time on seeing such a splendid sight. Like me, he was a bit disappointed by the fort itself 'very uneven, owing to former use'. He makes no mention of the baths, not a word. Then I realised. The baths weren't excavated till 1884 nor fully studied till 1930. He may have seen chunks of the Wall being pulled down which no one will ever see again, but overall we can see far *more* of the Wall and its structures today than ever he did. What other glories, one wonders, are yet to be uncovered?

The baths are a short walk down to the river bank from the fort. They stand as a complete entity, with every room clear, as if they'd only recently been evacuated. There is a ground plan in the fort guidebook and it's more than worth studying. Compared with the fort guide, in fact every fort guide, it's all so easy and straightforward. Baths are the best known feature of the Romans, as far as the general public are concerned. At Chesters there's the ideal chance to understand how they worked.

Every Roman town worthy of the name had its own public baths and every military establishment had its set of bath houses placed just outside the fort, for the use of the soldiers and eventually for the inhabitants of the vicus. (Inside the fort, the commandant had his own private bath suite.) Wherever the Romans went, they brought their baths. It was almost a fetish with them, yet a very practical fetish. The British in setting up their Empire in the far corners of the world took much stranger fetishes with them, such as cricket.

Hadrian, that great promoter of urban life, encouraged them to be set up. In towns they were erected at the expense of the town council and were open to all. All Romans took a bath daily and the leading Britons soon followed, as they did with other Roman customs. It's strange to think that baths became commonplace for the three hundred or so years that the Romans were here, yet once they'd gone, not just the habit but the *knowledge* of public bathing went as well. Throughout medieval England, until as late as the Victorian age, even the noblest in the land must have smelled a long way off. It's only relatively recently that bathing has become a regular habit once again.

Going to the baths was a social occasion for the Romans. Seneca in one of his essays describes what it was like if you were unlucky enough to live too near to the public baths. 'The sound of voices is enough to make one sick.' He had to put up with the groans of the weight lifters, the slapping of the masseurs as they pummelled away (with hands open or cupped), the splashings of the swimmers, the shouts of the arguers, the cries of the sausage sellers and puff pastrymen, singers singing, umpires calling out the score in a ball game and the howls caused by the removers of surplus hair. 'It would disgust me to give details,' he finally adds, making one wonder what else could possibly be going on.

The secret of the Roman baths was the hypocaust system of central heating, a secret which died with them. Hot air from a furnace was conducted through underground channels to a pillared vault beneath the room to be warmed. If they wanted dry heat, the furnace was stoked with charcoal. For moist heat, they used wood. If they wanted great heat, they not only heated the floors but the walls, using flues made of tiles. The principle is the same as today's central heating, though it was always hot air that was circulated, never hot water. We know the system worked, not just from the scores of baths which have been found all over the Empire, but from literary sources. There's a story related by the younger Pliny about the master whose slaves attacked him and threw him on the heated floor to see if he was still alive. He survived by pretending to be dead, though he nearly burned alive in the process.

The best-known Roman baths in Britain were, and still are, at Bath, or Aquae Sulis as the Romans called it. It's thought to have been the greatest bathing establishment in the Western Empire. It had three great plunge baths. The largest, the Great Bath, was fed by a natural hot spring and had an arched roof, thirty-five feet long. Visitors came from all over Britain and Europe, and around Bath sprang up some of the richest Roman villas in the country.

Chesters military bathhouse is much more modest by comparison, but it was typical of military bathhouses all over the Empire. There were none of the large plunge baths in which

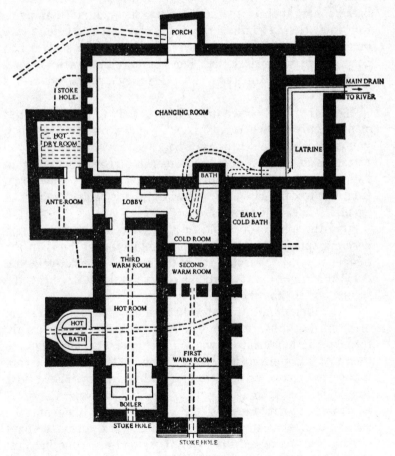

Chesters Bathhouse

you could actually swim, but the sequence of hot and cold rooms was repeated all over the Empire.

The bather entered the bathhouse through a porch (see diagram) which led into a large changing room, forty-six feet long and thirty wide. Here you got undressed and if you wanted, used the lavatory on the left. (This latrine had a large drain which took sewage down to the river.)

On the right wall of this changing room are seven beautifully carved niches, still intact today. The experts are divided on their purpose. Some say they contained the lockers where bathers hung their clothes. Others say they contained altars to Roman deities. I examined the niches carefully and could make out what I thought were grooves, where wooden shelves had been placed to hold clothes, but you wouldn't normally put clothes so high up on a wall. I decided they'd contained statues after all.

The bather then passed into a lobby, ready to enter the series of differently heated rooms. Looking down on the flagstones, you can see where centuries of bare feet have worn away the entrances to every room. The sequence of rooms varies from bathhouse to bathhouse, but the principle of being able to go from hot to cold, via tepid and warm, moist or dry, then back again, is the same everywhere.

From the lobby you could turn left into a cold room (*frigidarium*), splashing yourself from a cold washing bowl in the middle or lying in a cold bath in the corner. Alternatively you could turn right into two rooms reserved for hot dry heat, the second hotter than the first.

If you didn't want the immediate shock of a very cold room or a very hot room, you took it more gradually, going directly through the lobby into a warm moist room (*tepidarium*) and then into a hotter moist room (*caldarium*). This had a hot bath in a corner alcove which was lit by a bay window above, four feet wide, the opening of which you can still see. Clayton's excavators found traces of the window glass lying outside. Parallel to these rooms are a set of other warm rooms, perhaps overflow rooms when times were busy and everyone had just come off duty.

The idea was to get a good sweat up, open all the pores, and then have your skin rubbed with oils. The oil was scraped off with a metal flesh scraper known as a strigil. The Romans didn't have soap but they made ample use of sponges – both for washing and as lavatory paper. In the unctorium, where the oils were rubbed in, the masseur would be on hand to pummel the flesh.

There are signs at Chesters of many of the activities Seneca complained about. An altar to Fortune, the goddess loved by gamblers, was found in the bathhouse showing her with what looks like a cornucopia. They also found a gaming board, carved out of stone with little figures like draughts as counters. This is now in the museum and was probably used in the bathhouse.

As for the activities Seneca would not mention, it is known that from time to time things got pretty riotous in the bath-houses and the authorities had to step in to restore order and decency. Officially, women weren't allowed in the baths at the same time as men – they were supposed to use them at different times, as in present-day municipal Turkish baths. But some sort of intercourse must have gone on, judging by the number of times edicts were issued saying that mixed bathing had to stop. In the drains at several baths (notably further along the Wall at Vindolanda), women's hair pins and jewellery have been found, which would indicate that both sexes were allowed. The sheer size of the changing room at Chesters shows that it must have been a meeting place as much as anything else.

I finally dragged myself away from the baths, and the endless conjectures encouraged by such a fine building, and went into the stone-built museum. It was snug and warm inside and I realised I'd been cold standing in the bathhouse. It's a hand-somer building than the Corbridge Museum, which isn't saying much. It's teeming with treasures, almost to overflowing, and I found it fascinating. Everything is not only labelled but explained, such as the tiles which fitted together to make flues for the hot air. It's nice to have explanations with the actual materials. On the site of the fort, even though you can see bits of tiles and raised slabs, it's hard to see how it all worked.

One of the most important discoveries at Chesters is a diploma issued to an auxiliary soldier to mark the completion of twenty-five years service. It consists of two thin bronze plates hinged together. It was issued in 146 and mentions several of the units serving in Britain at the time, which makes it a vital source of information. It grants the auxiliary full Roman citizenship, now that he's been discharged, and legalises any marriage he might have made. For a long time Roman soldiers were not officially allowed to marry, but naturally many unofficial marriages took place. Their families moved with them from place to place, living outside the fort in the vicus. It's rather a long and wordy document and not much to look at. Only ten have been discovered in Britain. The one at Chesters is a replica, the original is now in the British Museum.

As at Corbridge, there's a fine collection of tools and instruments, pottery and jewellery, inscriptions and altars. Several of the largest statues are incomplete, such as a headless goddess standing on a headless and legless cow, which doesn't exactly make you want to rush off and look at it. In fact, it's surprisingly impressive. Despite the bits missing, it is vastly superior in workmanship to most statues found on the Wall. Birley, in the Chesters guidebook, says the motif is Syrian.

It was dark by now and the curator was getting ready to close for the night. I just had time to look at the pictures of John Clayton, begetter of Chesters and so much else, before leaving the museum and its lovely coke fire.

The huge mansion next to the museum is Chesters itself, the original home of the Clayton family. The central part is eighteenth century with the wings being added in 1890. Nathaniel Clayton, father of John, was having the field levelled in the 1790s to improve his view of the river when his workmen first came across the sunken strong room of the fort's headquarters building.

The estate was bought by Captain A. Keith in 1929 and today it is lived in by his son-in-law, Major John Benson. He gave me half an hour in his estate office. He's incredibly tall and looked every inch the country gentleman in his tweed plus fours. He went to Eton and then into the Black Watch. He appeared slightly suspicious, saying he didn't like being interviewed. He was simply a farmer, trying to get on with the business of farming, and didn't pretend to be an expert on the Wall. It just happens to run through the Chesters estate, the property of his wife and sister-in-law.

The estate covers three thousand acres of the Wall country, half of which is let to tenant farmers, and includes Chesters fort, the bridge abutment and other sites. Through his wife, he is related to Major Joicey, another great Wall landowner who lives near Haltwhistle. His brother, another Major Benson, farms the family estate centred on Newbrough. Between them, the three Majors, all related, have control of a major slice of the Wall country between Hexham and Haltwhistle, perhaps the most interesting section archaeologically and certainly one of the most beautiful.

'The Wall actually runs under the house,' he said. 'Good gracious no. I've certainly no intention of excavating for it. I have enough problems with the Wall as it is.'

From Major Benson's point of view, and it's very understandable, he's a bit ambivalent about the growth of interest in the Wall. So far that year, 106,000 people had come to look at Chesters fort. Naturally he worries about people straying too far into his fields. 'We have lost some cattle because the gates have been left open. I can't prove, of course, that visitors to the fort were responsible. The attendants are terribly good and I'm quite sure that no one has ever done wilful damage, but with so many people around, one or two can be forgetful. On a sunny Sunday you can have 1,500 in that field. It takes some controlling.

'One of the cattle we lost died through eating leaves from a yew tree. A gate had been left open and it had strayed amongst the trees. I would never stop people going on our land who want to look at the Wall, but it's very annoying when they don't close gates. There's a new law which makes farmers responsible for their cattle straying, even if it's not their fault.'

The Wall is a protected area, classified by the government as an ancient monument and therefore untouchable by anyone, even the owners of the land on which it runs. It means that farmers can't farm too near it, or even plant trees in the area without permission. 'Not that you'd want to plough too near anyway. It's all stony.'

His current worry concerned the possibility of one of the tenant farmers losing some of his grazing land. Just over a mile further along the Wall from Chollerford Bridge, a long stretch of the Wall (at Black Carts) was being uncovered and consolidated. If it proved a success with the public, Major Benson feared that the next stage would be providing car parking facilities. Two acres of ground could be lost if this happened. He'd had long legal discussions with the Department of the Environment and agreement had been reached whereby the tenant farmer would get compensation, if necessary.

'If the Wall could be moved two miles further north,' he said at one point, 'it would certainly take away a lot of problems for us.'

It was pitch black when I got outside again. With standing in a rather cold estate office in my wet clothes I was now feeling pretty miserable. I staggered round the grounds, trying to find my way out. I have a rotten sense of direction anyway (in the old days my wife carried the map as well as the rucksack), but with taking my mind off my bearings for half an hour I was completely lost. I bumped into several trees, hoping none of them were yews, and staggered into several courtyards, hoping I hadn't left any gates open.

Suddenly in the dark I came face to face with Major Benson, confirming no doubt his worst suspicions. He pointed me in the right direction for the gates, asking where I thought I was heading. I said I was booked into the Hadrian Hotel in the village of Wall, just a few miles along the road to Hexham, or it might be the Wall Hotel in the village of Hadrian. I was becoming rather confused. Oh, he said.

My rucksack felt a ton weight as I staggered along the road back to the bridge, looking for the road to Wall. It was too dark to read the map and find out if that was the right name of the village. I became ravenous and had to think myself into a trance to rise above it. I hadn't eaten all day, saving myself for the evening. My feet got to the stage where they became displaced persons, great lumps moving stiffly forward, not knowing where or how but knowing that stopping would mean being unable to start ever again. I realised almost I was enjoying the agony of being absolutely exhausted, of being an automaton, but I couldn't be, so I kept telling myself. I counted trees and shadows and car lights in the distance, tricking myself that I was moving and that I hadn't been sentenced to mark time for ever. What I wanted most in the world was a hot bath.

6
Langley:
Some Medieval High Jinks

About an hour later I was lying in a bath at the Hadrian, for such was the name of the hotel, in the village of Wall, and soon felt much better. My luck had changed. The hotel was on the road and had looked flat and boring from the outside but inside it was splendid, extremely comfortable with antiques in the corridors, more like a country house than a hotel. All the bedrooms had Roman numerals. Mine was number XI. On the landing outside was a spinning wheel and a stripped pine Grandfather clock. Inside it was old fashioned and elderly with a massive mahogany wardrobe and a rather creaky bed, but overall, it was the nicest hotel I'd stayed in so far, much better than Corbridge or Newcastle. My bedroom fire had been lit to greet me, though they'd no idea what time I would arrive. A very helpful girl was booking a taxi to pick me up later that evening. I'd decided once I'd recovered, to go to a medieval banquet nearby, one advertised in a local paper.

The longer I lay in the bath the more soporific I became and I realised that the advantage of the Roman baths was the change of heating and atmosphere which stopped you dropping off. Like a sauna bath or a Turkish bath (and Roman baths were both) you feel invigorated afterwards. With all those oils and pummelling you must have felt ready for everything. Another advantage was that you were constantly going into fresh water. The presentday system of taking a bath means lying in a pool of stagnating water. Having opened the pores, you then lie in dirty water. A shower, in theory, should be more hygienic. No doubt someone somewhere has done a survey.

Even with central heating, the constant problem in most houses is getting enough hot water to bathe the whole family at once. The bathhouse at Chesters must have needed an ocean of water to wash those five hundred Asturians. And as for heating the stuff, they must have had a regiment of stokers to keep the fires going. They must have thought it was worth it.

They must have thought a sumptuous bathhouse was worth it just for a cohort of auxiliaries in a far flung provincial border. They must have thought that such a large fort was worth it, that the whole Wall was worth it, that coming to Britain was worth it. They could easily have stayed at home. As I lay in the bath, I began to ponder one of the questions that has bothered Wall walkers through the centuries: what was in it for the Romans?

In the first place, there was a strong element of prestige in conquering Britain, another triumph for the Emperor, a public relations gesture to keep the critics quiet and the citizens happy. Most Emperors were very keen on a good public show. Claudius brought elephants with him to Britain in AD 43, which must have entailed some awkward transport problems. He was determined to conquer in style, though no doubt they were a pretty frightening sight to the ancient Britons. Julius Caesar on his campaigns, even when he was living under canvas, took tessellated and mosaic floors with him which had to be laid out every night. This bit of gossip went round the Empire and everyone oohed and aahed at such conspicuous elegance. It certainly impressed local barbarian chiefs when they were taken to his tent.

In some ways, conquering didn't need to be impressive. As long as it could be afforded, it almost went without saying, without needing to be justified. Since Augustus, the Romans had pursued a philosophy of world rule. It was accepted that civilising the known world was a duty as much as agrandisement.

Strategically there was much to be said for taking over Britain. Although Roman soldiers had originally been worried about leaving the known world, Roman geographers and politicians knew all about Britain. They knew that troublemakers in Gaul were finding refuge in Britain. There might come a time when Britain became positively anti-Roman, a large off-shore island threatening the stability of their mainland provinces. Conquering Britain might be a way of ensuring peace on the Continent. Britain was a natural progression from Gaul. On the face of it, controlling Britain would be a lot cheaper than creating an Atlantic frontier.

It's hard to say how the Romans costed the job in advance, either in military forces or in the revenues they might receive. Strabo, the first-century geographer, lists the primary products available in Britain – corn, cattle, gold, silver, iron, hides, slaves and 'clever hunting dogs'. He doesn't mention tin. In earlier centuries tin had been exported from Britain in large quantities but by the time Claudius came to conquer, the Romans had found an easier supply in Spain. On the whole, Strabo didn't think much of Britain economically. His opinion was that the taxes would hardly pay for the sort of garrison that would be necessary, such as one legion and a few cavalry regiments.

Despite Strabo, there seems to have been a gold rush feeling about Britain before the conquest. Tales of gold and silver and fine slaves had grown out of all proportion. It wasn't only prestige and strategy which brought the Romans. Until they landed, they were convinced it was Eldorado.

The reality doesn't seem to have changed their minds. Perhaps once they became committed it was too late. For a start, Britain turned out to be enormously expensive to conquer and then to control. Claudius arrived with four legions and a great deal of auxiliaries, a total of around forty thousand soldiers. For the next three hundred and fifty years there were three legions stationed permanently in Britain. No other province had more. Spain, for example, had a garrison of only one legion after its conquest, yet that conquest had been much more difficult than Britain and had taken almost two hundred years. The scale and proportion of the military investment in Britain as a whole helps to illuminate, if not explain, the scale of Hadrian's Wall. They'd put so much into Britain already that the frontier just had to be a good one.

All the same, a permanent Wall garrison of fifteen thousand still takes some explaining. Roman policy was always to make the army as self-supporting as possible. How did those fifteen thousand soldiers on the Wall manage to raise enough taxes, corn and other supplies to keep itself going? Until the Romans came, the Wall line was virtually unpopulated. It can only be assumed that England as a whole helped to support the Wall, directly or indirectly, in taxes and other levies. The Romans did well for troops out of Britain. We've seen already that the Wall's garrison came from every corner of the Empire. In its turn, Britain was the source for eighteen auxiliary regiments which were sent overseas.

The south of England did grow prosperous under the Romans, especially in the third century when there was almost a century of continuous peace – a rare event in the history of this island. Large villas were established, imperial and private estates produced and exported goods throughout the empire. Lead became the most important of the many minerals. Spinning and weaving was developed and British warms became very popular in Italy. A British tossia or plaid was considered a very smart gift. Corn was exported to Germany. British oysters went all over the Empire. British hunting dogs were considered the best. Jewels, salt, leather, seal skins were exported in great numbers. There's even evidence of bears being exported from Britain for use in the Roman arenas.

On the Wall, Corbridge was a supply centre and contained many factories. Carlisle's factories must have been even bigger, to support a larger military population, but little evidence has been found. Coal was worked in Northumberland and lead in Cumberland. So far, there has been little sign of large-scale farming or villa life around the Wall. The Wall continued to be very much what it had always been – a military zone with its village and civil population dependent on the army. The Romans were in this region for purely military reasons.

They had to have a Wall in the first place because they hadn't managed to conquer the whole island. So in one sense the Wall was a sign of failure. But from a military point of view, it was a success. Thanks to the Wall's strength, the three legions were able to withdraw to their headquarters further south, leaving the auxiliaries in charge, which made it therefore much cheaper to run. The legions could then get on with building towns and roads and generally bringing urban civilisation to the south. England prospered under the shelter of the Wall. Hurrah for the Wall!

I was beginning to feel exhausted, despite the recuperative powers of the bath. It can be rather tiring, going round in circles, thinking about the Romans. I got dressed and went downstairs to have a drink. I met the manager, a Mr White, who turned out to be the tenant. From the furnishings I'd presumed he was the owner. It was a tied house, which isn't usually the sign for much individuality, but he'd taken it over empty and had put in all his own furniture and ornaments. His menu looked good, prepared by two Portuguese chefs. His hotel is full most of the year, which I could understand, mostly people coming to visit the Wall country. He told me about some Italian writers who'd recently come to look for *Italian* influence in the Wall country, things like a way of ploughing which was more Mediterranean than English, people who looked Italian rather than Anglo-Saxon, just any little thing to show that the Romans had been here in such force for so many centuries. Naturally, they found nothing. As Roman baths didn't even continue after they'd gone, what chance had Roman ploughing habits. I'd been in Rumania the previous year and had been surprised to find that Rumanian is a Romance language, yet it's surrounded by Slavonic speaking countries, an isolated left-over from the Roman Empire. In the north of England, all that's left is the Wall.

After, my bath, the taxi arrived to take me to Langley Castle. The driver, Mr Batey of Hexham, spends most of his summer taking people up and down the Wall, especially Americans. He has regulars who come back year after year and send him Christmas cards. Three years ago an American honeymoon couple hired him for one day and kept him on full time for three weeks, paying for him to stay at every hotel. 'They were very good in the evenings. They never bothered me.' Mr Batey has nine cars, three hearses and two buses, so he told me, and will take anyone anywhere, but he doesn't like London. Like everyone who's never lived in London, he was full of stories about Londoners not knowing their own neighbours. It's funny to go back north and hear all the Northern inferiority complexes coming out. They protest just too much about their dislike of London and the soft sheltered life that Southerners lead.

The advertisement in the *Newcastle Journal* had said that Langley Castle was a genuine fourteenth-century castle and invited all to partake of 'ye feasting and ye merrymaking', all at £3.50 a head. I'd heard about these medieval banqueting castles which were springing up all over the North East, a strange regional growth industry.

Langley Castle is about five miles west of Hexham, right in the heart of the Wall country, so I thought it merited a visit, even if it turned out to be not exactly typical of Wall life today.

From the outside the castle looked very impressive, all lit-up and towering above the countryside. Inside, the walls were four feet thick, the panelling seemed genuine and some suits of armour in the entrance gave a metallic chink when I tapped them. I suppose I half-expected the castle would be mock medieval. I opened the door into the bar and the air of excitement almost knocked me over. There were about a hundred people already inside, most of whom seemed to be middle aged women, all in their best long dresses, their hair piled high, their jewellery flashing and their eyes aglow. More people were arriving all the time till there were about two hundred in all, most of them in large parties, all of them determined to enjoy themselves.

At eight o'clock, three gaily dressed flunkeys trooped in, to a gaggle of oohs and aahs, a trumpet was blown and a herald announced it was the feast of St Ursula, the patron saint of virgins (giggle giggle). Tonight's banquet was in her honour. He read out a list of the party leaders and each group marched out, self-conscious but very chuffed, except for those who wanted to go to the Knights' room or the Damsels'. On the half-landing was another suit of armour, this time made of plastic with someone inside who was goosing women and shoving plastic gold coins into hot surprised hands.

The baronial hall looked terrific, with the long tables sumptuously laid, the pewter plates glistening, armour gleaming on the walls, the candles glowing and the thirty serving wenches, all in medieval costume with low cut blouses and tightened waists, lined up and eagerly smiling a welcome. In one corner was a group of minstrels, playing away on electric harpsichords and violins, making a noise not unlike muzak. The audience almost burst into a round of applause at the very sight of it.

When we all got sat down, a herald told us that we were to be lords and ladies for the night and that very soon, our King would appear. He wanted us to give a big cheer for His Majesty when he appeared. Everyone held their breath. More trumpets sounded. The lights dimmed and in minced a short, dapper figure with blond hair, pouting and muttering 'Oh you are awful.' He tripped gaily round the tables, giving little waves. His very appearance brought the house down. The Jester shouted 'Get you'. In the half silence that followed I heard someone distinctly mutter, 'Haven't I seen him at Pontins?' Both the King and the Jester *had* worked at Pontins in a previous incarnation when they'd been known as Paul and Danny. The King said Pontins had been lovely, 'cept that they wouldn't let him do drag acts.

The King climbed on to his throne on a raised dais and, hand on hip, commanded everyone to say hello to the person on their left. If it was a woman, or even better, a man, give her a kiss. He said the tumbler in front of each person was full of mead. It was said to be aphrodisiac. If you drank it quickly it could give you a stiff ... neck (giggle giggle). He went round different tables, asking which part of his kingdom each party was from. 'Corbridge,' said the party next to me. They numbered forty-five altogether, all women from a keep fit class.

The menu was very long and impressive and each of the eight courses was announced with great ceremony and trumpet blowing. In between each course, and sometimes during, either the King or the Jester told jokes, sang songs, getting the lords and ladies to join in. Some of the wenches came up to the microphone to do a turn. One of the most successful songs was 'Blue is the Colour', that well-known medieval plain-song. For this the audience was divided in two and each side tried to sing it louder than the other. 'Lilly the Pink' was also very popular. A photographer, in full medieval clothes, went round taking photographs of the revellers, giving them an order form and his price list.

The King said he'd been in France recently and been 'grabbed by the Gauls'. The Jester told the story about the girl who asks a Scotsman if it's true that there's nothing worn under the kilt. 'Lassy, there's nothing worn under my kilt. It's all in good condition.'

Despite the phoney medieval names which each course was given, I enjoyed every dish. Soup was first, described as Royal Bruse. Langley Mamery, the second course, turned out to be a terrific pâté, home made and very rich. Imperial Fyshe was coquille St Jacques. Chanticleer was half a chicken. Then there were ribs of lamb, oranges stuffed with an icecream sorbet, cheese. The eighth course was billed as 'Crusaders' Ethiopian Elixyr' which turned out to be coffee, but excellent all the same. For £3.50 you'd be hard pressed to find an eight-course meal anywhere, apart from having all the professional comedians and musicians thrown in.

The mead, which was sweet and tasted like strong Ribena, was the aperitif. After that, beer and wine flowed freely throughout, as much as anyone could drink, and very soon several lords and ladies were trying to creep out quietly to the lavatory. The King, hooting over the microphone, stopped the first ones, asking them where they were going. 'Ladies, you must bow to my throne and say "Prithee, can I use your privee."

And gentlemen, what you must say is "Sire, may I slash on your stone".'

Audience participation, or audience humiliation, depending on which way you look at it, reached its height when several guests were dragged from their seats and locked in a set of stocks at the side of the hall. There were screams of laughter and howls of delight from everyone else. Apparently each party leader had been asked beforehand which of their members would be game enough to take part in such high jinks, without either having a heart attack or starting a real fight – but the persons concerned hadn't been warned. Every reveller was given polystyrene balls by the serving wenches and encouraged to throw them at the people in the stocks. This was the first night that polystyrene balls had been used. Up to now, they'd given out cotton wool balls which the smart alecks had dipped in their drink and turned into sodden and rather lethal ammunition. However, a few guests soon moved on from the harmless polystyrene balls to throwing bread rolls and chicken legs. Before too many glasses were broken, the King smartly moved on to the next diversion. This was a huge bear which went round tickling the women in embarrassing places. After that the audience was taught the words 'Oh Sir Jasper do not touch me'.

Each item brought roars of applause and genuine cries for encores. The meal and the entertainment went on for almost four hours, by which time my ears were numb and my throat sore. I'd come to scoff but I'd been carried along with all the activities and obvious enjoyment of everyone present. The King and the Jester hadn't wasted their years at Pontins. They had the audience eating out of their hands the whole evening.

Not since standing in the Park Lane end at Tottenham have I seen an audience so carried away. At times it was almost obscene, as very respectable looking middle-aged women stood on the tables and literally screamed, yelling on their side in the singing competitions, shouting back responses at the King or the Jester, or holding themselves in agony, convulsed with laughter at yet another saucy joke. None of the jokes were actually blue, just a bit rude. As for all the gay jokes and camping it up by the King (or the Queen as the Jester kept on calling him), that was no different from any TV variety show. They were still high on their own excitement when they trailed back into the bar for a last drink. The King and Jester looked exhausted.

In the bar I met one of the directors, Duncan McLellan, formerly an executive with the Newcastle and Scottish Breweries. He'd been to the other medieval banqueting castles in the North East, at Lumley near Chester le Street and Seaton Delaval, as well as others in Edinburgh, Manchester, Wales and Eire. He'd liked them all but considered that the other ones in the North East were a bit sedate. 'They have excellent and authentic medieval music, madrigals and such like, which go on throughout the meals and are very beautiful. But personally I think they're too formalised. I think people like a bit more participation. When an old time squire gave a party, it was an orgy. People let themselves go. I wanted this place to be bawdy, not stylised.'

They've spent over £160,000 on making the physical style as authentic as possible, getting real pewter plates and the right ornaments, as well as twentieth-century style such as thick pile carpets and central heating.

They'd opened six months previously and had had full houses ever since. Two hundred people for every banquet, six nights a week, every week of the year. At that moment, they had twenty-two thousand advance bookings. They have to turn bookings away now, unless people are prepared to wait six months. Just think of a normal restaurant telling you to wait that long. They've also had lots of offers from backers, wanting to put money into the project, but they've been turned away as well.

You'd think with three medieval castles putting on banquets in the same catchment area there wouldn't be enough customers to go round, but each North Eastern castle reports huge waiting lists. Most of the people I talked to at Langley Castle had tried unsuccessfully to book the others and had come to Langley instead.

'It's different,' says Mr McLellan. 'That's the secret. You must admit that every hotel lounge looks very much like any other hotel lounge, but this is special. It's a genuine castle. People are encouraged to potter around and explore.

'We did think of having medieval music, but it's not very sing-along is it. And as for medieval food, it looks good written down, like pheasant or venison, but people would go Ugh if it was put before them and we'd have sixty per cent sent back.'

I went round some of the revellers in the bar and they all said it was even better than they'd expected. They were definitely going to book up again. They came from as far afield as Carlisle and Dumfries, Leeds and Scarborough. Only one little group, a quartet of local gentry from Hexham, said they thought it was a bit rowdy. They stood to one side, a bit superciliously, but three of them said they were booking up again, despite the noise.

Tommy Bates, whose family have owned Langley Castle for the last hundred years, is one of the three directors. Having an empty fourteenth-century castle was a bit of a problem, till Mr McLellan came along and suggested the banquets.

'I was hoping that one day a Texan millionaire would go past and say I must just have that dinky castle, and take it from me for a million dollars. It's not uncommon in Northumberland to be burdened with a medieval castle.'

Now, he's obviously delighted by its success and turning away offers of further financial help as people realise that history can be a good investment, if used properly.

'The secret is encouraging people to have a good time,' said Mr McLellan. 'We want them to have a bawdy evening. How many English hotels encourage you to do that?'

Perhaps those Italian journalists, if they'd been looking for true heirs to Roman orgies or bathhouse high jinks, should have visited Langley Castle.

7
Carrawburgh:
A Night with Mr Bates

There was a thin drizzle and Black Carts was absolutely deserted. For about half an hour I climbed over and round a brand new stretch of the Wall, about a hundred yards of it, brand new in the sense that it had obviously just been uncovered, so new that I could see the whites of the tree trunks where they'd had to cut away the undergrowth to get at the facing stone. I felt very excited, as if I'd made the discovery myself, as if no one else but me had seen this stretch for centuries. On top of the new hard core I found an empty Tom Thumb cigar tin, thrown away the previous day by a Department workman. Next time they came it would be buried and delight some archaeologist around the year 3000 AD.

The drizzle suddenly turned to hailstones and I made a dash for a hut I'd noticed beside the site. I banged open the door with a crash, surprised that it wasn't locked. Inside were four workmen, all asleep. I'd been convinced I was the only person on the site, in fact the only person for miles around. I was more amazed than they were.

Taking the scene in slowly, I realised only one had been definitely asleep, a young one curled up on a bench. Another had his head in his arms and was slumped at a little table, that morning's copy of the *Sun* spread out in front of him. A third had been sitting upright, arms folded, eyes closed. But the fourth had been far from asleep. He was deep in a massive ornithological volume, *The Birds of Scotland*.

The young one slowly uncurled himself, yawned and stretched. The other two looked a bit guilty. The ornithologist looked coldly impassive, annoyed by my interruption. I apologised for barging in. I felt like the West Wind in that children's story, who arrived mysteriously under the door. I burbled on about walking the Wall for a book, throwing off names of Department of the Environment people I'd spoken to, trying to justify my existence and prove I wasn't a spy from head office. They didn't reply.

'Seen any good birds on the Wall recently,' I said to the ornithologist, trying to make conversation. The young one tittered. I hadn't meant to be facetious.

'No,' said the ornithologist. 'Have you?'

'No, no, I haven't,' I said hurriedly. 'Having that book, I thought perhaps you'd be well up on what you see at this time of the year . . .'

'Seagulls,' he said, blankly. I could sense he was being sarcastic.

I said what a good job they were making, how this was the best bit of the Wall I'd seen, much better than most, especially that awful bit at Denton. From a previous workman, I knew they'd like me to criticise Denton, as it wasn't their responsibility.

'I spent many a day at Denton before the war,' said the oldest workman. 'Sweeping up the tram tickets on the site. It was scruffy even in those days.'

In a corner I could see a little calor gas stove, a kettle, a toasting pan, some bread, all beautifully neat and tidy. I felt terribly hungry. It was a particularly attractive hut, almost a caravan. I wondered if the ornithologist kept it clean.

'Don't you think it would be a good idea to build up a new bit of the Wall, perhaps on this site,' I said eagerly. 'Just to let people see what it really looked like. Perhaps a turret, or even a fort?'

There was silence. It obviously wasn't a topic which occupied their minds.

'No,' said the ornithologist. 'If you built a new fort on the site of an old one you'd ruin the foundations for ever. If you moved the fort somewhere else, then it would be false. A fake.'

The others waited to see how I'd reply to this. I was getting nowhere. Any chance of being invited for a cup of tea was disappearing fast. I turned to the old man and asked him if he'd ever found any coins.

'Yesterday we found a bit of glass, that's about all.'

'No coins?' I asked.

'You wouldn't find coins in the Wall,' said the ornithologist. 'People didn't throw their money into a Wall, any more than they would do today. You find coins where there's been habitation.'

I asked how much more they had to do. The old man said they were now working on the Scotch side. The English side has been uncovered for quite a bit. The others smiled. I asked what the joke was. They exchanged looks.

'It's what we say in our gang,' said the old man. 'We call one side the Scotch side, the other the English. Just our joke . . .'

The ornithologist looked at him, as if he'd let out a secret, or even worse, a titbit which I might pounce on. The young workman was lying down again, his eyes open, watching me. They were all waiting. I knew I had to go. I'd ruined everything. The ornithologist obviously had strong ideas about the Wall, but I'd never prise them from him now. I said thank you very much. Sorry I barged in. Cheerio.

I marched on quickly without turning back and in about ten minutes I came to Limestone Corner. This is a sharp left turn in the Military Road, a dangerous bend for traffic and even more dangerous if you're standing at the roadside, map in hand, trying to work it all out. This bend was for almost three hundred years the northernmost point of the Roman Empire. It's an area of the Wall which has kept archaeologists in speculation for a long time. I must confess my main reaction was confusion.

On the left is the Vallum. It's right beside the road, an amazing deep gorge, cut out of sheer whinstone, overgrown with ferns and bracken. I stepped into it and it was like another world, eery and mysterious, a place where strange flowers start creeping out in the Spring. The rock walls have been cut sheer and smooth. The Roman engineers had no dynamite but worked with iron wedges, driving them into any faults. Sometimes they used wooden wedges, soaking them to make the expansion break the rock, hoisting it all out with pulleys.

It's at this spot that the Ordnance Survey proudly proclaims in black letters, 'Ditch unfinished owing to hardness of rock.' I had some trouble finding the ditch. I couldn't see it from the road but had to clamber into the field on the right. I eventually found some big rocks, still lying in the ditch, one large with a number of holes in its top surface, holes which the Romans had drilled, ready to put in the wedges. They had started but given up. Why?

If the rocks had been too hard, as the Ordnance Survey map says, they couldn't have cut the Vallum, only a few yards away. It might have been the end of the season. The Romans built the Wall and its structures in the good weather months, packing up for the bad winter months. Until very recently, most people in Northumberland did the same. That taxi driver, Mr Batey, had been telling me that when he was a lad, at the beginning of every winter his mother got in a sack of flour, a sack of potatoes, and that was their food till Spring.

Perhaps a new gang took over the ditch in the next season, starting again further on, refusing to finish off the previous gang's botched job. Perhaps this was the last bit of the ditch to be dug when the plans were changed. It's a guessing competition anyone can enter.

Despite the romance of it being the Romans' Land's End and all that, I found the area rather depressing. There is a feeling admittedly of being on top of the world, but a rather flat, boring bit of the world, with not much vegetation. Ahead, it looked terrific. I could see wonderful tree-covered ridges running across the skyline, with further hills in the distance. I knew that once I got to those proud ridges, I would be rid of this beastly road for ever.

My next stop, just another mile ahead, was a fort I'd been looking forward to, Brocolitia or Carrawburgh. This was the fort where John Gillam found that famous temple of Mithras, the peak in a lifetime of studying Roman Britain. This was the fort where John Clayton opened up Coventina's Well in 1876 and discovered one of the most remarkable hoards in all Roman Britain. The well's existence had been known for several centuries. The Rev Horsley in 1732 had written an account of it but said he couldn't give the exact depth 'because it was almost filled up with rubbish'. Over 140 years later, Clayton decided to have a look inside and found 13,487 Roman coins (four gold, 184 silver and the rest bronze), carved stones, altars, jars, pearls, brooches, incense burners and other objects. It is thought that someone in a panic had thrown the altars away. The coins on the other hand had been offerings, thrown into the well to bring good luck. Coventina, after whom the well is always known, was a local water goddess. A lot of the treasures are now on show back at the Chesters Museum. There would have been even more but during the weekend in which Clayton found the hoard there was a raid on the site and many coins were stolen.

Over three hundred of the coins which Clayton managed to secure were from the reign of Antoninus Pius, the Emperor who succeeded Hadrian – the one who built the Antonine Wall in Scotland. These commemorate a pacification of the north after disturbances in 155 and show a very dejected-looking figure of Britannia, her head bowed, her banner lowered, her shield cast aside. It contrasts with the proud figure of Britannia used on coins under Hadrian – he had her sitting up armed and erect on what looks like a bit of stone, probably signifying Hadrian's Wall. Like Roman inscriptions, coins served many purposes, such as publicity. When Emperors start boasting about achieving concord on their coins, it's a sure sign there's been trouble. When they go on about the Health and Glory of the Empire the decline is probably setting in. Usurpers particularly tried to further their own causes on their coins, boasting of their conquests and laying their claims to be the real Emperor or Governor or whatever. Britannia rampant or recumbent, therefore, indicated what had been happening around that period.

On today's 50p piece, Britannia is still there, complete with Roman helmet, her shield beside her at the ready and her trident spear in one hand. It's nice to think in this day of Womens' Lib that for almost two thousand years the symbol of Britain has been a woman – and a fighting one at that.

Today at Carrawburgh (pronounced Carrawbruff) there are no coins to be seen nor any trace of the well in which the coins were found. There's a huge car park beside the site of the fort, which leads you to believe there must be something worth parking for, and a very pompous notice put up by some private landowner warning you to keep dogs on a lead. There is no need for cars or pomposity. The fort is simply a bumpy, grass-covered field. There are no Roman remains.

However, if you go through the field and follow a path you come to a hollow and the site of the Mithraic Temple. The foundations have been excavated and are neatly laid out and cared for, if a bit bare and sunken. The altar stones are fakes, copies of the originals now on show at Newcastle. Personally, I found the suburban temple at Benwell, the one surrounded by all the semis, more interesting and certainly more amusing, but archaeologically this temple is of extreme importance.

There's a very learned paper by Professor Eric Birley in which he deduces almost complete life stories from the names of the three prefects who put up the Carrawburgh altars. A Roman citizen normally had six elements in his name. Amongst other things, they indicate the benefactor through whom the family originally received citizenships, the Emperor of the time, father's tribe, town of origin. There are also fashions in names which can be dated and placed. Omissions from names, forms of abbreviations, can provide other clues. This name analysis by Birley is only one part of a whole load of information which the temple has provided. It's all in the academic books and papers for those interested. Unless you're on a car-parking tour of Northumberland, there's no real reason to stop.

I didn't stop for long. Just two miles after Carrawburgh the line of the Wall at long last leaves the Military Road, one of the nicest moments for anyone walking the Wall. I couldn't wait to get there. Old Hutton describes how he 'quit this beautiful road and the beautiful scenes of cultivation and enter upon the ride of Nature and the wreck of Antiquity.' The road from Newcastle might have been beautiful in his day but it certainly isn't now, not for walking along. But Nature was definitely in sight.

I could see the crags and tree-covered ridges of the Whin Sill stretching invitingly ahead, flowing up and down, a magnificent ship sailing onwards into the distance. I knew that on this ridge was the Wall itself, in its greatest glories, just waiting for me. I left the rotten old road, too scared to climb the crags, to go its own nasty way, for ever I hoped, till it disappeared up its own exhaust and choked on its own fumes.

I was so carried away with the turf beneath my feet instead of tarmacadam, that I stumbled into turret 33B, an exquisitely excavated turret, before I realised where I was. On the map, it's in red, meaning you can't see anything. I dug out my notebook and yes, turret 33B was Roger Miket's turret, the one he'd helped to excavate, so he'd boasted to me those months ago in Newcastle. I smiled at the thought of him. To celebrate, I sat down and had a bar of Kit Kat. When I started again, my pack felt that much lighter.

I was climbing hills all the time, gazing round in wonder, making out the dark grey glints of water to the right. I was now in an area where with confidence I could imagine the Romans looking round at similar views. Nature stretched in every direction. Only the Wall was man-made. But even it looked natural, as it started to appear in bits and pieces, green and grassy on the top.

On the crest of the hill I turned left and followed the Wall into a farm. It looked a rather grim setting. Old Hutton thought the same in 1801. He was well received by the farmer, who took him to see some ruins, but he described the farm as being 'dreary' and the land 'better adapted to the teeth than the plough'. He thought the whole area of Sewingshields crags much the same. 'A more dreary country than this in which I now am can scarcely be conceived. I do not wonder it shocked Camden. The country itself would fright him, without the Troopers.'

The next few miles of the Wall, climbing up and down the crags of Sewingshield towards Housesteads, contains many excellent stretches which can be seen and walked – you can get up on top of the Wall and actually walk along it. I don't know why Hutton thought it was dreary, though the area is dramatic, not to say frightening. You look from the top of the Wall, perched on the crest of the crags, down a sheer two-hundred-foot drop on the northern face.

By Troopers Hutton was referring to the Moss troopers, one of the many gangs of Border raiders who hid out in this area, terrorising the inhabitants for many miles around, scaring travellers like Camden.

It's not just an area rich in rugged natural beauty, it's rich in stories, factual and legendary. Perhaps they go together. Dramatic scenery inspires dramatic stories. One of the strongest concerns King Arthur. Despite what they say in the south, Northumberland lays great claim to have been the true home of Camelot and the Knights. Every writer on this part of the Wall recounts the Arthur stories and I always make a point of skipping them. My interest quotient on legends is, alas, rather low, though some of the local ones are quite funny in their awfulness. There's one about Guinevere who's sitting combing her hair when she says something to annoy King Arthur. He picks up a huge rock and chucks it at her. She's three-quarters of a mile away at the time, and the rock weighs all of twenty tons, but when you're Arthur, you can do anything. Clever old Queen catches the rock with her comb and it lands at her feet. There it is to this day, so local legends say. And sure enough, down below the crags, there's a giant twenty-ton rock.

There are other Arthur stories equally daft, though some more chivalrous. Hutton was filled with his share. The farmer at Sewingshields took him to see what he was told was 'King Ethel's chair', a pinnacle of rock shaped like a seat. Hutton says that Ethel was an abridgement of either Ethelred, Ethelfrid or Ethelrick, all Saxon Kings of Northumberland. Later experts have said that Hutton might have misheard – for Ethel read Arthur.

Sit Walter Scott helped with other legends of these crags by using Sewingshields Castle (an ancient castle, now gone, which stood at the foot of the crags) as a setting in his *Harold the Dauntless*.

As I walked along the top of the Wall from the Knag Burn to Housesteads fort, I could see a little group of figures, huddling from the rain in the middle of the fort. They were the first people I'd seen all day, since those workmen in their hut. One of them was holding a large umbrella while the others crowded round him. I drew nearer, watched a gust of wind catch the umbrella and turn it inside out. As they scrambled to retrieve the umbrella I saw that they'd been huddling round a TV camera, trying to protect it from the rain. They were from Blue Peter, the BBC children's programme. Valerie Singleton, the interviewer, was huddling inside a large sheepskin coat. When the rain slackened slightly they got the camera lens dried and took up their positions again. Valerie was speaking her words to the camera, all about what the soldiers must have thought, being sent from Spain to serve on the Wall in this sort of weather.

She went through her words several times, as the wind howled and the clouds rushed across the sky. It wasn't yet two o'clock but they had a lighting man, valiantly shining his lamp on Valerie's face. They were all shivering and looked very miserable. Valerie kept on changing the last few words of her stuff, but told the director not to worry, she would dub it on later as commentary. Suddenly the cameraman slipped on the greasy surface and both he and his camera went slithering down a muddy slope. There are many ways of announcing a Wrap, as they say in the business, meaning an end to the day's shooting, but that was about the most dramatic.

The director said everyone could adjourn to the fort museum

for lunch. I said hello to the sound man, whom I recognised by chance from some BBC programme I once worked on, then I stood around trying to look hungry. Miss Singleton graciously invited me to join in their humble BBC repast. It wasn't at all humble – the PA (producer's assistant) produced hot soup out of large thermos containers, coffee, chicken, rolls, sandwiches and biscuits. The sugar cubes were the familiar green wrapped BBC ones, used in all their canteens. I felt overcome with nostalgia, as if I'd been ten years in the Arctic and just been rescued.

I asked Miss Singleton if they were going to do Chesters bath houses, saying that kids would love it, but she hadn't heard of it. I said what about Vindolanda. I hadn't reached there yet but I knew that was where all the digging was going on these days. She hadn't heard of that either. She'd just arrived from London, been given the script which had been written and researched by someone else, and had been instructed to read it to the camera. This was one of the reasons she was looking forward to leaving Blue Peter. Not that she didn't like it, but after ten years she was planning to move on to new things, perhaps taking part more in the creation of programmes.

The director, Harry Cowdy, and cameraman eventually reappeared to say the camera still wasn't working, so that was definitely a Wrap for today. It was getting darker. With sitting inside for an hour in wet clothes I was feeling cold and shivery. I had intended to make for Vindolanda that day, but it was now too late and I didn't feel up to it. I hitched a lift with Miss Singleton in a BBC car to Haydon Bridge. They were going on to their hotel at Hexham. I told them if they had the evening free, they should go to the medieval banquet at Langley Castle. They'd find nothing like that in London. (They did – and agreed they'd seen nothing like it anywhere.) As she left, Miss Singleton pressed a Blue Peter lapel badge into my hand, to give to my kids, and drove off. I'd brought many presents home so far from my Wall trips, like postcards and reproductions and other bits of Roman memorabilia, but a plastic Blue Peter badge, that would really surprise them.

I stood around Haydon Bridge in the rain for some time,

trying to get a taxi. I found it a depressing little town, not a
patch on Hexham, in looks or in life. All the taxi drivers were
out ferrying school kids home. I chatted to an old man who
asked me if I knew how the Romans managed to build the Wall
so straight. I said no, tell me how the Romans managed to build
their wall so straight. Smoke fires, he said. They lined up the
two columns of smoke, then marked out the route. He said this
information had never been written down. A very old man had
told it to him. I said how fascinating. It just showed how
history could be passed down verbally from generation to
generation. Where had the old man come from – Haydon
Bridge or Hexham? 'He was an American. Came over here on a
package tour. The Americans know more about the Wall than
we do . . .'

I got a taxi to Langley, not to the castle this time but to the
home of Mr and Mrs Tommy Bates, the owners of the castle. I'd
met him at the medieval banquet and he'd kindly invited me to
spend the night at his house. It had been rather a bitty day so
I'd decided to give history a rest and have a look at the locals.
Apart from being a large landowner in the Wall country,
with a three-thousand-acre estate, Mr Bates is a Hexham
councillor.

I hadn't had much success with the gentry so far. My last
encounter had taken place in a cold outer office and had been
conducted standing up. The signs this time looked more
promising. It was a smaller, more homely-looking but affluent
farmhouse. I rang the bell at the Bates' house and a young
American called Karl, who'd met Mrs Bates in Greece the year
before, welcomed me in saying he'd run a bath for me right
away, hot or warm, with Badedas or without.

I was given Annabelle Bates' bedroom for the night, one of
their six children, away at school at the time, where I changed
into clean clothes and came down to find Mr Bates dressed like
a farm labourer, with a dirty old cap and worn tweed jacket.
The previous evening at the banquet he'd looked very dashing
in a velvet jacket and silk cravat. He was holding the latest
Private Eye which had arrived while he'd been in the fields.

Mr Bates' great-uncle was Cadwallader Bates, the noted

nineteenth-century historian. In his *History of Northumberland* he said that part of Hadrian's Wall had been built of turf, a prediction later proved right by the discoveries of Simpson and Richmond. Cadwallader Bates bought and renovated Langley Castle in the 1880s. Since Cadwallader, the family have produced soldiers and sailors rather than historians – Tommy's grandfather was General Sir Loftus Bates.

After Tommy left Oxford, where he read law, his father suggested he should enforce the law rather than learning it so he joined the Metropolitan Police. He was a constable for two years, largely in Downing Street and at Buckingham Palace, when his father died, leaving him the estate. He resigned the force and came straight home to Northumberland. He's now Deputy Commandant of the County Constabulary – a far cry from his Oxford days when he was fined £2 for being drunk and disorderly after a Varsity cricket match.

He admits that the country society he moves in these days is a small and enclosed world. The fact that he's amused by himself liking it, aware of himself playing a part in it, doesn't lessen his enjoyment. He tries to be a good landowner, looking after his tenant farmers, improving the land, trying to carry out his duties to the area at large.

'There are more and more business executives from Tyneside moving into the area, especially ones who've been sent up from the south. Instead of living in the suburbs of Newcastle, they want to have a nice house in the country. But they cannot always become part of a county society. Naturally, we're growing smaller and smaller. It's a very limited circle. You meet the same people at all the same parties and one is greeted the same way, "What have you killed today." But I like it.'

He went to get dressed for dinner, giving me some sherry and an old cuttings book to amuse myself with. The cuttings were mainly from his Oxford days in the early fifties, though they seemed centuries older. The clothes looked positively thirties. I recognised one of his Oxford friends, Anthony Blond, the publisher. They were involved in bringing out an undergraduate magazine, *Harlequin*, which lasted about two issues. There were cuttings about deb parties, balls, engagements of friends, funerals of relations. His summons at Bow Street in July, 1950, and his fine of £2 was pasted in very carefully.

There was a telegram from the BBC, saying they were going to use his question on Round Britain Quiz. His question had a lovely period flavour, so different from today's vulgar TV quizzes: 'In the eighteenth Century if you went from Newcastle to Devonshire and then back to Newcastle, where would you go next?' (Answer: the Isle of Bute. They were a series of Prime Ministers.)

It was interesting to see the cuttings becoming more serious as the years went on, from the jolly undergraduate pranks to long and terribly serious letters, signed T. A. Bates, published in the *Newcastle Journal* and the *Hexham Courant*.

As I was reading, Mrs Bates' brother, Sir Richard Musgrave, joined me for a sherry. He and his wife were staying at the house. The name Musgrave is still very common in Cumberland, as well as appearing in ballads by writers like Sir Walter Scott. He said his family were the original Cumberland Musgrave family, but they'd moved to Ireland in the eighteenth century. He now devoted his time between his house near Dublin and his villa in Greece which he rents out in the season. Like his sister, he has six children. 'The problem is educating them. This villa idea is to make enough money for that purpose. I use my name as much as I can, but it becomes rather hard to be all pompous with my rich American guests when my sister arrives with her hippie friends.'

When Tommy Bates was ready, he drove his wife down to the castle so she could help out in the bar. Mr Bates takes no part in running the castle, being a full-time farmer, but his wife likes to lend a hand. The rest of us were left to get the dinner ready for their return. Three grouse had been laid out, shot on the estate the previous day. Sir Richard and his wife had long arguments about how to do them. He said he wanted his blue while she wanted hers well done.

It was a huge farmhouse kitchen with a solid fuel stove, at least a row of stoves. From the direction of one stove I heard a baby-like whelping. For one minute I thought the grouse weren't just blue but alive and kicking. Underneath I discovered five chihuahua dogs playing in a wooden box. The house seemed to be overrun with dogs.

Over dinner I'd meant to get them going on living in Northumberland, what they liked and didn't like about it, but with both Sir Richard and Tommy having the problem of six children to educate, before I knew what was happening we were arguing about education. Well-behaved house guests shouldn't argue. I suppose in the circles they move, it is rather quaint to hear someone advocating State schools.

However, by the time coffee came round, we were ensconced in front of the telly (watching Spurs play Red Star of Belgrade in the UEFA Cup) and Tommy's wife Lizanne was talking about being a deb. She was turning over the posh cuttings and invitations I'd been looking at earlier, saying they were a facade. She and her mother had come from Dublin for the season and had had to do the whole thing on a shoestring. They took the cheapest flat and when her boy friends sent flowers, they were put in jam jars.

Next morning over breakfast I returned to the problems of the Wall. Tommy was at that time chairman of Haydon Bridge parish council and vice-chairman of Hexham Rural District Council. The Wall is one of their constant concerns. They have about fifteen miles of it running through their area.

'I welcome the trade the Wall brings, but many people don't. They resent all the visitors. The Department of the Environment pays for its upkeep, but there is the problem of servicing the visitors. Who pays, for example, for the loos? Haltwhistle has been arguing with the Department for a long time about putting a loo at Housesteads. It's very expensive because of the problem of water disposal. Our council has put in several rural loos, but they attract vandals.'

Caring for the Military Road is probably the biggest worry. Most plans to widen or improve it lead to opposition, either from the Department or from the preservationists, worried that the Wall underneath will be disturbed. Even when it's a matter of public safety, they still have trouble, such as the new roundabout at the Portgate, or Stagshaw as it's known locally. This is the site of the important Roman crossing.

'We wanted to widen the road and build the roundabout, but

the Department was intransigent. In the old days, we would try and play off the Ministry of Works against the Ministry of Transport and often get some results, but now that they're all one huge Ministry it's very difficult to get round them.

'Something desperately had to be done because of all the accidents. The trouble was the fact that the A68, the north to south road from Scotch Corner up to Edinburgh, had to give way to the B road, the east to west road. Motorists belting up from Scotch Corner, coming to the first intersection for miles, saw it as a B road and presumed they had right of way. The result was a collision of opinion which ended up in Hexham Magistrates Court. No matter how many signs we put up, we couldn't stop the accidents.'

In the end, the Department gave permission, as long as the new roundabout was moved twenty yards further north, leaving the archaeologists to dig up the Wall foundations one day and look for the original Roman gateway. All parties, it would appear, are now satisfied.

'But the next time we have a traffic problem in that area it will start again. I'm afraid the Wall is always going to be one of our greatest headaches.'

After breakfast, he drove me back to Housesteads, calling in first at his own railway station, now a post office, to see if his morning papers had arrived. He bought the station and two miles of railway for about £400 from British Rail when they were closing the line. 'Nobody at the time thought it worth anything, apart from farmers who owned the adjoining land. It was handier for them to have it than anyone else. Now the Ramblers' Association have realised what marvellous walks could be made, right across Britain.'

He stopped the car on the hillside just below Housesteads fort so that we could look back across the South Tyne valley to his estate. He sat for a long time, just looking at it, taking in the view.

I set off in the morning sun across the fields to Housesteads fort, the best known Roman military site in existence, leaving him to go back to do the PAYE forms for his men's wages and get some sheep ready for the sales. Later on there was a council meeting. It was going to be a long day.

8
The Army:
How the Professor Won the War

The Roman Empire was the Roman Army and the Roman Army was the Roman Empire. It's impossible to think of one without the other. The size of the Empire depended on the size and efficiency of the army. The quality of the army decided the quality of the Empire. Yet the Roman Empire wasn't a military state, not in the oppressive, totalitarian sense in which we think of military states today. The Roman Army was so much more than a military force. It was a force for civilisation.

As the first regularly paid, full-time, professional army the world has known, it has been copied ever since. As a fighting force, they were successful for almost five hundred years, give or take a few local difficulties. As victors, they handed out peace, created order and established what they considered civilisation. The Roman Army built roads, bridges, houses, baths, temples and towns; made pottery, clothes and tools; codified the laws, set up courts, acted as policemen. Many of their officers went on to be poets and historians, magistrates and politicians. To be a Roman army officer was a preparation for life.

To understand Roman civilisation you only have to think of what life was like outside the Empire. 'All the Britons dye their bodies with woad,' wrote Caesar in his *De Bello Gallico*, 'which produces a blue colour. They wear their hair long and they shave the whole of their bodies except the head and upper lip. Wives are shared between groups of ten or twelve men, especially between brothers and between fathers and sons.'

This was probably a slight exaggeration. There's evidence that in the south of England there were many pockets of civilisation before the Romans came. And as fighters, the Britons gave the Roman Legions some nasty moments. Boadicea and the Iceni tribe annihilated seventy thousand when they recaptured London from the Roman Army. But the Romans, back in Rome, liked to think smugly that all the Britons were painted blue, long after the army had made England as civilised as any other part of the Empire.

The legions were the heart of the Roman Army. The number varied between twenty-five and thirty, with three being stationed in England. Each legion was around six thousand strong, including officers and non-fighting soldiers like orderlies, clerks, priests, doctors and surveyors. At the top as commanding officer was a legate. He could be relatively young, around his early thirties, and his previous career would have included non-military service, as a magistrate and politician.

The legionary legate was always of senatorial rank, the highest class in Roman life. As a rule, at least in the early centuries, you had to be born into the senatorial class, just as in medieval days you had to be of aristocratic birth to get anywhere, in politics or the army. A similar class system still operates today in Britain – you don't get many secondary modern lads who become Guards officers.

Inside the senatorial class, the Romans managed their own form of meritocracy. The best youths of the senatorial class were picked out very early while the poorer ones retired to the estates. The chosen ones, having come through all the tests, then embarked on a public career which was very strictly marked out for them. A legate would still be hoping for even higher things, such as a provincial Governorship.

Below the legate were six tribunes, one of whom would be of senatorial rank – in other words a legate in the making, doing his bit of military service. The others would be of equestrian rank, the landed gentry rank, still pretty smart, though not quite blue blood. Several of these tribunes would be relatively young, perhaps little more than twenty-one, all hoping for further promotions, perhaps to be commander of a cavalry regiment. Some might already have been commanders of an auxiliary cohort. Service as tribune in a legion was considered to have the higher staus.

It was always possible for a soldier to push his way up, regardless of his birth. You could jump into the senatorial class from the equestrian, if you caught the Governor's eye, or best of all the Emperor's by distinguishing yourself in some way or simply by knowing the right people. Your rise meant that your sons, if they were of the right quality, started off from where you left off. As the centuries went on, many provincials whose forefathers had probably been conscripted native soldiers rose to be top legionary officers. It's not known how many Britons attained high rank – very few, judging by the evidence that has survived, though several became centurions. It's thought that one of the Commanders of the Praetorian Guard of the second century, Macrinius Vindex, was born in Colchester, but there's no positive proof. (The Praetorian Guard, about five thousand strong, were the cream of the cream, and were the Emperor's personal army, stationed in Italy, not in the provinces.)

Under these senior officers came the centurions, the real backbone of the army. There were sixty in every legion and they had enormous power and responsibility, in war and in peace. They carried a vine staff as a swagger stick, the symbol of their office, and were entitled to inflict corporal punishment, which they did. They wore gleaming decorations showing all the battles they'd been in and the service they'd seen.

Most centurions had risen from the ranks, working their way through the many levels of non-commissioned officers. Soldiers could rise above the basic grades relatively quickly, getting some special qualification or position which gave them extra privileges, pay or more time off. It was hard for a centurion to rise much higher, apart from becoming a senior centurion, or at the most, the camp prefect. But he was quite content with the power a centurion had, as it gave him control of the legion's training and discipline. As so many senior officers served for only three- or four-year periods, the centurions were vital to ensure stability.

The centurions were often feared as much as admired, but they held the legion together. There must have been at times some friction between them and the younger, almost amateur officers, who acted as tribunes above them. Tribunes were civilians doing a spell in the army. Centurions were regulars.

Roman life was constructed on military ideals so you could still be outwardly a civilian and yet instilled with all the right qualities. Having youth and movement at the top meant a flow of new ideas as the tribunes tried to establish and improve themselves. The middle ranking old sweats lower down, the centurions, had the job of making it all work. In many ways it's a good system. The creatively energetic part of most people's lives is between twenty-five and thirty-five. Once you start reserving the top jobs as a sort of reward for experience and age, then it can begin to ossify as those in power desperately want to hang on, to keep the status quo. However, experience is necessary in every walk of life. With the Roman Army, it was the centurions who gave it.

Each centurion was responsible for eighty soldiers – not one hundred as one might expect. (Presumably a century originally did contain one hundred men – including clerks and orderlies and such like.) His century of eighty soldiers was divided into ten units of eight men each, a contubernium. The units of eight arose from the sleeping arrangement in a tent which always contained eight men. The tents were made of best quality leather and Roman soldiers talked of sleeping under 'skins' as opposed to under canvas. A tent was known as a 'papilio' meaning butterfly. It was rolled up very tightly to be carried by the mules, and when unfolded looked like a butterfly grub emerging from the chrysalis. Even in a permanent fort, the barracks were divided into eight men dormitories.

Everything about the Roman Army worked to a pattern, a centralised system whereby identical legions built identical forts. You can almost recite the structure of a legion like a multiplication table: eight men equals one contubernium, ten contubernia equals one century, six centuries equals one cohort, ten cohorts equals one legion. (This makes a total of 4,800 fighting *soldiers*, in case you're adding it all up. Including officers, specialists and the one hundred and twenty horsemen which every legion had to act as scouts and messengers, the total number in a legion then rises to six thousand.)

Legionaries, like auxiliaries, signed on for twenty-five years. On retirement, they were given a lump sum and sometimes a bit of land. When an auxiliary retired he automatically became a Roman citizen – which meant that his children could join a legion. Only citizens were allowed in a legion, but in 213 all free men were made Roman citizens which made the legions open to almost everyone living in the boundaries of the Empire, if you were good enough.

Recruits were chosen in the first place for their height, strength and intelligence. Once conscripted, they were put through several months of rigorous square bashing. They had to be able to march twenty Roman miles in five hours in full kit. They ran races, jumped ditches, climbed walls, did weapon training and took part in mock battles. Once they'd passed all the tests, they took the oath as a Roman soldier, committing themselves to twenty-five years service.

Each legionary carried a sword – a short one, two feet long, called a gladius, for cut and thrust fighting – and a long javelin known as a pilum. The pilum was seven feet long and had a pointed iron head on a wooden shaft. In battle they carried a rectangular curved shield which was made of wood, covered with leather and panelled with iron or bronze. These shields could be interlocked together so that soldiers could crouch beneath them and move forward together, either into battle or against the walls of an enemy stronghold – a method of attack known as the testudo or tortoise.

On their heads they wore a helmet made of iron which came down to protect the neck and shoulders. On their bodies they wore a short woollen tunic, just like a gym slip, protected by sections of body armour made of leather and metal. The normal footwear was a heavy sandal. Looking at Roman soldiers on duty, as they're depicted on Roman statues and pottery, they look fierce and efficient but for duty in the northern climates they would have been pretty cold if they'd worn those open sandals with long bare legs. Their British wear wasn't normally depicted but we know for Wall duty the soldiers had long British-made cloaks and boots to cover their sandals.

Every soldier had to play his part in erecting camps and forts. His standard pack contained a saw, a hook, a piece of rope and a straw basket for carrying soil, plus his mess tins. The specialist soldiers, the surveyors, masons and carpenters, did the expert building work but each soldier was meant to act as a sapper, labouring to the skilled men. A soldier must have spent half his life digging ditches.

Even when there was none to be done, the centurions got them out digging practice ditches. The Vallum must have been a way of using up labour, keeping their bodies occupied, as much as anything else. All work, even mock work, was inspected and careless work punished.

The Romans were very fond of full-scale manoeuvres which were conducted as energetically as real battles. 'To the Romans, real battles are simply manoeuvres at which blood is shed,' wrote one observer. When it came to the real thing, very few of their enemies had much chance against such a disciplined, well-trained, well-protected army. Their heavy weapons were marvels of ingenuity. Here again, they were issued with standard manuals with different weapons and different tactics for every possible situation. Their heaviest piece of artillery was an onager or donkey, so called because of its kick. It was a large contraption which had to be wheeled around on an ox cart. Basically, it was a heavy wooden frame upon which was mounted a thick length of rope, or hair or perhaps animal gut. This was twisted by four men, using a series of levers. Sticking out of the rope was a long arm which contained the missile in a sling. When the tension was released, the missile was sent flying at the enemy. It was remarkably accurate and very effective in breaking down walls. Each cohort (i.e. a unit of five hundred men) had one onager but there were many smaller variaitons which could be moved around more easily. A ballista, for example, was a smaller version which fired stones.

The catapult, which was built on the crossbow principle, shot long bolts or darts. Each century had at least one catapult.

The largest artillery weapons were not used very often in the north of England as the native tribes didn't go in for large fortified hill camps the way they did in the south. But the Romans had many other ways of attacking enemy settlements. Under cover of the tortoise, they would dig under the walls or build mounds of soil outside and then climb over. Perhaps the most ingenious was their assault tower, a tall multi-storey mobile tower on wheels, heavily protected, which could be pushed against the walls and then a high drawbridge lowered to let the soldiers cross over.

The legions were the most heavily armoured sections of the Roman Army, which was why in battle they were always protected on the wings by the auxiliary forces – hence ala, meaning wing, the name given to a unit of mounted auxiliary troops.

The structure of the auxiliary troops was similar to the legions, with cohorts, centurions and tribunes. The ordinary auxiliary soldier was less well paid and had less status than his counterpart in a legion and at the top, the senior officers were from the equestrian class rather than senatorial, but discipline and tradition were just as strong.

While the legions had the specialist craftsmen for building the Wall, and specialist heavy artillery troops for laying siege to towns, the auxiliary forces included many specialist fighting units such as the archers from the Eastern provinces, slingers from the Mediterranean, Moorish horsemen.

When the Roman Army was on the march the auxiliary cavalry came first, followed by the auxiliary infantry and their baggage. Then came the legions with their high ranking officers to the fore, plus their baggage. Lesser auxiliary units brought up the rear. There were three types of encampments – a marching camp for overnight stops, a permanent garrison like the forts on the Wall for the auxiliary troops, and the great legionary fortresses such as the one at York. Once again, whether an overnight handful of tents or a massive stone-built legionary fort covering fifty acres, the basic arrangement was the same. A Roman soldier could walk into a fort anywhere in the Empire and know his way around.

When a site had been chosen by the surveyors for a camp, the soldiers got to work building a ditch round it, even for just an overnight stop.

Inside, the commander's tent had pride of place – the praetorium, as it was known. Beside it was the principia, or headquarters tents, with in front of it an open space where the standards were placed. This was the pattern with a group of tents or with any military fort, such as Housesteads.

Housesteads is the best Roman fort to be seen, not just on Hadrian's Wall but in the whole of Europe. Since the eighteenth century it has been the biggest attraction on the Wall – and still is today. It has natural beauty and must count as one of the most photographed sites in the British Isles. The Wall on either side of the fort has appeared in countless glossy guides, picture books and postcards.

Old Hutton knew it as 'the grandest station in the whole line – in some stations the antiquary feeds upon shells, but here upon kernels.' We see much more than Hutton did, thanks to John Clayton who bought the site in 1838 and got his workmen to uncover the fort walls and gateways and some of the interior. Work has gone on at regular intervals ever since – and it's still going on today.

The plan is the archetypal Roman fort plan, rectangular in shape with the corners rounded, like a playing card. Its only unusual feature is that its long axis stands east to west. The normal Wall fort is turned the other way round, with its long axis going north to south, but at Housesteads they chose a site perched on the edge of a ridge which is long and narrow.

It covers just over five acres and in the third and fourth centuries the garrison was the First Cohort of Tungrians, who'd been raised originally in Belgium. A detachment of legionaries were also garrisoned there for some time, as was a unit called a numerus. In later centuries, when the auxiliaries became full Roman citizens, with almost the same status as the legions, it became necessary to create a new type of Roman soldier, the numeri, the latest raw recruits from the provincial border lands.

As you go through the main gateway (the east gate) you can see, just as every Roman soldier could see when he entered a Roman fort, the headquarters building, facing straight ahead, at the end of the via praetoria. If you look carefully in the gateway, you can still see the wheel ruts where the Roman carts entered the fort. The width between them is 4 feet 8½ inches, the same gauge as today's railways. British Rail didn't pinch the measurements from Housesteads – it's the measurement used from the beginning of railways. George Stephenson took his width from the horse drawn coal waggons which in

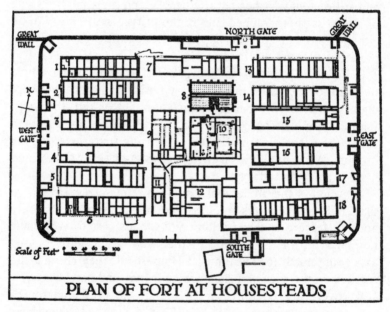

PLAN OF FORT AT HOUSESTEADS

Key:
1 – 3	Barracks	10	Headquarters building
4	Workshop	11	Unidentified building
5 – 6	Barracks	12	Commandant's house
7	Unidentified building	13–14	Barrack-buildings
8	Granaries	15	Mess-room with baths
9	Hospital	16–18	Barrack-buildings

turn came from farm carts. But who decided in the first place how wide a farm cart should be? In the absence of other evidence, it can only be assumed that a cart width is one more thing bequeathed to us by the Romans.

There are four gateways at Housesteads, and each gateway can be clearly seen today. Unlike Chesters, the fort has been revealed as an entity. It's still not completely excavated inside, in fact probably about fifty per cent of it is still grass, but there is a feeling of a living community as you walk round the streets and buildings. It is still of course a series of foundations, like all the Wall buildings today, but in many places the walls are up to ten feet high with only the roof missing.

Perhaps the most interesting interior building is the latrine block, the finest example to be seen in Britain. You've got to use your imagination with the hospital, and just accept the fact that it was a hospital, but with the latrines you can see how it was used. Timber seating covered the deep sewer channels on either side of the central platform and there are basins where the Roman soldiers cleaned their sponges after use. The sewer was flushed by water from the adjoining tanks and the effluent drained down the hillside. Like their baths and central heating system, it's again surprising to think that such refinements should have been lost for centuries.

This was the main latrine and wouldn't have coped with the thousand-man garrison, so presumably the individual barrack blocks had their own toilets, just as the Commanding officer had his. In his private latrine a gold ring was found, trapped in a crack in the sewer. There must have been some pandemonium in his household as family, servants and slaves turned the place upside down to find the missing ring.

The granaries aren't as impressive as the ones at Corbridge but you can see clearly the underfloor ventilation system which was used to keep the garrison's corn supply dry. Dried meat, fish, olive oil, lard and wine were also kept in the granaries. There's a serving doorway where carts unloaded and where each centurion would come and draw out the rations for his men.

The site museum isn't as big as the one at Chesters, nor does it contain as many objects, but it's bright and airy with the exhibits simply laid out. It's built on land presented by Dr G. M. Trevelyan, the historian, who also bought Housesteads farm. The fort itself and the adjoining few miles of the Wall were presented by John Clayton's descendants, to the National Trust. They are the present owners but the site is, once again, cared for and run by the Department of the Environment.

The custodian, Mr Turnbull, was very helpful, though in the height of the summer he would no doubt have had less time to chat. He'd had 145,000 visitors the previous year; like every year, a new record. In the winter months there is only himself and an assistant but in the summer there are five custodians on duty. He lives in a house beside the museum, the only house for miles around. 'We've just had electricity put in this year. I feel much more in touch.'

Of the foreign visitors, the Americans had once again been the most numerous, followed by the French. 'I think the Common Market has brought them in.' Foreigners generally seem more clued up about the Wall's history than the British. Children as well as adults are always saying to him 'That little bit of Wall couldn't have kept the Scots out for long.' He then explains at great length that it's only the *remains* of the Wall. The original was up to five times as high.

Mr Turnbull was originally a foundry worker, working in a factory at Byker, and had no knowledge of the Romans or the Wall till he got the job. He's been mugging it up ever since and is now a fund of information, reading all the latest archaeological reports as he feels it is his duty to keep in touch and be able to answer questions.

He gets highly aggrieved by the popular misconception that being sent to guard the Wall was some sort of punishment. 'Rudyard Kipling helped to spread that story. It's just not true. The auxiliary soldiers were *pleased* to be here. They were just barbarians living in huts, weren't they, before the Romans conscripted them into the army. They get sent over here, get all their food, wages, uniform, all found, well, they're bound to be pleased. It was a good life for them, compared with home. This wasn't the back of beyond either, which is what people think.

There must have been at least forty thousand people living along the Wall. It must have been the most populated part of the North of Britain.

'They didn't have much fighting to do either. After the Severan troubles, there was continuous peace for a hundred years. Tell me a hundred years when Britain wasn't at war somewhere or other?

'They were wonderful people, the Romans. They could do anything. Brain surgeons, everything. I've seen a skull that's been dug up with scalpel marks where the Roman doctor had operated. Wonderful.

'I read every book that comes out, but of course you can't beat Birley. Young Robin is following on in a similar way. He's really put a light under them, the way he's building up Vindolanda. I know some people don't approve, but I'm all for it. On my day off I often go and see how he's getting on. But his father, the Professor, he's my hero. When it comes to Roman Britain, you can't go past Birley.'

It's not just through the fort guidebooks that you meet Professor Birley at every corner; he's been the life force for so many generations of Roman Britain historians. I decided to give him a ring at his home in Hexham and ask if he would see me. He said come right over. Having looked at the greatest military fort in existence it seemed only right and proper to see the greatest expert in existence on the Roman Army.

In 1931 Eric Birley became a lecturer in archaeology at Durham University, a new post created especially for him. He had six pupils in all, five in Newcastle and one in Durham. (Durham University, in those days, consisted of Newcastle and Durham, now they're two separate universities.) In 1971, when he retired, there were a hundred and forty undergraduates at Durham alone taking a course in Roman Britain history and archaeology, plus twenty-four postgraduate students. What on earth do all those undergraduates do with their knowledge of Roman Britain when they get into the big wide world?

'A lot become school teachers and set up local archaeology societies, but there's a lot more jobs for professional archaeologists than you'd think. I've got former pupils all over the country, in museums, universities, government departments, galleries, from Exeter, Cardiff, London, right up to Scotland. My mission to Scotland is proving very successful at the moment. I've heard of lots of promotions.'

Professor Birley is an enthusiast. He'll enthuse to anyone, expert or layman, and will go to great lengths to encourage others in his excitement about Roman Britain. I spent the rest of the day with him at Hexham, though I'd just dropped in for a chat. He has a neat little white washed cottage near the Abbey, tucked in behind the gates of a park.

He first became interested in the Romans when he was at school at Clifton. After he went up to Oxford he managed to meet all the leading archaeologists of the day, getting himself invited to tea with R. G. Collingwood, joining Dr R. M. Wheeler (Sir Mortimer Wheeler) on digs during the vacation in the City of London and helping Simpson up in Northumberland.

After Oxford, he started digging on the Wall on his own, supporting himself from his private funds. It was in 1929 that he did his excavation of turret 7B, the first one to be seen coming out of Newcastle and still one of the best.

One day in 1929 he was working on Milecastle 9 when during the lunch break he heard some people discussing the forthcoming sale of a house near Bardon Mill and a nearby farm of some two hundred and forty acres. On this farm was the site of the Roman fort of Vindolanda, though no excavation had been done. He contacted his father, discussed it with him and got his agreement to sell some shares his father had given him. He bought the farm for £4,000 and the house for £400. As an amateur archaeologist, just starting in the field, he was in the pleasant position of owning his own Roman fort. A year later he was taken on at Durham and became a professional.

His father had been a director of Charles Mackintosh's raincoat firm in Manchester, the company which gave the world the name Macintosh. In 1921 they were taken over by Dunlop and Eric Birley's father received a goodly sum for his shares. It's interesting to note that Eric Birley (raincoats) and F.

G. Simpson (shoes) were helped to become archaeologists by profits made from High Street shoppers.

He taught himself German when he started specialising in the Roman Army because he needed to read what the German scholars in the field had written. In 1939, when war broke out, he was taken into Military Intelligence. On the face of it, a lifetime devoted to archaeology doesn't sound the perfect qualification for fighting a war, even if he could read German. When the war had broken out he'd been working on his own card index system of compiling information about the Roman auxiliary troops. Almost overnight, he was using the same cards for the German Army – piecing together the information from captured German documents and other sources, in the same way that he'd assembled excavated Roman inscriptions. In both cases it's a matter of chance what turns up. What it needs is skill in arranging, analysing and deducing.

When he worked out his answers, or his prognostications as he called them, he contacted his counterparts in French Intelligence. Their estimate of the German Army were wildly different from his, so were the results from another part of British Intelligence, MI 6. He estimated, at the end of March 1940, that the Germans had a hundred and thirty divisions. The French had a figure which was no more than ninety. There were such wild differences that hurried consultations took place. Birley persuaded everyone that his methods and his deductions were the most logical. It was on Birley's estimates that many major decisions were based.

After the war, by which time he'd risen to be a General Staff Officer with the rank of Lt Colonel and was in charge of the Research Division of Military Intelligence, his figures were proved to be correct to within two per cent both in manpower and in the number of divisions. The actual total of German divisions in March 1940 turned out to be a hundred and twenty-eight.

He says the main reason for his success with the German Army was not just his method of assembling information but that his study of the Roman Army had helped him to get into the *minds* of the German Army. 'They were both based on logic, both highly organised, both working on centralised plans. Even the German system of promoting generals was similar to the Romans. When a high general was killed, I had to work out the likely generals who would take his place. I'd studied the stages by which other generals had been promoted, what their experience had been. From that evidence, you can give a fairly good prognostication.'

Perhaps his most vital prognostication was one he was called upon to make for D Day. The date and the place was being fixed, but it had been realised that if the Germans could mass fifty or more divisions to confront the allies, then it all might have to be changed. It was partly on his demonstration that the Germans' fifty divisions in the west in 1940 were of a reduced size, and represented less than the normal fifty divisions of the planners' calculations, that the plans went ahead.

The big thing about researching the German Army, unlike the Romans, was that when it was all over, the *real facts* became known. Every ancient archaeologist works for ever in the dark, never knowing if his theories are right. Col Birley, being head of British Military Research, was called over by the Pentagon when the war was over. In Maryland he was given three hundred tons of captured German documents to analyse, plus forty-nine high ranking German officers which he'd had selected, all kept in a cage. German officers, like officers anywhere, were rather snooty to find he wasn't really an army officer. ' "Are you a regular?" they always asked when I was cross-examining them. They were very surprised when I said I was an ancient historian.'

All the German officers but one were above the rank of captain. The only junior officer was a captain who received a smaller weekly wage than the others. 'As the captain was the odd one out of forty-nine we thought at one time of promoting him. We had all the insignias, forms and legal documents and technically we could have done it.'

The officers, in the event, weren't really such a source of information, not compared with the documents. On interrogation most of them genuinely knew less about the arrangement of the German Army as a whole than Birley did.

It's noticeable how other historians did well during the war. Mortimer Wheeler reached an even higher rank than Birley, becoming a Brigadier. Trevor Roper was one of the stars of MI5. Birley agrees it's interesting but doesn't prove much. One of the best women he had on his staff was in civilian life a flower arranger. No doubt it takes a logical mind to arrange flowers as much as German documents.

The spur to his confidence as an archaeologist was evident when he returned to academic life. He now *knew* that his methods were correct. Unfortunately in his own field there wasn't much left to explain. 'By 1945 most of the major problems of Roman Britain had been solved.' Instead of excavating he turned more and more to discovering talent and encouraging it to go out and excavate. 'A good archaeologist has got to be a good detective. You don't just excavate for the sake of excavating. You must have a reason for digging, some theory or other piece of evidence which points to the dig being fruitful.'

Birley, in his retirement, is still involved in Roman Britain, continually giving lectures and running courses, mainly to adult students. He's chairman of the Vindolanda Trust which his son Robin directs. He sold off most of his Chesterholm property some time ago to pay for the education of his sons.

He tries to revise and update all the books and booklets he's produced over the years about Roman Britain, such as the official guides he's done for Corbridge, Housesteads and Chesters, three sites which in the first place owe a lot to his endeavours. I said how I'd enjoyed his Corbridge guide, even though it recommended the Black Gate Museum, now full of bagpipes. He said that was being corrected.

He first wrote the Corbridge guide back in the 1930s when he was working on the site. He'd been a bit worried about how to catalogue the many Roman tools being dug up, several of which he didn't know the English names for. He went into Corbridge and got a catalogue from the ironmongers. In it he was able to identify many tools he'd never seen before, such as leather working tools, and give them the correct names.

Through his family as well as his students, Professor Birley has been pushing the cause of Roman Britain. His wife was one of his first students of archaeology in Newcastle back in the 1930s. Both his sons are archaeologists. Robin is the one currently digging and organising and hitting the headlines with his excavations at the Vindolanda site, further along the Wall. Anthony is a lecturer at Leeds University and the author of the excellent *Life in Roman Britain*, the best general book on the subject on sale today.

A few archaeologists think the Birleys are just a bit too much, the way they've apparently carved up the subject, becoming the first family of Roman Britain. There are several who would dearly love to disprove some of Eric's old established theories, such as the 197 invasion. Luckily, there are several new archaeologists not out of the Birley stable who are taking over, particularly the whizz kid of them all, Barry Cunliffe. (The plodders in the field are now turning any jealousy on to him.)

At twenty-seven, Cunliffe was made professor at Southampton and he's now Professor of European Archaeology at Oxford. He's a more broadly based archaeologist than Birley, whose main subject has always been the Wall and the Roman Army – a subject in which a new giant has not yet appeared.

Like Cunliffe, Birley has always been an expert and at the same time a brilliant populariser, able to make things clear and simple, yet backing it up with immense research. In a field in which the experts tend to be plodders, plodding on regardless of the public, Roman Britain needs all the populariser and enthusiasts it can get.

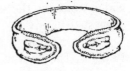

9
Vindolanda:
The Reproduction Business

If Corbridge is the front parlour of Hadrian's Wall, all prim and proper, with everything laid out neatly and clinically, then Vindolanda is the back kitchen. It seemed at first sight to be a chaos of activity, with half-open excavations all over the place, mounds of earth, machinery, huts and most dramatic of all, a life-size hunk of Hadrian's Wall taking shape before my very eyes. I couldn't believe it, though Professor Birley had said I would be surprised. The Wall's measurements are as familiar to him as his own birthdate, yet he'd got a shock when he'd first seen what a fifteen foot high wall really looks like in the flesh.

There was a stone mason working on it, fixing some hand-made wooden scaffolding which had been roped together and erected in the same way as the Romans must have done. For the first time in almost two thousand years, here was a workman building Hadrian's Wall. Once again, I couldn't understand why it had never been done before. All the Department of the Environment will say is that their job is to conserve the Wall as they find it, not to rebuild or recreate it in any way.

The workman, Jimmy Biggs, is a freelance mason, not one of the Department's men. He works for the Vindolanda Trust three days a week. Ten years ago he was a local coal miner till he hurt his back in an accident. He took up dry stone walling to support his family and did some work for Mrs Archibald, owner of the surrounding land. When she gave over the field which contains the site to the Vindolanda Trust in 1970, she suggested Jimmy as a good stone workman.

'The tools I'm using are similar to the tools used by the Romans. They haven't changed over the centuries. There's only one big difference – the cement mixer. But the Romans didn't need one. Their masons had all the labour they needed to mix their mortar for them. I need the mixer as I'm on my own and have to do everything. It was probably *easier* for the Roman masons than for me.'

I walked round the Wall, half of which is in turf and the other half in stone, and found it almost frightening as it towered over me like the hulk of a great ship, marooned by some freak tidal wave. Its size alone must have alarmed any barbarians who ventured near it. I climbed a flight of stone steps to the top and gazed over the parapets at the surrounding site and up the hill towards Housesteads, two miles to the north-east.

In re-creating this stretch of the Wall, building it the way the Romans did, using original facing stones, they've discovered many details of the construction which only experience can give, such as how quickly the stones could be laid. They've calculated that a gang of eighty men needed thirty-two wagons and sixty-four oxen to keep it supplied with stone, lime and water. The two sections meet at right angles, stone running into turf. The turf had to be cut by hand as no cutting machine could cut the turfs to the necessary depth. No real bits of the turf Wall are left today, unlike the stone Wall, so they had to assemble the turf by trial and error, deciding for themselves the right slope and thickness.

Vindolanda is not on the line of the Wall – the Department would not have allowed the Wall to have been re-built if it were. It's a mile to the south, one of the old Agricolan forts on the line of the Stanegate road from Corbridge to Carlisle, and therefore has a longer history than Housesteads. But it's always included as part of the Wall fortifications.

Vindolanda today is really two sites. There's the fort itself, looked after by the Department of the Environment, and beside it the site of the town. This town is now being excavated and is the scene of all the excitement, including the reproduction Wall. The Vindolanda Trust, a private charity, are the owners of the land on which the fort and town stand and they are the ones doing the excavating in the town.

The fort, firstly, has already been partly excavated, thanks to Professor Birley's work when he owned it back in the 1930s. It's fairly small, only three acres in area, and the remains to be seen can't be compared with the fort remains at Housesteads. But the different layers of occupation and rebuilding make it a valuable site, if rather difficult to unravel. Strategically, it wasn't as important a fort as Housesteads, containing a garrison of only five hundred (the Fourth Cohort of the Gauls were there for some time). When Housesteads was built, it was probably left empty for some time, but was then rebuilt towards the end of the second century.

The outline of the fort is on the traditional playing card lines, but the only major building to be seen today is the headquarters building. The regimental chapel inside the headquarters has a sunken room, a strong room where the soldiers' money was kept. The standard bearers not only looked after the unit's standards and badges, which were treated with great reverence and included in religious ceremonies, but were also the paymasters. You can see the counter, with a stone which contained a screen like a banker's grill, over which the paymaster handed out pay, less deductions for things like a burial club, and took in the soldiers' savings or gambling winnings.

The civilian town site, the vicus, is where everything is happening. It's much larger in area than the fort, probably no less than fifteen acres which is what they're working on at present. And it has already proved what has been suspected for the last ten years or so – that the soldiers on Hadrian's Wall were not condemned to a life of military isolation, stuck out in the wilds with no civilian amenities.

It was as recently as 1958 that Richmond mentioned the existence of vici at thirty-four forts in the north of England.

Until then, many archaeologists still believed that there were no civilian settlements north of York, apart from Corbridge, the supply station for the Wall. Even today, there are still text books keeping the old myths going.

The Vindolanda vicus is the only one on the Wall currently being excavated. The findings can be assumed to be typical of the other Wall forts, even if so far they have been seen only from aerial photographs, if at all. One of the luckiest finds at Vindolanda has been the remains of the first century timber fort, incredibly well preserved. They've had to do a lot of pumping as the hole has been filling up with water seeping from an underground stream. Because it has contained a lot of decaying vegetable matter, unusual chemical conditions have stopped the normal decomposing processes. For example, many absolutely perfect leather sandals have come out of the dump, looking brand new and showing no signs of disintegration. Even more exciting, two wooden writing tablets were found the week I arrived. They had been sent to Durham for Richard Wright, the epigraphic expert, to analyse, but already they'd been hailed as the most exciting discovery in Roman Britain for many years. Only inscribed stones have ever been found in England, papyrus having disintegrated almost from the beginning, so finding an inscribed wooden tablet is a unique event. One of the problems with the tablets, as with the sandals, leather goods, textiles and other objects dug out of the hole, is that once exposed to the atmosphere they can fall to pieces almost at once if not carefully sealed and protected.

They've also had a lot of fun with the bath house. This was where they found in the plug holes some women's hair pins and other female ornaments. Had women been allowed to use the baths? As Roman baths were the social centre, women had probably been brought in to join in some of the unmentionable activities – at least that's what some people like to think.

Professor Birley thinks the Vindolanda civilian community will prove to be one of the best examples in the whole Empire. There are Roman civilian remains in Italy much more impressive, such as the Colosseum, and in North Africa there have been some freak discoveries, such as a Roman bath almost in working order, thanks to being buried and preserved for centuries by the sands of the desert, but at Vindolanda it will be possible to unearth the remains of a *complete* Roman village, with houses, workshops, temples and baths.

The activity all around the vicus site gave the impression of a living village, as little groups went about their jobs in the houses and shops. Little is known for certain about what actually went on in the past. The civilian population must soon have outnumbered the military as the centuries went by, if the area of the Vindolanda vicus is any guide, but military records are by far and away the most numerous. Officers put up stones to commemorate the slightest achievement and even ordinary soldiers, by saving with the burial clubs, could afford a tombstone, but only wealthy civilians went in for such mementos.

It was a butcher going round the Vindolanda vicus who identified a butcher's shop – recognising a gutter in the rear of the shop where the blood from the carcases ran away. The excavators had identified it as a shop from the counter but didn't know what it had sold. Other shops and taverns have been discovered. A handsome mansion has been found, a large inn used for official travellers as well as tourists or merchants, a reminder that Vindolanda was on a main Roman road, the Stanegate. Army officers going to a new posting, tax officials, census officials, representatives of the Governor or even the Emperor would stay there in some comfort. Excavation has shown a large open courtyard with three bedrooms on each side, a dining room, lavatories and a bath suite. There was probably stabling facilites as horses were changed or rested.

Vicus life at Vindolanda, however large, would revolve round the army. The majority of civilians, apart from merchants and traders, would be the dependants of the soldiers. A boy in Vindolanda would have expected to go into the army.

What language did they speak? In the army itself, the official language was Latin. Officers spoke it all the time and civilians with any pretensions educated their children in the Latin manner. In the early years, ordinary auxiliary soldiers kept their native language amongst themselves, whether Greek or Germanic or from the East, but even they would have a grasp of simple Latin, just as in the old days of the British Empire, Indian troops would pick up a smattering of English. As they settled down and the centuries rolled by, everyone, regardless of their origin, became a Roman Briton. When in Roman Britain, do what the Roman Britons do. In this case the language of the locals was a form of Celtic. Celtic was spoken in the vicus and no doubt became the everyday language for everyone – except the Latin-speaking officers and upper classes. Perhaps the wooden tablets will reveal all when they are analysed.

Literacy in Roman Britain was wider than one might expect. The Roman senators and equestrian classes brought their schools with them and the wealthier Britons were encouraged to use them, but it looks as if some of the ordinary workmen could often read and write, judging by the odd bits of graffiti scribbled on tiles or stones in idle moments. There's one saying puellam (girl) and another satis (enough), and another longer rather hurried message telling someone to 'turn the slave into cash'.

The houses were stone built and solid, well drained and many of them heated, palaces compared with the native Celtic round huts. It used to be said that the Roman legionary soldiers were vegetarian – usually by vegetarian organisations who liked to boast about the fact. (How to not eat meat and conquer the world.) On campaigns they ate corn meal baked into hard biscuits, porridge and various pasta sounding dishes. Their vegetables were limited, mainly beans and cabbages, far less choice than today. Tacitus makes an interesting reference in an account of a campaign in Armenia during which he says rations were so short they had to eat meat dishes to keep starvation away. It's now presumed that in the later centuries the legions picked up the meat-eating habits of the auxiliaries – being originally barbarians, they naturally ate meat. All auxiliary forts on the Wall contain masses of bones and so do the legionary fortresses further south. From the bones it looks as if beef, mutton, venison, chicken, game were popular. Oyster shells are everywhere and must have been imported by the cart load. In the vicus they drank beer and wine in the fort. Instead of sugar which the Romans never discovered, honey was the universal sweetener. No doubt they sat on couches at the best tables, as they did in Rome, but the eating habits of the native Celts have not been recorded. Neither civilians nor soldiers had forks – they used knives, spoons or their fingers.

It's always stated that life expectancy was short in Roman times. Analysis of tomb stones found in Britain shows an average age at death similar to the rest of the Empire – both men and women rarely surviving beyond the early thirties. Yet if conscription was always at least for twenty years, this would indicate a certain confidence that a boy joining at fifteen would be expected to reach thirty-five at least. As the majority of the population didn't have a tombstone, average ages can only be guessed at.

Women in Roman times didn't have too bad a life. The Greeks certainly were surprised that the Romans treated their women with such equality. They participated in banquets with their husbands and had equal legal rights in most circumstances. Divorce was easy – and very frequent amongst the aristocracy. The native Britons must have given women a fairly high status as well, judging by the number of queens in command of the native tribes when the Romans arrived, such as Boadicea of the Iceni and Cartimandua of the Brigantes. (It was with the coming of Christianity that women were encouraged to take an inferior position.)

Village life must have been fairly pleasant and prosperous, especially in the third century when there was peace for so long. There was a constant army to feed and constant soldiers with money to spend, constant employment, and constant entertainment. Calling the Vindolanda vicus a town is perhaps a bit presumptuous – the Romans were rigid in the categories accorded to every settlement. A town, such as Corbridge or Carlisle, would have meant magistrates and a town council and lots of regulations. Vindolanda, by the feel of it, was a little market settlement, living off the army. But one never knows. Of the fifteen acres of the vicus known to exist, only two acres have so far been properly excavated. The best must be yet to come.

After I'd looked round the vicus, and popped into the

museum and bought some souvenirs, I called at Codley Gate Farm, the house beside the site, where Robin Birley, director of Vindolanda excavations, was then living.

He was brought up in the bigger house nearby, Chesterholm, now owned by a solicitor. At one time, Professor Birley lived there with his family when he owned the site but he gave up the house in 1939 when he went off to the Army. Little work had been done on the site, in the fort or the vicus, since the 1930s, until Robin Birley returned in 1969 and the Vindolanda Trust was set up in 1970.

Unlike his brother Anthony, the university lecturer, Robin has moved around. He deliberately read modern history at Oxford, partly as a revolt against his father. It might not seem much of a revolt to an outsider, when ancient history and modern history sound much the same, but for a Birley, it was almost sacrilege.

When he graduated, he moved out to Canada, where there's not much ancient history, and became a teacher. Then he moved to Scotland, still as a teacher, and became senior history master at Gordonstoun where he taught history to Prince Charles. It was partly thanks to Robin Birley's encouragement that Prince Charles got such good A-levels in history and went on to read archaeology at Cambridge. (All archaeologists hope this interest will bear fruit in the years to come. Genuine Royal patronage has been notably missing from history and, in fact, from the arts and culture generally in the last few decades.)

He then moved to a teachers' training college at Alnwick in Northumberland where he met his second wife, Pat. As a teacher, she plays a vital part on the educational side of Vindolanda.

Robin has all his father's enthusiasms. Not only thinking of new ideas and ventures, but seeing them through, but he's probably more direct and outspoken than his father. He's moved at a great pace since helping to establish the Vindolanda Trust, bringing in help, money, publicity and, most of all, visitors from all over. And as for the archaeological work, each booklet he writes on Vindolanda is out of date by the time it's finished. So much is going on that they have a notice board in the Museum to carry all the latest news. When you consider that at Corbridge and Chester little work has been done for the best part of sixty years, Robin's return to his fatherland has in three years been something of a whirlwind.

Technically, the Department is in charge of the maintenance of the fort, while Robin and the Vindolanda Trust have the site of the town. He had running battles with them earlier on, when he refused to back fill a site when told to do so.

Mrs Birley invited me in, laid out my wet boots to dry and gave me a sherry, saying she hoped I'd stay for lunch. Robin was out on the site with some Department officials. He does a lot of digging himself, cutting and fetching, and labours when necessary to Jimmy the mason.

As we sat talking, the phone rang. Mrs Birley looked upset as she answered it. 'Who is it? Who is it?' she demanded, then the phone went dead. Later it happened again. She eventually explained that she'd started to get threatening telephone calls, meant for Robin presumably, but he was usually out on the site so she had to take them. Sometimes it was a young voice, swearing at her, sometimes an older woman.

'I don't understand it. Someone has got a grudge against us coming here, but I don't know who or why. We've had no rows. I know a few locals are a bit worried at all the visitors coming to the site. They would like things left as they've always been. When it's a government site, like all the other forts and sites, then they have got no one to blame. But with Vindolanda they know that Robin's name is attached so they have at least a person to take their spite out of. But these nasty calls. They're more than spite. Someone is definitely a bit touched.'

This part of Northumberland is rather strange. At the top level, the county society keeps itself tight and withdrawn. At the village level, they can be equally feudal, suspicious of outsiders. I'd been in several pubs in the Bardon Mill district and been met with distinctly stony stares. It's not just out-siders. They can be the same with each other. You can say a wrong word to your neighbour and not be spoken to for years. And as for new people, in Northumberland and Cumberland, the locals never rush things. You winter them, you summer them, you winter them again, then you might say hello.

All along the Wall I'd come across opposition to new things and new people. Though many like and want tourists, there's a hard core who wish they'd go away and leave Northumberland alone. (That's if the Wall has to stay where it is and can't be moved out of the way somewhere else.) It would be tragic if anyone was seriously trying to jeopardise such excellent projects as Vindolanda.

When Robin returned his wife didn't mention the phone calls. Over lunch I was telling them about meeting the Blue Peter TV team. Robin was suddenly very upset, firstly at them filming in bad weather, making it look as if it always rains in Northumberland, and secondly for repeating the myths about the rotten life of the Roman soldiers. Like the custodian at Housesteads, he feels personally insulted when going to Northumberland is made to look like a penance.

'You'd think it never rained or snowed in the south, the way people always go on about our weather. The weather is terrific. You should see it in the snow. It's breathtaking.'

There was a knock at the door, not a threatening caller but a man come to service the huge deep freeze which takes up almost half their kitchen. They'd been snowed up for seven days last year and had lived off the deep freeze.

I happened to use the term 'private enterprise' about his Vindolanda work, which also didn't please him, though it's one that many people use. 'It makes people think we're in some sort of business. We're not. We're a charity. We have a terrible struggle making ends meet.'

Thinking about it, this could be at the root of any local opposition. People get it all wrong and think the Birleys are making money out of the site. I could see by the house that they live frugally, though a bottle of wine was opened in my honour for lunch.

'We'd be much better off if we were both teaching,' said Pat.

Robin was born into the world of archaeology while Pat, coming in as an outsider, finds many of them a bit strange, not to say eccentric. 'They have tremendous enthusiasm but they can also be very destructive about others. One of their problems is turning an opinion into a fact and for this they need their colleagues to agree with their evidence. Well, you should see them demolishing each other. They tear each other's work apart. I went to a lecture in Newcastle last night where one archaeologist was presenting his theory that milecastles had *two* watch towers, one at each end, not just one as is normally thought. They really went for him. But I suppose archaeologists are no more vicious than any other closed-in professions.

'But I think they could help each other more. Robin is OK. He's got this going on his own, though his father is always there with advice and help. But lesser connected or lesser established people have a lot of trouble in getting help from the experts, even when they're doing excellent work.'

Vindolanda has two major objects – to excavate and display the site's treasure to the public and secondly to provide facilities for training school children in excavating. It's with this latter aim that Pat Birley is most involved. In many ways, it's their most worthwhile object. You can see Roman remains at other sites but nowhere else does a deliberate policy of education take place.

In just three years, they've built up the educational side from scratch. Now they're booked up completely for two years ahead. From March to September each year they have a party of twenty to thirty school children on the site every week. The children, aged fifteen to eighteen, are charged £4 a week for their tuition fees, paid for by the local education committees. Accommodation has to be arranged by the schools and has nothing to do with Vindolanda. Many schools put their kids into the nearby Once Brewed Youth Hostel. Gateshead has its own camp school. Gateshead has been particularly keen and so have Newcastle, Northumberland and Cumberland education authorities, all of them sending regular parties of school children.

They both teach on the courses. Up to now they've had a marquee erected on the site as a temporary classroom but next season Gateshead was presenting them with a large mobile laboratory. Eventually, they'd like permanent classrooms.

Half the children's time is spent excavating, under supervision. It means that Vindolanda gets free and very willing labour, hence so much activity and progress in a short time, but it's also teaching children how and what to look for. It was the girls who carried all the turf for the Wall while the boys did the cutting out.

If there were more staff, and more accommodation, they would take more pupils. The demand is there but they can't satisfy it. One problem is paying for staff of the right ability to teach the children.

'You couldn't expect teachers to give up their jobs and be like us, with no security and no pension rights,' said Pat. She is the only full-time paid employee of the Vindolanda Trust. Jimmy the mason is part-time and Robin, though director of excavations, is officially a consultant for which he receives a modest annual fee. He augments his own income by writing and lecturing. They were without a museum custodian the day I was there. She'd just resigned, feeling it was too lonely out of season. Pat and Robin were taking turns at guarding the treasures and serving on the book stall. In three years, they already have enough inscriptions, jewellery, tombstones, statues and other bits for a museum five times the size.

To augment the school kids' labour they take on what they call volunteers every season. Some are adults ranging from doctors and miners, but most of them are usually older children or possibly students, many of whom have previously been to Vindolanda on the school parties, received tuition and been so excited by the work that they've wanted to come back. They don't have any tuition but simply excavate. For this they are paid £4 a week. They're allowed to camp on the site and in the summer it becomes positively festive, with the tents aglow and teenagers everywhere.

Perhaps this was what some locals objected to? Pat said no. They weren't those sort of teenagers. There were no drugs, little drinking and no orgies, though she didn't exactly go round each tent at night to inspect the occupants. Every volunteer had to be over sixteen. What they did after the day's work was their affair. (From my knowledge of archaeological students, who tend to be highly sober and serious, I'd be very surprised at any unmentionable activities.)

Robin picked up the topic of local opposition and said it didn't worry him too much. It was sad, but he'd become thick skinned. 'Farmers are upset, I know, when gates are left open or litter left around, but we do our best to stop it happening. I know I get attacked personally but I'm afraid I expect it. The government is impersonal and not worth attacking. Whatever you do, there's bound to be someone against you. I had to throw out one visitor from the fort last season when I caught him climbing in at eight o'clock. He swore at me, saying it was disgusting, closing the gates at eight o'clock at night, typical of private enterprise. I told him that all the Department forts close at six. But he didn't believe me. We had forty thousand visitors last season, so I know some are bound to be upset. It's unpleasant to be criticised unfairly, but you've just got to put up with it.'

Though the educational side of their work is patently the most worthy, the part which I enjoyed most was their reproduction work. The bit of Wall already mentioned, built at a cost of only £750, is just the beginning.

'People want to see real buildings. It's only through buildings that they can imagine what the people were like. Personally, if I were the Department, I wouldn't keep uncovering so many little bits of the Wall. I'd build up from scratch a big new bit, to let everyone see.'

'Oh, they've got to keep working on the Wall, Robin,' said Pat. 'That's vital.'

'Oh, I don't know. There's so much of the Wall to see already. I'd rather they had a go at reproducing some fort buildings.'

Robin has already interested many people in his plans for reproduction work. The English Tourist Board is very keen and has given money, hinting that it might contribute forty-nine per cent of any future repro-work. A newspaper had promised to furnish the inside of a museum, if he can ever get the money together for a new building. (The present Museum is a Nissen hut.) He would like the museum to be housed in a reproduction headquarters building, to let people see what the most important military building inside the fort looked like.

They have high hopes of several wealthy people making individual contributions. Major Cussins, of the soap family, visited the site and was very impressed, saying that if they put up a turret, cost around £2,500, they could send him the bill.

They would also like to put up a signal tower. There is the foundation of one nearby on an adjoining hill. If built to its full height of sixty feet, it could be used by the public to look down on the Vindolanda vicus and fort. A milecastle would cost about £60,000 to build and the biggest and most ambitious scheme of all, building a complete headquarters block, would cost in the region of £160,000.

However, they have enough practical and educational work to go on with while they wait for the grander schemes to materialise. Continuing to excavate for eight months of the year and using fifty helpers at a time, they have enough digging in the vicus to keep them happy for seventy years.

10
Crag Lough:
A Youth Hosteller Remembers

The Wall between Housesteads and Crag Lough is like walking through a picture postcard. So many photographs have been taken of this section that I felt I already knew it intimately. In the summer it can be like the M1, with standing room only on top of the Wall and a queue of people waiting to get on. It soars up and down along the crest of the crags, commanding the countryside for miles around. You've got to be pretty agile and, in bad weather particularly, you need good strong boots. Old Hutton was very proud of himself. 'I had now the severe task of creeping up rocks and climbing stone walls, not well adapted to a man who has lost the activity of youth.' In his day, the Wall was in isolated sections and in poor condition. Thanks to the Claytons and the Department of the Environment workmen, it stretches solidly for many miles and is easy to walk.

Milecastle 37, just half a mile west of Housesteads, is by far the best preserved Milecastle of them all. John Clayton excavated it in 1853, clearing away the rubbish, and found part of an inscribed stone set up by the second legion saying they'd built this section of the Wall under the governorship of Aulus Platorius Nepos. He was the Governor appointed by Hadrian and given the job of carrying out the building of the Wall.

As I followed the Wall to Crag Lough up and down, but all

the time clinging to the summit of the Whin Sill, I could see that the north face was much straighter and smoother than the south side – the English side, as those workmen called it. The north line was marked out for the centurions by the surveyors and they had to keep strictly to it. On the inside, you can see where one century's work meets another and sometimes awkward joins had to be made.

This stretch of the Whin Sill is known locally as Cuddy's Crag, a name which derives from St Cuthbert. I came down one little slope of the roller coaster Wall top path and came to a magnificent gap in the crags where I noticed a rather battered wooden signpost. It pointed due north to the Pennine Way. I could see the route stretching romantically ahead, down the face of the crags and away into the distance, straight as an arrow, skirting forests and zooming up hills. It looked so tempting that I half wanted to follow it. The Pennine Way is one of the wonders of our age, if you consider it a wonder that so many national and private landowners should finally have been persuaded to allow walkers to cross their land. The Pennine Way is a public path which stretches for two hundred and fifty miles from Edale in Derbyshire across the Border to Roxburgh. It was completed in 1965 after thirty years of campaigning by Tom Stephenson of the Ramblers' Association.

As the Wall began to veer left the view changed and I found myself suddenly looking down towards Crag Lough, the most beautiful of all the Northumberland lakes. I'd never known there was a Northumberland Lake District until I'd started this walk. Many of the loughs I'd already spied from the top, such as Broomlee and Greenlee, seemed a bit flat and barren looking, almost like reservoirs. Crag Lough is more like a Lake District lake, lush and green with dramatic steep crags and beautiful trees. I stood for a long time admiring the views. To the north east I could make out the Simonside Hills and beyond them the Cheviots.

Turning south, over the other valley, I worked out where Langley Castle must be, scene of all those medieval high jinks. Further south I could see the Pennines rising on the horizon, grey peaks that must have been Cross Fell and Cold Fell. On a clearer day I could probably have seen Skiddaw and the Lakeland summits.

I breathed in deeply, inhaling the freshest air in England. According to a recent survey on the growth of lichen, which can only survive on pure air, the only two areas in England (not Great Britain) with absolutely unadulterated air are Dartmoor and this central section of Hadrian's Wall.

Coming up the Wall, walking on top of it, I could make out a long line of walkers. As I got nearer, I could see they were all school children. Very politely, they stood to one side, waiting for me to pass. The Romans didn't build laybys on their Wall. I wondered if there were casualties on really busy days, when people must fall off the Wall trying to squeeze past each other. There was a male teacher at the head with a lady teacher bringing up the end of the crocodile. They were from Harraby School, Carlisle. The coach had dropped them an hour earlier and had driven on to pick them up an hour later at Housesteads fort. I asked the kids what they thought of the Wall so far and they said it was great. 'But a bit battered.' I asked them how many forts there were on the Wall, how often you got a turret and how high the Wall was originally. They knew all the answers and the teachers smirked. I told them if they hurried they might see Valerie and the Blue Peter team filming at Housesteads. Talking to them about Roman Britain had been easy. It was all around them. Suddenly switching to the present day confused them. You what? Peter who? I produced my badge, fresh from Valerie's hot hands, and they shouted with delight and set off at a very brisk pace.

I went down to Crag Lough to have a look at it, hoping to see some water lilies. Those on Greenlee Lough are supposed to be white and Crag Lough's yellow, but I was too early in the year. I met a man on horseback, looking for some sheep, who said he'd never noticed the colour of the lilies. The fishing club might have ruined them. The club, who rent the fishing rights from the National Trust, had drained the Lough the previous year, so the horseback shepherd told me. They wanted to catch all the pike so their trout would have a better chance. 'No sport', he added contemptuously, riding off.

The National Trust own and lovingly care for the Lough and the surrounding farmland and over three miles of Hadrian's Wall stretching west from Housesteads and we should all be very grateful to them for their care and attention. (They also own Housesteads fort but let the Department of the Environment run it for them.) Ever since leaving Housesteads, I'd noticed neat little green National Trust notices, asking the public to take care.

The National Trust don't get much publicity for owning probably the nicest and certainly the best-known part of Hadrian's Wall. One tends to think of them owning stately homes and forgets that they're the biggest private landowners in England, owning 400,000 acres. They have two hundred and thirty houses and gardens in England, visited by four million people a year, and three hundred miles of unspoilt coastline. They rely for their income on endowments and entrance fees (getting nothing from the Wall as it's free) and the £3 annual fees which their 350,000 members pay. They're an independent body and not a government department, despite what most people think.

In Northumberland and Durham (their local region), they don't have many properties – only eighteen in 1973. In Surrey, a much smaller area, they have forty-seven separate properties. One of the reasons is that Northumberland land owners have traditionally managed to hang on to their very big estates. But they have some very choice properties, perhaps their best known being their islands.

The Farne Islands, where St Cuthbert died, are now bird and seal sanctuaries, open to the public most of the year. Then there's Holy Island and Lindisfarne Castle, one of the most dramatic and beautiful spots in the whole of the British Isles.

The Trust's major chunk of Hadrian's Wall, including Housesteads fort, was given to them in 1930 by the Clayton family. They also received land from Dr G. M. Trevelyan. In 1951 they placed the fort in the guardianship of the Ministry of Works, now the Department of the Environment.

But the Trust does look after its three miles or so of the Wall to the west of Housesteads, employing its own mason to keep it in trim. And all the time it's trying to buy up more land in the area. In 1942 it bought Hotbank farm and in 1972 High Shield farm which was when they took over all of Crag Lough and the surrounding farmland. They lease the farmland to tenant farmers who run it. The Trust always aims to make its estates self-supporting, but their prime prupose is to care for the land and make it open to all.

The National Trust's local chairman is yet another of those Northumberland majors who seem to be behind so many aspects of North Eastern rural life – though this time he's not a landed major, owning only seven acres, and for once a major with a genuine crusading spirit to open up the countryside.

Major Peter Orde lives in a large house in the village of Newbrough, midway between Housesteads and Hexham. He's been chairman of the National Trust's Northumberland and Durham region since 1964. It's a voluntary job – though the Trust does have several professional staff in the area, such as a full-time land agent to look after their properties. Major Orde works for a living as a stockbroker in Newcastle, commuting from Hexham every day on what British Rail grandly call its non-stop 'Executive Express'. It's the usual dirty train which I'd travelled on many times in the last few months, with windows so grimy you can hardly see out and seats so dirty you daren't sit down. 'I'm not sure who the executives are,' says Major Orde. 'Most people seem to be typists.'

Major Orde is naturally very proud that the Trust owns such a good piece of the Wall. 'It's not just an archaeological treasure – it's a chance for everyone to enjoy some marvellously unspoiled countryside. When I took Lord Antrim along it – he's our national chairman – he described the experience as "high drama". That's just what it is. It was looking marvellous that day.'

Major Orde's wife Lavinia is a great-great-niece of John Clayton, the Wall's great benefactor. She's an active member of the county set and a keen huntswoman. Though she can appear rather High Tory, she's in fact considered radical and liberal and can be very funny about her own circle. At least, I was amused. Perhaps it was all deadly serious.

'No one who's anyone in Northumberland ever marries anyone from Cumberland,' she said, rather haughtily. 'People in Cumberland marry either people from Westmorland or people from Lancashire.' She appeared to give a little shudder at the very thought of Lancashire.

'In Northumberland we marry people next door or at a pinch, people from Durham or North Yorkshire. It's all to do with that lovely limestone we have in Northumberland. It's so good for breeding horses. They don't get the same type of grass in Cumberland. You need lime in the grass to make good bones. Look at Malaysia. You can't breed horses in Malaysia. I just throw that in by the way ...

'You see, the Pennines make a natural division, separating us completely. People on our side in the North East are very conscious of what they've suffered. They've had different reasons for their hard times than, say, Lancashire. In the same way we have different reasons for being rich. Our money came from coal and lead, steel and shipping, not from cotton. We have different social structures over here, at all levels.

'Unfortunately, our nineteenth-century coal owners and industrialists did dreadful things to the countryside. Having made a fortune exploiting the workers, they moved out into rural Northumberland, bought up the beautiful eighteenth-century houses and then knocked them all down. What they wanted with all their new money was something really vast. There are hideous Victorian mansions everywhere. They get turned into institutions like Cheshire homes because nobody can live in them. My relations have a delicious Georgian house. I presume they didn't have enough money to pull it down.'

Unlike Tommy Bates, Mrs Orde doesn't think the new arriviste breed of business executives particularly want to be part of the old established county sets – either the ones based on nineteenth-century industrial money or the older ones to which she belongs.

'The new groups have their own circles. They've got aeroplanes and fast cars and Mediterranean villas, as well as a home in Northumberland. They can move around the world very freely. They're not tied to the land. They haven't got the sort of responsibilities which the older families have.'

It is of course a sense of responsibility, which bodies like the National Trust and individuals like Major Orde both have, which makes them devote such attention to the countryside. So far, such new money which has arrived doesn't seem to have been put into local causes, either rural or archaeological. Perhaps when Vindolanda becomes nationally famous, it'll start rolling in.

Back on the Wall, I carried on from Crag Lough, still on National Trust property, this time heading for the Once Brewed Youth Hostel, I picked my way through the trees and over Crag Lough and soon started the familiar switchback ride, up and down the crags, following the Wall. The wind was strong on the top and every time I reached a summit it suddenly tore at my ears and into my skull. Yet down in the hollows everything was still, eerily still, so that I began to imagine I could hear voices, people talking round the next crag. When I got to the top again, and was met by a howl of wind, I could see nobody. Once again, I could sympathise with Romans and anyone for that matter believing in local deities and spirits. When you're alone for any time on the heights of the Wall you begin to think you might even be a spirit yourself, invincible and ethereal, able to throw yourself off over Crag Lough and just float to the heavens. There are few suicides on the Wall, despite all the dramatic cliffs and crags. Perhaps suicides haven't got the energy to drag themselves all this way.

At the end of Peel Crags there's a large gap, almost a valley, with a road through it, the first road which crosses the Wall for six miles. I'd been so used to the luxury of untrammelled walking that I'd forgotten the dreariness of those miles on the Military Road. It's just a little road crossing the Wall at right angles, running south down to Twice Brewed. I was so busy staring across the gap that I started to slither down a series of very steep steps, the Cat Stairs they're called locally. The melting snow had turned them into a treacherous ski slope. I was sliding down helplessly on all fours until I managed to grab hold of a wire fence. At the bottom, when I'd cleaned myself up and walked across a field to the road, I found another climber who had been watching me. He said people fell down those steps in all weathers. Rock climbers came from all over to practise on them. Why, in just two hundred feet or so, you could experience almost every type of rock climb you'd meet in the Alps.

Twice Brewed is a handful of houses strung out along the Military Road. There's a pub, a guest house called the Bognor (built while George V was convalescing at Bognor Regis), a garage and the Youth Hostel. It's miles from anywhere and seemed surrounded by rather menacing looking fells as I walked in half darkness down the half mile or so to the Military Road.

General Wade is supposed to have stayed here at one time. He wasn't very pleased with the beer that was brought him at the local pub, saying it wasn't strong enough, and made them brew it again. That's the story normally given for the name Twice Brewed. Old Hutton records in his *History of the Roman Wall* that he had a lot of trouble getting into the pub in 1801. Twice Brewed was apparently a very popular overnight stop for the carriers carting goods between Newcastle and Carlisle. Being half-way and the only inn for many miles, it was always full up – as Hutton found to his cost.

'Can you favour me with a bed,' so Hutton enquired.
'I cannot tell till the company comes.'
'What, is it club night?'
'Yes, a club of carriers.'
A pudding was then turned out, about as big as a peck measure, and a piece of beef cut out of the copper, perhaps equal to half a calf. 'You must be so kind as to indulge me with a bed. I will be satisfied with anything.'
'I cannot, except that you will sleep with this man,' (pointing to a poor sick traveller who had fallen ill upon the road).

'That will be inconvenient.'

'Will you content to sleep with this boy' (about ten years old).

'Yes.'

Having completed our bargain and supped, fifteen carriers approached, each with a one-horse cart, and sat down to the pudding and beef which I soon perceived were not too large. I was the only admitted and watched them with attention, being highly diverted. Every piece went down as if there was no barricade in the throat. One of these pieces was more than I have seen eaten at a meal by a moderate person. They convinced me that eating was the 'chief end of man'. The tankard too, like a bowl lading water out of the well, was often emptied, often filled.

It sounds almost as gluttonous as my twentieth-century medieval banquet, the one I had further back along the road. Old Hutton obviously enjoyed himself in the end. Luckily, he didn't have to sleep with the ten-year-old boy. When the guzzling was finally done the Twice Brewed landlady, as is often the way with landladies, suddenly found that after all she did have a bed for old Mr Hutton, much to his delight.

The present Twice Brewed Inn looked an attractive enough place – it does do bed and breakfasts – but having stayed at pubs and hotels so far, I'd been determined to get into the youth hostel. The Once Brewed Youth Hostel (as it was jokingly named when it was first opened in 1934) is one of the best known in the north of England and is a centre not just for Hadrian's Wall walkers but also for Pennine Way hikers.

As a youth, I spent many holidays in youth hostels, though I never stayed in this one. A lot of the time was usually spent waiting for them to open up at five o'clock. In the mornings, my wife and I were always last out, usually not speaking to each other. We had terrible rows in youth hostels, or terrible silences. She once poured a bowl of cornflakes over my head at Uig in the North of Skye. It was a particularly good hostel as well – one of those lovely rare ones where the warden didn't sleep on the premises but went home every night. I used to be terrified of most of the English wardens. They always seemed dour blunt Yorkshiremen who stood no nonsense. I remember one at Patterdale who never ever smiled. One evening I heard sounds of hysterical laughter coming from his private quarters – or, I'd thought, it might have been screams as he beat up some poor hosteller who'd forgotten to sweep the dormitory. I crept over and heard the voices of Eccles and Bluebottle and Minnie and Henry and Neddy Seagoon. He was human after all.

We used to do our own cooking in hostels, in the members' kitchen, as we couldn't afford hostel meals however cheap. It meant we were forever scratching round the dusty shelves of some isolated village store for tins of stew. I can still smell the Nescafe which somehow always had a special smell in youth hostels.

We were always pretty snooty in the members' sitting room at night, keeping ourselves to ourselves and ignoring all the Lancashire hearties in their thick woollen socks and Marks and Spencer jumpers who were determined to be friendly and make us join in their sing songs by the log fires. In the mornings we always seemed to get stuck with some wizened old walker who'd been everywhere and done everything and insisted on setting off with us when all we wanted was to be alone.

The last night of hostelling was always the worst. She would say we've only got five bob left so we can either have a good meal tonight and go home tomorrow or have no meal and stay one more night. I always chose the meal, which was why we always went home not talking.

I'd rejoined the YHA specially to stay at the Once Brewed Hostel. When I was a teenager, twenty years ago, I remember paying only half a crown a night. It's still amazingly cheap. The 1973 price at Once Brewed was only 62p. a night. It's a Superior Hostel, one that's been custom built for hostelling, complete with mod cons such as central heating. The standard youth hostel charge for adults is 55p, a night.

The YHA in England and Wales has over 250 hostels ranging from shepherds' huts to Norman castles. They seem to be getting larger and better equipped all the time. The biggest is

Ambleside with 240 beds and its own landing stage on Lake Windermere. By joining the English YHA you automatically become a member of YHAs in forty-eight foreign countries. There can't be a cheaper or easier way to see the world – or your own country. It's as good a way as any of touring the Wall as there's a hostel at Acomb and at Carlisle.

They'd changed one of the rules since I was last a member, much to the horror of the traditionalists. The basic philosophy, then as well as now, is the same – to provide cheap accommodation for young people exploring the countryside. They used to state categorically that on no account could hostellers travel by car – you were meant to be under your own steam, walking, cycling or canoeing. In 1972 they came into line with Scotland and the rest of Europe and allowed hostellers to arrive by car. They did it quietly, with no announcements, but from all accounts the YHA is still split as pressure groups try to get the rule put back. The traditionalists say it's ridiculous for the YHA, a countryside body, to encourage people to bring their cars into the country. The official attitude is that as many hostellers have always arrived in cars, despite the rules, you might as well make it legal. If you want to come up from London to Northumberland for a few days walking then the cheapest method is by car. (The way the local trains and buses run, it'll soon be the *only* way.)

Another big change is that individual hostellers are more and more being outnumbered by organised parties. It has changed the atmosphere of many hostels but from an economic point of view it makes sense. Large-scale catering can be planned efficiently and popular hostels can be open all the year round, even remote ones like Once Brewed.

In many ways, the rise of the school parties is a return to the youth hostel origins. The first was set up in 1909 in Germany by a schoolmaster whose idea was to take parties of town schoolchildren into the country. They reached England in the 1930s – Once Brewed being one of the first. My youth hostelling days, in the 1950s, happened to be the period when individual teenagers and wizened walkers were at their height.

One thing definitely hasn't changed – the YHA still has its

endearing socialistic, egalitarian outlook. Even in these days of Hilton-type hostels and arriving in motor cars and a record membership of over two hundred thousand, everyone is still equal under the YH roof. You have to do your morning job, such as sweeping the dormitory floor or washing the dishes. The National Trust, an equally worthy body, has a rather pukka upper-class flavour. The youth hostels are in the best traditions of working-class self-help.

Barry Hudson, the warden of Once Brewed, is thirty-two, comes from Lancashire and was formerly a coal miner, an armourer in the Navy, then a fireman. Three years ago he and his wife Ann decided they were fed up with industrial life and wanted to get back to the simple life. As youngsters they'd both been keen hostellers. She'd had a sequence of different jobs – as a teacher, a librarian and at the biological warfare station at Porton, which she hated.

They were sitting in the members' common room, which is also the dining room, in front of a large log fire with their two young boys and his mother and father beside them. It's only in the midweek winter months that they can stretch out, have relations to stay, because from March to October every year they are hard at it, seven days a week, looking after fifty-six hostellers. In the winter they're closed from Monday to Thursday, though they will open up if specially requested, as they did for me.

Ann was sitting sewing sleeping bags. A warden and his wife have to decorate and look after the building, clean and repair the bedding – all without any paid help.

He was sitting with graphs and lists, working out the bookings for the year ahead. So far they had firm bookings from fourteen different school parties, each of about thirty children, from Somerset and Exeter to all the northern counties. There were many foreign bookings, including a group of Swedish walkers and a party of American cyclists, both coming for the second year running, plus those local educational authorities (such as Cumberland and Westmorland, Newcastle, Gateshead, Northumberland) who use the Hostel for their children going on the Vindolanda archaeological courses.

They'd had record bookings the year before, cooking over thirteen thousand meals and filling ten thousand five hundred and thirty bed nights. They now boast that the profits from their hostel helps to subsidise the smaller less frequented hostels in the rest of their region. Neither of them had any previous experience of catering, yet they plan and cook and serve those thirteen thousand meals on their own with the help of one part-time assistant warden in the summer season.

I made a booking to come back at Easter with my two kids in order to experience the full horror, or perhaps surprising delights, of eating and sleeping with fifty-six excited school children. Ann said the eating at least was terrific, if you took into account that there was nowhere else you'd get a three course hot meal for 38p.

Their first hostel was at Canterbury, taking the post to get into the YHA, though they wanted to be in the north. There's always a waiting list to be a warden, despite the arduous life and the low pay. Their basic wage at Once Brewed is £500 a year, but having got over the magic ten thousand mark in bed nights, their coming year's salary was going to be £1,000. Salary increases are tied to bed nights – there's nothing in it for them financially in doing all those meals or running a thriving hostel shop. All part of the service.

'Canterbury was a bit like a transit camp,' said Barry. 'They were mainly foreigners beginning a hitch-hiking tour of Britain and just spending one night. Here we have mainly parties who stay for five days or individual walkers who stay for up to three days as they explore the Wall country. We're right in the middle of two of the most popular hostelling routes in the country, Hadrian's Wall and the Pennine Way. From Easter to October, there's no slack period.'

'It's a tiring life,' said Ann. 'And very tying. One of us has always got to be in for deliveries, even in the middle of winter. We haven't been out together for a meal for two years, but that's as much with having young children as anything else.

'I quite enjoy the cooking, and so does Barry. He's become very good at it. I would like to do more varied meals, but the school kids don't want it. If I did fresh fish with white sauce it would be all back in the bin. They only want fish fingers or beef burgers. They won't eat fresh vegetables either. We need the school parties financially but they're a lot of work. Some of the kids these days can't even butter their own bread – you're expected to be their cook, waitress, nurse, doctor, taxi driver and information officer, all rolled into one.

'The private school children tend to be more mature, used to things like dormitories and being independent, but they're like all kids, not much use at things like washing up. Kids don't seem to do it these days. It's a job for six hostellers, washing up after every meal. But some of these kids can take two hours over the job! They expect butter not margarine. Oh, you have to put up with a lot of complaints. On the whole, I think the Americans are the worst at complaining. They expect to be waited on hand and foot.'

'Not all Americans are like that, just the spoiled rich ones,' said Barry. 'We got an awful lot at Canterbury. Many of them pretended they weren't Americans – sewing on maple leaves and passing for Canadians, all because of the Vietnam war. They felt ashamed to be Americans.'

'When I used to go hostelling myself I was scared of the wardens,' said Ann. 'They always seemed very severe. But the kids these days aren't scared of anything – least of all their schoolmasters. Discipline's gone completely. We sometimes have to take over to keep them in control. The teacher just gives up.'

'You can tell the minute the coach drives up what sort of party it's going to be,' said Barry. 'If the teacher makes every kid stay in the coach while he comes to the door on his own, holding a pad of notes and with a list of questions ready, then you know you're OK. But if they just all pile out together, rushing in a horde for the door, knocking each other over as they barge in, then you're in for a hard five days. For a start, you can't find the teacher. Kids are bigger than the teacher these days and he gets knocked over in the scramble.'

'You should see the faces of the teachers when they discover they've got to sleep with the kids in the same dormitory! They get very upset.'

'All you can do is fill the kids up with pop and nutty from the shop and hope for the best.'

'It's a harder life all round than we thought it would be, but we just struggle on. We can't go back to a humdrum town life now. It's so nice to be independent, running our own show, even though we'll never be rich.'

They do of course get free accommodation and live in a new, centrally-heated building in beautiful countryside. They are virtually their own bosses and do have the satisfaction of helping others, but they would like more time off. There's supposed to be a relief warden scheme, but they haven't been relieved yet. They find their little flat, which runs off the main kitchen, too small with a growing family and would like to buy a cottage nearby, if they could ever scrape £2,000 together or raise a mortgage. They want to retreat for at least one night a week to the peace and quiet of a separate house and escape the noise of the school parties. Ann says she finds it very hard to relax, living on the premises. I don't fancy their chances – not with Newcastle week-enders snatching up even tumbledown barns for £2,000.

As they had babysitters for the night, with his parents being there, they broke a lifetime's habit and agreed to come out with me for dinner. Such excitement. And such a choice range of gastronomic delights to choose from. There was the heady pleasure of the Bognor Guest House, sandwiches at the Twice Brewed pub or a twenty-six-mile drive to civilisation to Carlisle and the nearest Chinese restaurant. Barry is very fond of Chinese food. When you think that 150,000 visit Housesteads fort every year, and probably about half a million visit this area of the Wall, you'd expect at least one decent restaurant or hotel within a radius of twenty miles. In the end, they chose the Milecastle Inn, a pub about three miles west along the Military Road which does very enterprising meals at the bar. It's known locally as the Jerry, though nobody seemed to know why. Barry suggested a German had once run it but Ann said it was something to do with the fact that in the old days it only had a beer licence, not a spirit licence. Such places were called Jerries, though she didn't know why.

For a Northumberland pub, it was certainly enterprising. It's run by a London born ex-chef and I had a very tasty oxtail casserole in a nice earthenware pot. He's opened up the pub, laying the stone walls bare, and was aiming to add bedrooms for sixteen people. He got out his building plans with great pride. The Hudsons capped this by saying their hostel was also having an addition built – increasing the accommodation from fifty-six to eighty beds. Old Hutton would certainly have more choice on the Military today.

It was strange that night to sleep in a youth hostel again, in an empty dormitory with acres of bare floor all around. I'd had to ask them to lend me a towel and soap, which of course all good hostellers always carry with them; I'd got so used to hotels all these years. It was lovely and warm, I admit, thanks to their central heating, but they still haven't spoiled hostellers by putting in things like carpets. I had to make up my bed in the morning but they let me off the breakfast dishes, which was kind.

II

Great Chesters:
Down with the Wall,
Up with Farmers

At the far end of the car park a group of workmen were in a
huddle examining a noticeboard. They were laughing and
nudging each other and didn't hear me as I approached. It was
another dry but very cold late January morning and yesterday's thaw hadn't quite melted all the snow. They jumped in
the air with surprise when they suddenly realised I was behind
them, rushing to their shovels and brushes, looking very guilty,
and busily got on with laying a new tarmac surface. From time
to time they gave me little glances, stopping and staring like
startled sheep, not quite sure where I'd come from.

I went over to the noticeboard and found a large map of the
Wall and the Pennine Way. I couldn't see anything funny
about it. I studied it for some time, though I knew it backwards, as I could tell they were watching me. Then I walked
back across the car park, glancing only to admire the prize-
winning lavatories.

Steel Rigg Car Park is so discreetly screened by fir trees and
carefully positioned off the road that you could easily miss it,
unless you were looking for it. I could see why it's won so
many plaudits. It's right on the line of the Wall yet carefully
created to cause the minimum of fuss. It's a perfect spot to
leave a car and explore the Wall, either going east over Crag

Lough towards Housesteads, or climbing west to Winshields Crags, the highest crags on the Wall. Though the car park itself can hardly be seen, you can see everything from it, which in itself is an achievement. The little road beside it doesn't appear to have a number – it's just the one that crosses the Wall at right angles, coming up from Twice Brewed. That was the way I'd come. Now I was heading west for the heights.

I was out of breath by the time I reached the top but it wasn't really hard going, despite the remnants of snow. There's a trig point to indicate the summit, all one thousand two hundred and thirty feet of it.

In the Lakes you're always getting to the top of much higher hills, which on the map look enormous, only to find you're dwarfed all around. Winshields seems much higher than its one thousand two hundred and thirty feet. From every point of view it feels the dominant hill on the horizon. Looking south there was bright sunlight. I could see the Military Road very clearly and the valley of the South Tyne with the hills rising again on the other side. The snow was lying in the gulleys on the valley slopes, like white ribbons tying up huge green Christmas parcels. To the east there was Crag Lough and the familiar line of the Wall, going up and down on its journey to Housesteads. I couldn't see much of the Wall to the west because of a low mist but in the distance there was the beginning of the Lake District peaks.

While everything to the south seemed very clear, with smoke curling across the valley from dotted farmhouses and a different shade of green for every field, the North seemed at first sight completely barren, much as the Romans must have seen it, looking out beyond what they considered the limits of civilisation. Then through the mist I made out a tower about three miles due north. I took it at first to be part of Spadeadam, the Blue Streak rocket establishment. Yet Spadeadam should be much more to the west, towards Carlisle, and their towers are concrete. This one looked metal, a sort of Eiffel Tower, a latticeworked Post Office Tower. There was no reference to it on the map or in any guide books.

It was much later that I discovered what it must be – one of the Post Office's mysterious communication towers. It was put up so discreetly, with no fuss and no explanations that many locals are not aware that it's there. There's apparently a string of them round the country, usually on high ground. Officially, with a lot of pushing, the Post Office will tell you they're telephone and TV relay stations. In fact they're part of the government's air defence warning scheme, put up in the late fifties when we thought the Russian nuclear bombers were about to attack us any day. They're supposed to be the vital links between a series of secret hideouts to which provincial authorities will flee in the event of invasion. Perhaps out there in the mists there's a monster concrete dugout, just waiting for Newcastle's Lord Mayor and other civic dignitaries, helmet and gas mask at the ready.

This particular tower is situated in the middle of a piece of nowhere called Hopealone, which is nicely named. It's on a lonely moor called Henshaw Common surrounded by those monster forests which the Forestry Commission is growing over half of Northumberland and Cumberland. The next secret Post Office tower to the west is in a built-up area, but equally unexplained and unpublished, on top of a hill in Harraby in Carlisle.

Once again, the Romans did it all first. Their signal turrets followed the selfsame route – and probably passed messages along just as quickly, always assuming you had good eyes. On the Wall, the turrets were the signalling points. On top of Winshields Crags there's an excellently placed turret, T 40 A, which no doubt linked up with watch towers out in the field, perhaps even at Hopealone, and with other turrets along the Wall to Carlisle. Not many Roman watch towers have been found – only one on the Wall so far – but they are known to have been set up in the heart of South Scotland, giving an early warning of any Caledonian advances. The only one known today on the line of the Wall, at Pike Hill, was built before Hadrian, probably under Agricola, but incorporated into the Wall defences.

Every army lives on its lines of communications. One of the reasons why most medieval battles were such a shambles was lack of information – they'd hang around for weeks, looking for an enemy to fight. The Roman Army, being the most successful fighting force the world has known, had it all worked out. We don't know precisely what the signals were – except that it wasn't blowing down magical speaking pipes – but one look at the map of the Wall turrets and milecastles shows it was a communication line as much as anything. Even though the Wall's HQ was at Carlisle, right on the west coast, they obviously felt confident of controlling troops up to seventy miles away. Even further away was York, the legionary headquarters for the whole of the north. In this case they had a direct system of watch towers along the Carlisle–York road.

Several Roman signalling methods have been suggested, based on scraps of literary information or from studying Trajan's column in Rome – this is covered with a series of sculptured drawings showing the Roman army at work, a mine of information for all Roman army scholars. On the column are three watch towers with signal torches sticking out of the windows, and a bale of hay and a pile of logs. It's thought the hay or logs were for urgent messages, like Help, while the torches were for more detailed but less urgent work. One early Latin writer describes a system of semaphore using two torches. The alphabet is split into groups of five letters and the position of one torch tells which group is meant. The other torch indicates which letter in that particular group is being spelled. It sounds workable, but there must have been simpler ways. There's another system whereby a beam is lowered or raised in front of the burning torch, like a morse code.

Every unit of the army had its code book, though none of them survives and like the daily watch words used by the guards on duty, they were changed all the time to stop the enemy interpreting them.

After Winshields Crags, I followed the Wall as it soared up and down over other giant crags, sometimes on top of the Wall itself and other times beside it, marvelling at how it managed to hang on to the edge by amazing feats of engineering, even when presented with great crevices in the crags. They all have splendid names, like Bogle Hole (Bogle meaning ghosts?), Bloody Gap, Thorny Doors, evidence of a nasty past and a rather dramatic present. A lot of the Wall still stands proud and erect today, squat and rather low, rarely more than six feet high, but impressive nonetheless. This is the sort of area where you'd expect the Wall to survive – since Roman times there's been no habitation on the crag slopes.

After Milecastle 41 another little road crosses the Wall and beyond this I came across another party of workmen, this time Department of the Environment men, opening up a new section of the Wall. So much is happening on the Wall these days that the Ordnance Survey's archaeological map of the Wall, first produced in 1964, which is very recent as maps go, is already out of date. All along the Wall I'd been discovering new stretches and new turrets not on the map. I'd got the 1964 map without realising a new one had come out in 1972. It's strange to think that an archaeological map, a map solely concerned with structures almost two thousand years old, has dated in less than ten years. Hadrian's Wall is a living wall, not just for the local inhabitants, but for tourists and archaeologists, a living, breathing, expanding, growing wall.

'Not a movement in it,' said one of the workmen. 'Look at yon bit. Marvellous.' He'd just sliced away and cleaned a new section and was standing back admiring it. He bent down and pointed out the Broad foundations, showing me where the Narrow Wall had been built on top, explaining it all slowly and very seriously.

'Stop your lecturing,' shouted a voice from the other side of the Wall. A younger workman stuck his head over and jeered.

'Take no notice of him. He's soft in the heed.'

I thanked him, slowly and seriously, for his information, and walked on. Just after the next milecastle, number 42, which stands over eight courses high, I came to where a great gaping quarry had bitten a giant chunk out of the Wall. If I'd been Hutton, I probably would have cried. I'd been thinking what clever conservationists we were in these days, uncovering so much of the Wall, far more than Hutton ever saw, until I came to this gaping hole. It's one of several quarries on this stretch of the Wall, all of which have had many genuine tears shed over them in the last few decades. Most of the battles have been lost, so far, but this one, I later learned, has been won. The quarry in question, Cawfields, has recently been bought and in 1974 Northumberland County Council plans to spend £50,000 turning the great chasm into an artificial lake and the surrounding tips into landscape gardens. In the meantime, I could make out a couple of bulldozers, chugging away below. I followed a line of notice boards which said 'Danger, go no further' and worked my way with some difficulty round the noisome, nasty quarry. It was like coming across a bomb crater in the middle of Kew Gardens, an office block at the end of Lock Lomond, a Wimpy bar on the top of Helvellyn.

As I crossed the Haltwhistle Burn, hurrying to get away from the quarry, I took a quick look down the valley for any signs of the small Roman fort, Halfwhistle Burn fort, which stood half a mile away on the line of the Stanegate. It's thought this was a pre-Hadrian fort, evacuated when the forts were built onto the line of the Wall. There's nothing now to see, except its ditches, though around this area remains of several camps have been revealed by aerial photography, temporary camps set up to house the troops and labour forces during the construction of the Wall.

I hurried up the path on the other side of the little valley and found a chalk arrow on the side of a barn and was soon approaching an isolated stern looking farmhouse called Great Chesters, the next fort on the Wall, a fort with an occupant I was looking forward to meeting.

It's always been called Great Chesters, very confusing. People come to see it believing that it's the same as Chesters, the one that's in all the guidebooks, the big one with the terrific bathhouse and the museum, miles back along the Wall beside the river at Chollerford. There's no museum or bathhouses or indeed very much at all to see at Great Chesters. The 'Great' bit is thought to date from the eighteenth century when this fort still had thirteen-feet-high walls, being in a remote area. Chesters itself, being more rural, was at that time losing out to the farmers, till the great John Clayton arrived. But at Great Chesters today there is Councillor Ted Woodman.

Councillor Woodman is one of the few people who actually live and work on a Roman fort – much to his displeasure. His farmhouse and the farmyard *is* the fort, the whole lot being enclosed by the rather dramatic remains of the fort's ramparts and walls. As I approached I could see the ramparts and the south and west gateways. Inside the fort walls there are mounds everywhere, indicating the buildings beneath, though now they're left to his cows who graze over them. Only one bit of the internal structure can be seen, the fort's strong room. It has an almost complete stone arch, now lying flat on its side in the grass.

The south gate yielded a famous hoard of jewellery, particularly a golden brooch in the shape of a hare, a masterpiece of Celtic art, and many Hadrianic inscriptions. The west gate is unique amongst all the Wall forts in showing exactly the successive blockings of the different Roman periods. Altogether it's a complicated site, but rich in information about the history and purpose of the Wall. The arrangements of the ditches, the relationship of the Broad Wall to the Narrow Wall, have been studied, but not fully. By the number of grassy mounds, they would appear to be relatively easy to unearth. The site is ripe for plucking, though not while Councillor Woodman has his say.

There's also a fascinating aqueduct here, a series of water pipes which brought drinking water to the fort from six miles away, down and round the hills from the head of the Haltwhistle Burn. 'One of the most remarkable and best preserved military aqueducts in Britain,' according to Sir Ian Richmond. The fort was built on the site of a milecastle (MC 43), one of the vital bits of evidence to prove the secondary stage in the Wall's structures – when a change of plan moved forts onto the Wall. The fort covered just over three acres and was a small- to medium-sized infantry fort, the main purpose being to guard the Caw Gap – where the Haltwhistle Burn crosses the Wall and the modern quarry has been built. At one period the garrison was a detachment of Raetian spearmen who came from the Upper Danube.

From what I'd heard of Councillor Woodman in advance, I half-expected to have a spear thrown at me as I carefully went through the south gateway of the fort, I mean his farmyard, and tiptoed past the barracks, I mean the lawn in front of his parlour window. At first I could see no sign of life, apart from the cows paddling round the muddy mounds, feeding from the tops of the grass covered granaries which lie beneath, then eventually his wife came to the back door and led me into the kitchen where I took off my muddy boots.

This same farmhouse was here when Old Hutton arrived, but he didn't glean much from it. 'All the doors I found open and none to guard the premises but a child from whom I could gain no intelligence. There was no danger of a thief, for in this solitary place, he must come a great way to take a little.'

Councillor Woodman's family have farmed Great Chesters farm for eighty years, though he has only been there four years, having come a few miles up the hill from his birth place at Bardon Mill. He's a tenant farmer – the first one I'd talked to properly. He's short and rather intense and stares into your face when talking. His accent was broad Northumberland, unlike the estate owners I'd met so far with their public school accents and off.cer backgrounds. The owner of his thousand-acre farm, which he works with just two men, is the Blenkinsop Estates, which means Major Joicey. Having left Major Benson territory behind I was now on to Major Joicey land.

Mr Woodman had been a Haltwhistle Rural District Councillor for ten years. He'd just been made chairman of the Housing and Planning Committee. He's also an active member of the National Farmers Union. He has two children, fourteen and eleven, who go to local schools, not away at boarding schools like the owners' sons. His particular grievance at that moment was Vindolanda. I'd barely got my boots off, and was sitting in my stockinged feet in his parlour when he launched into a tirade.

'The most important thing in this area is farming. The Wall comes second. It must never be allowed to take over, which is why I'm having a battle over Vindolanda. They want to build a new road right to front gates of the fort which will go right past a local farmer's house. They want to turn his path into a public highway, bring thousands of visitors across his fields and traffic roaring by his front door.

'If land has been bought purely for archaeological reasons, as Mrs Archibald has done (the lady who presented the Vindolanda fields to the Vindolanda Trust), then that's one thing. But the rights of farming people should come first and the likes of Vindolanda second.'

He took my map from my hand and pointed out the farm in question and where the proposed road would go and how he'd brought it up at the council meeting and helped to get the proposal thrown out. It had now gone back to Northumberland County Council. Everyone was waiting impatiently to see what the result would be.

'Young Birley, on his own admission, has said that he expects as many visitors as Housesteads in the next year or so. That's one hundred and fifty thousand! And eventually he hopes to double that. If he gets just one hundred thousand, and half of them walk and half drive, then at two people in a car that's twenty five thousand cars in an eight month season. If they come in coaches at thirty to a coach that's eight thousand charabancs! What's more important – archaeology or the lives of the local farmers?'

I said I thought that the pleasure of a hundred thousand seemed to be more important than the minor discomfort of one farmer.

'It's not *minor* discomfort. They leave gates open, damage fences. Farm land has to be given up and the noise will be terrible. I know that ninety per cent of people stick to the country code, but there's ten per cent who don't. When I go to town I obey the town code. I park where I'm told. I don't mind town people coming to the country. If I lived in Liverpool or Manchester, I'd want to come to the country. But it's only people who *live* in the country who realise the problems that tourists bring. It's not just appertaining to the Wall. All National

Park areas have the same problems. Tourists are spreading all over the countryside. They're taking over!'

He calmed down a bit and explained, very reasonably, that he wasn't simply being negative and obstructive. He'd suggested two other possible roads that could bring visitors to Vindolanda. 'If there was really only one way to Vindolanda, then I'd say hard luck, that's it. Building a new road past Causeway farm isn't the only way. My two suggestions would stop a bit short of the fort, and that's not too much of a hardship. But no. Young Birley wants them dropped right at the gate which will mean a big car park and even more land lost.

'If it goes through, then naturally the value of the farm goes down. Who wants all those problems and inconveniences? In that case, the farmer should be well compensated. He would be compensated in the town if a new motorway was being built. When do they think of compensating farmers, tell me that?'

I said I was sure he would be compensated. I quoted Major Benson who had told me that he'd agreed legal terms which would help one of his tenant farmers, if the new bit of the Wall at Blackcarts ever became a tourist attraction and meant a loss in farm land. That's as may be, said Mr Woodman. What really got him was that archaeologists and tourist people *expected* to push the farmers around, putting them into second place.

His wife came in with some coffee and biscuits. She looked much younger than her husband, slightly plump and quietly amused. I was asking him what he would do if the archaeologists came to open up Great Chesters.

'You'd be all right, Ted,' she said. 'You'd get a job digging.'

Her husband gave a wintry smile. That would really be the end, he said, if his farm became another Vindolanda.

'It's bad enough as it is. All summer they trail past my front window, great lines of them. The teachers are at the front and the last kid through leaves the gate open. I then have to go and sort out the right cows with the right calves. If we went into the towns and had picnics on their front lawns, we'd soon hear about it. But they do it here. They don't realise that I'm going to cut that grass for hay. In one of the guide books it says that the path goes round the back of my house, which is all wrong. So I get them both ways. They knock at the door, asking to see the museum, thinking this is Chesters.'

'What a trouble we had building the cow shed,' said his wife. 'That went on for months.'

'Two years it took to get planning permission,' said her husband, grimacing at the memories. 'It's a cubicle shed for wintering ninety-six cows, one I designed myself. We had to have it. Well, they came up from London to have a look at the foundations, archaeologists came to poke around. Seemingly the Wall went right underneath it. They said it would be an eyesore. It's no more an eyesore than the electric pylons and you soon get used to them, don't you. Anyway, I had to put it round the side, not where I wanted it.'

Mr Woodman rears cows and sheep – on his sort of hill farm there's no land worth ploughing. The farmers on richer soil in the valley grow the crops and in turn fatten up the cattle and the sheep which he has reared on the hills. He has a hundred and forty suckler cows and just over six hundred black faced sheep. A suckler cow has one calf per year. They're kept together all the time and never used for milking. Gates left open, separating a suckler cow from its calf, is therefore very inconvenient.

'I get a government subsidy of £30 a year for every suckler cow I keep. Before the war, hill farmers let their land go because it wasn't worth it, but during the war the government gave grants to encourage breeding on the hills. Hill farmers couldn't have got the capital otherwise. It's paid off now, with the national shortage of beef.'

He used to do his calving in the spring but since he built his big cow shed, giving them a proper home for the winter, he now starts calving in the back end of the year, in October and November. It means he now has much bigger calves for sale when the annual sales come round. The previous year he'd got between £100 and £120 for his calves. The farmers in the valley get about £200 a calf, after they've fattened them for a year and sold them to the butchers.

To buy suckler cows themselves, the heifers had cost him last time about £160 each. With reasonable luck, they should produce a calf a year for ten years. The biggest single expense is the bulls – he has four Hereford bulls which cost him between £600–£1,000 each. A good Charollais, a very popular bull in this part of Northumberland, can cost up to £2,000. His six hundred ewes cost him £20 apiece.

Mr Woodman was being particularly forthright about his finances, when you consider how close and tight the average farmer is supposed to be, to illustrate a point about the large amount of capital tied up in farming. Considering he's a tenant farmer, not an owner, it did seem enormous.

'The amount of capital I've got tied up in my farm at the moment, just in the way of stock, is between £40,000 and £50,000. Do the sums yourself – buying a hundred and forty cows at £200 each would cost £28,000 and six hundred ewes at £20 is £12,000. That's £40,000 before you count the bulls.

'Every year I sell about £30,000 worth of produce. Let's say the average farm produces £10,000 a year as mine's a fairly large hill farm. There's about two hundred farms in the Halt-whistle area which makes in all £2 million. Just around Halt-whistle – £2 million! It's by far the biggest industry, far bigger than tourism, yet it's the least thought about. We keep the country going. But what do we get out of tourism? Nothing.'

I said what about those famous one hundred and fifty thousand visitors at Housesteads, not to mention the hundreds of thousands at other parts of the Wall. They must bring a lot of money to the area.

'Have you watched them? They come in their cars, have a picnic and drive off, what do we get out of that? A few bed and breakfast places make a bit of extra, but that's about all. I could do it here, with all the folks I get walking round my house. I could get a grant as well. I might manage to put up thirty people here, bed and breakfasts, but I'd have to forget farming. I work seven days a week on the farm as it is.'

I told him about the Once Brewed youth hostel, serving thirteen thousand meals last year. Admittedly they went to Carlisle for bulk frozen produce, but most of the food was bough locally. Indirectly, and in many cases directly, the farmers must be gaining. And if the area wasn't so ill-prepared in the way of restaurants and hotels, they could gain a great deal more. Since leaving Newcastle I'd only come across one hotel which I could recommend to someone wanting comfort and good food. Haltwhistle in particular is a barren area.

'Accommodation is difficult, I admit that. Tourism takes time to build up. We're worried about it on the council. We wrote to all the big breweries about this but we haven't got very far. I'm not against tourists. Don't get me wrong. I just don't want them having precedence over farmers.

'The North East tends to get missed out on most things when the government is spending its money on improving things. The North-East has got one of the highest drunkenness figures in England, so I'm told. They're on strike all the time. Look at Swan Hunters. There's another strike on now. No wonder the area's got a bad name. You get three inches of snow and the electricity stops working. We get the second best of everything. Yet are we less efficient than the south?'

I tried to ask him where he got his facts from, but he was moving on, summoning up fresh ammunition. After all, what people imagine can be more damaging than the truth.

'Afforestation, that's the new thing. I think it's gone too far already. You can't eat paper, can you? Only farmers feed the population. What happens to all that paper anyway? Refuse. One of our biggest expenditures on the council is cleaning up refuse. And what about Spadeadam. They've spent millions on that, and what have we got out of it? Have some shortbread.'

Half-jokingly, I said he couldn't be doing so badly at the moment, with the high price of beef. He soon put me straight. He might be getting good prices when selling his calves, but he's continually having to restock his herd and he in turn has to pay the big prices.

'I don't gain. Cows are £40 more a head than they were last year. If I was buying two hundred now I'd need to spend £8,000 more than I would have spent on the same cows last year. That's £8,000 extra capital. Where do I get that from? Returns are not what they were.'

Then there's the problem of grass staggers, which can

decimate herds at any minute. (Using decimate in its proper Latin sense – killing one in every ten.) It sounds very nasty. Officially, it is called hypomagnesium and it can cause beasts to stagger and die in five minutes. 'If you catch them in time you can pump magnesium into them, unless the heart's gone. It's a deficiency of magnesium and personally I think it's caused by modern fertilizers, though the vets don't think so. It was unknown years ago. Once you start forcing too much out of the land you upset the balance.'

So a farmer's lot is not a happy one, even at the best of times, what with staggers and high prices, folks bringing roads and cars to the countryside, others getting drunk, gates left open and sucklers getting mixed up, not to mention being lumbered with a Roman Wall, the ever present complaint.

He's undecided whether to carry on as a councillor when Haltwhistle becomes part of the big new regional council, though he's had approaches. It takes up a lot of his time and in the future it will mean even more travelling.

'Few are willing to stand for the council. Local businessmen get worried that they might offend customers. I'm a Conservative but I stand as Independent. There's too much damned politics these days – decisions get made for political reasons and nothing else. What should matter is common sense and economics. It's politics on the TV all the time, but little common sense.'

I said I liked the idea of turning the nearby Cawfields quarry into a lake – that seemed a victory for common sense and aesthetics – though it was tragic that the quarry had ever been worked in the first place. He said that it was all the Romans' fault that the quarry was such an eyesore.

'The reason for that great deep scar at the edge of the quarry is that they got to the milecastle and had to stop. If the Wall and the milecastle hadn't been there, the quarry men could have gone right along the crags and flattened everything. They had to go down much deeper instead. It would have been quite level today, but for the Roman Wall and Milecastle on top. I don't know why they're bothering to landscape it anyway. It'll cost thousands and won't benefit the countrymen. There's no return on landscaping.

'There's no return either in the Wall, not for me. They tell me it was a great feat. They reckon it took a lot of doing. A ton of stone had to be brought by horse and cart for every yard of Wall. All I know is that whenever a bit falls down it's another problem for me. I've got stock either side of the Wall. I have to run barbed wire along the top to keep them apart. It's a blinking headache to me, that's what it is.

'I've got ten thousand yards of fences to look after, most of it stone walls. It costs £2 a yard to rebuild. I need more stiles put in the walls to stop people climbing over, but who should pay for them, me or the tourists? I didn't ask them to come.

'My children are interested in it and know all about it at school but to me, the Roman Wall is nothing, just a confounded nuisance. The past is supposed to give you guidelines into the future which is probably true. As a farmer I try to benefit by the mistakes I made last year. If it bites into my pocket, then I try and change. But the past, I don't care about delving into the past. The present is too important.'

However, Mr Woodman is sure the conservationists, archaeologists and such like won't be kept away from Great Chesters for much longer. 'It's Major Joicey's, but some day they'll make him give it up. They'll just come and say, we're taking it over for excavations, out of the way. That'll be the end for me.'

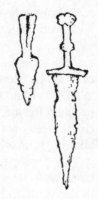

12
Border Wars:
The Government Inspector

I was never cold when walking on the Wall, even in the middle of January. I was often cold when I stopped and rested, either in a dip in the switch back to take a breather from the wind or on the tops to admire the views. I was always very cold on the occasions I tried to hitchhike back to my overnight stopping place, though a sensible Wall Walker should have his route and bed places planned to avoid hitchhiking. But when actually walking, I was never cold.

I was never wet when walking on the Wall, even in the middle of rain storms. I made myself dry for an outlay of £1.50. I bought a plastic mac from Woolworths for 50p. and a pair of plastic leggings from the Headquarters and General for £1. I wasn't the smartest best-dressed walker on the Wall that year, but I was certainly dry. I did contemplate one of those super luxury anoraks that all the best walkers wear when walking through the best advertisements, but then I remembered my teenage walks in the Lakes. My wife had one of those expensive anoraks and she indeed looked terribly impressive. I looked a jerk in my plastic mac but come opening time at the next youth hostel, I was always dry. She still looked impressive but it let water in and she weighed twice as much as when she'd started.

The big advantage of a cheap plastic covering is that you can stuff it easily in a pocket. When the sun comes out, and the sun does come out in Northumberland, then you're not lumbered with walking all day like a refugee from the last Mount Everest expedition. The secret of keeping warm and dry is to have as many light layers of clothing as possible. Two cotton T-shirts are warmer when walking than an Arran pullover and weigh half as much. Over these I wore a leather jacket which buttoned up high against the wind and kept off the lighter showers. When the heavy ones started, out came the plastic. My only real expense was £10 on a pair of light leather walking boots with thick rubber soles. Your feet deserve the best.

The weather and how to deal with it is always going to be a problem for anyone contemplating the Wall. Personally, I don't think there's such a thing as bad weather in England. If you're equipped, there can be pleasure in any weather. Soft snow, I have to admit, is hard to walk in, but wonderful to look at.

I've spent winters in different ends of the Mediterranean, in Malta, Tunisia and in Portugal, and I've never had such cold, damp, miserable winters in my life. In each place we got up to three weeks at a time of very cold, incessant rain. (In Portugal we also got an earthquake, which is one thing they haven't had in Northumberland, not so far.)

The Roman soldiers, as we know, didn't come from Rome, and hardly even from Italy. Most of the ones stationed in England came originally from central Europe, from places like Germany, Austria and Rumania, where the winters are far harder than anything we ever get in England. It's an engaging speculation to say that any Roman soldiers were actually *delighted* to be posted to Hadrian's Wall, which is what the curator at Housesteads maintained, but it's fair to say that for most of them an English winter would be no surprise, except perhaps in its mildness. We know they wore winter cloaks to protect their summer bare knees, and that their forts had all mod cons, so there was no need for them to have been either cold or damp.

If the Northumberland winter can be a pleasant surprise it would be hard to make a case for the summers. You've got to be quick to catch them. They must have been a terrible disappointment for any soldiers from southern climates. There just is no month, week or even day when you can guarantee it won't rain. Personally, I prefer it that way, having experienced the insufferable boredom of endless sun. For months on end in Malta it never rained. Eventually we'd wake up, look at the spotless sky and feel the enormous heat and say 'God, not another perfect day.'

There must be something innately perverse about Empire builders. The British couldn't wait to get out of their lovely temperate climate and start sweating it out in Africa and India. The Romans made a bee line for Central Europe, for the winter snows of Austria, Germany and Britain.

I did make one mistake about the weather. I never got myself a proper hat. Since leaving Wallsend I'd been wearing a rather floppy suede cap which my wife bought me as a Christmas present several years ago. It never let in the rain, but during those days of incessant drizzle, such as the one I ran into after Great Chesters, it began to sag lower and lower round my ears till eventually my neck was creaking under the weight. At each little town I tried to buy one of those fishermen's oilskin hats which I decided would be the best head covering, but I never found one. So I persevered with my ridiculous, entirely unsuitable suede hat, convincing myself that if I was going to look a jerk from below the neck at least my headgear was expensive.

With fussing about my hat, I missed a few minor archaeological goodies on the way to Walltown crags, though even in perfect weather I'm sure I would still not have spotted them. There's supposed to be a short stretch where the Narrow Wall and the Broad Foundation go their separate ways. Richmond presumes that the Roman engineers thought for once that the Broad Wall foundations weren't deep enough so they built a bit of the Narrow Wall from scratch.

I did intend to look for a spot on the map named as Walltown, though even in Hutton's day there was no town, or even a village. 'We arrive at Wall-town,' so he wrote, 'if a single house deserves the name. On each side the door stands a Roman altar, used for washing hands, kettles, dishes, etc, and has at last the honour of supporting the dish cloth.' I couldn't see this single house or any signs of habitation. How strange to call an empty bit of moorland a town.

I did look hard for chives and other signs of herbs amongst the crevices of the Wall. In the sixteenth century Camden wrote that it was the practice for Scottish surgeons to come down once a year to replenish their supplies from the Wall crevices. 'That the Roman souldiers of the marches did plant heere every where in old times for their use certaine medicinable hearbs to cure wounds; whence is it that some Emperick practitioners of Chirurgery in Scotland flock hither every yeere in the beginning of the summer to gather sich simples and wound herbes; the vertue whereof they highly commend as found by long experience, and to be of singular efficacy.' The Romans did introduce many herbs and spices to Britain but I could see no sign of them.

However, I didn't miss the Wall at Walltown Crags, one of the best preserved stretches of all, in height and in length, with an excellent turret, 45 A. Hutton says at this stage that he was obliged to crawl on all fours, but he must have been feeling his age, or perhaps the after effects of his half a cow at Twice Brewed. The walking is easy and for once mostly downhill, until suddenly another quarry rears its ugly head and cuts off the Wall in its prime. At one moment it's rich and lush, twelve courses high, then you're brought up short before a deep pit and a notice saying 'Quarry danger Blasting'.

I blame the quarry for the fact that I lost Carvoran fort, the next on the line. I turned left, scrambling down the hillside to a farm track and a wood, working my way round the quarry to get to Carvoran. It took me so long to get my bearings that I never found it. I tried to console myself for miles afterwards, when I'd given up and walked on, by saying that anyway, it's a rotten site with nothing to see. Even if I'd found the right field, it would just have been another field. But I felt very guilty. Losing a fort is nothing to be proud of. After all, I'd found the previous non-existent forts. I'd traced out the lines of Wallsend fort, where there's nothing but Victorian terraced houses. I'd seen service at Benwell, in and out the semis. I'd done my bit in the rutted field that is now Haltonchesters fort, been frightened by geese in the farmyard that used to be Rudchester and scoffed at the huge car park which is Carrawburgh fort. I now can't say with honesty that there's nothing to be seen at Carvoran because I didn't manage to stand there and see with my own eyes that there's nothing to be seen.

It was just a little fort (excuses, excuses), only three and a half acres and is actually not on the Wall line, being a few hundred yards to the south on the Stanegate. It could be argued that it wasn't a Wall fort in the normal sense because the Vallum goes to the *north*, making a big loop round. (If the Vallum was a military boundary line, which is the presentday thinking, then Carvoran fort was excluded from the military zone of the Wall.) In the past, a few reasonable bits and pieces have been found on the site, such as Hadrianic inscriptions, proving it was occupied and used at the same time as the Wall. One of the few tombstones to a legionary soldier found on the line of the Wall was dug up at Carvoran.

Under Hadrian, the garrison was the second cohort of Dalmatae, who came from the mountains of Jugoslavia. I haven't wintered in the mountains of Jugoslavia so I can't vouch for its climate but I'd guess Northumberland was a good posting, weatherwise. Later in the second century, the garrison was the first cohort of Hamii from Syria who have achieved fame in Romano-Britain studies through being archers – the only record of a detachment of archers known in Britain. Auxiliaries from far flung parts of the Empire who had any special skills or weapons were always encouraged to keep their native methods, especially the horsemen.

The use of archers and cavalry is interesting because the Romans themselves didn't apparently rate them very highly, except for specialist jobs. They were relegated to the wings during the big battles, guarding the real fighting soldiers, the heavily armed legionaries, or to frontier work. Yet for centuries afterwards, throughout the middle ages in fact, archers and horsemen became the vital men in any army. That's how Harold lost his eye at the Battle of Hastings. That's how Henry v won at Agincourt. And as for the soldiers on horseback, the Knights, they became the elite. Yet the legions spurned bows and arrows and horses. On coins or sculptures, you never see an Emperor on horseback.

The Roman legions knew all about mounted soldiers – they fought them enough times and often found them very difficult. It took them some time for example to devise a technique for the likes of Boadicea and her chariots. The Romans had never encountered such things in Gaul and on first landing in Britain Julius Caesar had been confused by the speed of their attack. Chariots had one driver and one warrior and were drawn by two ponies. Constant practice taught the driver how to drive with great speed over rough ground. With the warrior hanging over the side swinging his sword or hurling his javelin, they could cause confusion and panic in any battlefield. Chariots in essence combined the mobility of cavalry with the directness of infantry. The Roman legionaries, weighed down with their heavy armour and disciplined to stick in strict formation, could never run after them. When the Roman cavalry were set against the British chariots they at first appeared to flee, enticing the cavalry away from the supporting foot soldiers, then the warriors got out and hacked down the cavalry. As Caesar eventually learned, the best way to counter the chariots was to keep the cavalry and infantry constantly in touch, one lot protecting the other.

Incidentally, there's no evidence that Boadicea's or any of the Celtic chariots had axle-scythes sticking out from the side, an image beloved by all schoolboys and even a few historians. Julius Caesar never mentioned them, and he describes the British chariots at first-hand very fully, nor are they supported by any archaeological finds. They were known in Persia and it can only be assumed that later Roman historians, knocking out their graphic histories of the Empire without ever leaving Rome, worked them in to add a bit of colour.

After Carvoran and its archers, or where they should once have lived, I came to a ruined castle, Thirwall Castle, which towered perilously over me on a hillock beside the stream. I asked an old man feeding some hens if he wasn't worried it was going to fall down. 'There's an 'al booger of eighty in yan hoose. When his faither was a lad, they thowt it was ganna fall doon.' His accent was a peculiar mixture of Northumberland and Cumberland, with bits of Border Scots. He explained that Thirlwall meant Through Wall – as the castle was built in a gap through the Wall. He pointed out a Roman inscription, in an outhouse in front of one of the cottages, just above a blue door. It is mentioned by Richmond in the Handbook but I hadn't been able to find it. It was upside down but the lettering was very clear, Civitas Dumnoni, indicating that a British tribe, the Dumnonii from Devonshire, had been drafted up here for some Wall work, probably for repairs.

He said he was going for a 'coop of tea and a wesh' and then to see his son who was just about to get married. They'd got a two-roomed cottage to move into and he was trying to get them to give up one room for bed and breakfasts. 'They're nowt but an arse kick away from the Wall. They could make a canny bit for themselves, but he won't do it. Tourists are here to stay. Ah divn't understand his mentality.'

Heading on towards Gilsland I began to notice a definite change in the landscape. After sixteen miles of glorious road-free crags and hill and moorland, the Wall was creeping back to cultivated civilisation. The Central Section of the Wall is by far the richest archaeologically – for obvious reasons. The Irthing Valley I was now beginning to enter, and beyond that the Cumberland plain, have had centuries of continuous ploughing which has destroyed almost every trace of the Wall.

Gilsland is a pretty area of neat rolling fields, bright streams and deep green valley gorges, yet somehow unappreciated, almost a no-man's land. The village looks towards Carlisle, not Newcastle, as its Big Brother, the nearest town to supply such necessities of life as Chinese restaurants and frozen foods in bulk, yet Carlisle doesn't really care about Gilsland, not any

Overleaf The Wall, looking west over Cawfields Crags.

Above left Remains of Roman columns at Corbridge, the first important site to be seen today on the Eastern side of the frontier. Corbridge was the second largest town and the main supply base for the legionary craftsmen who built Hadrian's Wall.

Left The Bathhouse at Chesters fort on the banks of the North Tyne. This is probably the best remaining military bathhouse in Europe and the best preserved of all the buildings along the line of the Wall.

Above Vindolanda. Students helping to build a reproduction section of the Wall, in turf and in stone, as a tourist and educational attraction. Until now, nobody in the last fifteen hundred years or so had seen Hadrian's Wall at its full and original height.

Following page Vindolanda.

Above A decorated spoon bowl of silvered bronze from Vindolanda.

Left Sheep safely grazing at the Knag Burn, looking east from Housesteads fort.

IOM
△▽△▽△▽△▽△▽△
CETERISQVE
DIISIMMORT·
ETCEN·PRAET·R·
QPETRONIVS
Q·F·FAB·VRBICVS
PRAEFCOH IIII
GALLORVM

EX·ITALIA·
DOMOBRIXIA
VOTVM·SOLVIT
PRO·SE·
AC SVIS

Left Seated mother goddess – stone relief from Vindolanda.

Right An altar to Jupiter from Chesters Museum (IOM stands for Jupiter Optimus Maximus, Jupiter best and greatest).

Lady with a Fan, Carlisle. Though on the west of the Wall, Carlisle was the biggest frontier town and had beside it Stanwix, the Wall's largest fort. This elaborate tombstone of an unknown lady gives an idea of the quality of local life. Was the fan to protect her from the sweltering Cumberland summers or to denote her status?

more. In Victorian days it was a popular spot for Sunday jaunts, a holiday spa attracting visitors from all over the north who came to take the waters. Now the spa is no more and Carlisle day trippers take their Ribble Mystery tours elsewhere, to the Lakes or to Silloth and the Solway. Gilsland, for all its prettiness and former glories, is now decidedly in the sticks.

It felt rather strange, coming down from the rugged, barren heights into such a lush green backwater. It might be truer to call it a watershed area than a no-man's land. It literally is a watershed – you can see on the map where the streams suddenly get fed up flowing east to the North Sea and decide to try their luck with the Irish Sea to the west.

Geologically, it's a watershed, as the Romans found, with the Red Rock Fault splitting the country from north to south. To the west, the limestone runs out, which would explain why the Romans originally built the western part of the Wall in turf. (At least until some clever archaeologist comes along and proves that they *started* the Wall in turf, working from the west, and turned to stone after crossing the Red Rock Fault.)

Archaeologically, the River Irthing at Gilsland is the dividing line of the Broad Wall Foundations. After the Irthing, the complications of Narrow Wall on Broad foundations cease as it becomes Narrow on Narrow.

Gilsland is on the border of Cumberland and Northumberland – the village is actually in Northumberland – and it's around the Gilsland area that there's a sudden change in accent. Defenders of the genuine Cumberland dialect, who definitely produce their own dialect poems and booklets and have their regular meetings, consider themselves very different animals from the Northumbrians. The accents become quite different to the ear in only a couple of miles. In the same way, the differences in a few miles from Scotland into England are equally startling to hear. That people should live so near, look so alike, even have the same surnames (you get English Grahams, for example, and Scottish Grahams), yet sound so different is quite amazing. Borders always have the effect of exaggerating differences.

Right from the beginning of the Wall walk, and all the way

still to go to Carlisle and the west, the area has had hanging over it the effects of four hundred years of Border wars. The history of both Newcastle and Carlisle, and of every church tower and barnyard in between, has been dominated by the centuries of strife between the two peoples.

In Elizabethan times, when the Border raiding, raping, arson and general gangsterdom was at its height, there was a move to resurrect Hadrian's Wall. Once and for all, it was thought, the fighting could be stopped by copying the Romans and building an eighty-mile long wall, with skonses (or castles) at every mile. The anonymous writer of this proposal to the Queen, put forward around 1587, estimated that the cost would be £30,000. It was never followed up.

If anybody, it was Hadrian who started it all – by building his border from the North Sea to the Solway to separate the Romans from the Barbarians. The present-day western Border runs only ten miles or so to the north – over on the east it's further north, going up at an angle to follow the Tweed not the Tyne.

Border history is full of romantic tales, most of them tarted up for genteel consumption by Sir Walter Scott. There were indeed gallant Young Lochinvars but most of the incidents were sordid, full of pointless acts of vengeance, cattle stealing simply to kill cattle. The Borders had protection rackets long before Chicago invented them. It was from this region that the term blackmail crept into the English language, a rather ignoble claim to fame.

The Border families who spent so long killing each other are still there on either side – the Armstrongs, Grahams, Forsters, Fenwicks, Nixons, Musgraves, Lowthers, Kerrs, Carrs, Bells, Ridleys, Johnstones, Maxwells. Every telephone book along the Wall is full of them. In my class at school in Carlisle, we had eight different Grahams. It's a wonder any of them survived, not just survived but spread throughout the rest of the world. The last two presidents of the United States had Border blood in their veins, which no doubt accounts for their strong survival instincts. There's one historic photograph of Nixon and Lyndon Johnson with two other American heroes with Border blood – Billy Graham the evangelist and Neil Armstrong the astronaut. (Last year Mr Armstrong came back to his fatherland and received the freedom of Langholm.)

The tragedy about all the Border families who spent so many centuries trying to kill each other is that they are all kinsmen – they come from common stock. You only have to set down in print a Border accent, from Dumfriesshire or Berwick, Cumberland or Northumberland, and you see at once the uniformities.

Professor J. D. Mackie has demonstrated that the Border was essentially an artificial *political* creation, a line dividing people of the same tongue and the same stock. The characteristic place names, occurring on either side of the Border, give away the common origin and most interesting of all, the common ancestors of the present-day Border inhabitants. Place names are vital in tracing origins because they don't change, not the way people change. On either side, you come across such words as fell, meaning the upper slope of a hill, beck and burn both meaning stream, haugh meaning flat land beside a river, holm an island in a river, hope a sheltered valley and moss meaning peat bog. All of these words are of Norse origin, proving once and for all that the Borders were invaded and settled by Scandinavians. A central island of Norse-speaking people grew up who were gradually encroached on two sides. From the south, the Saxon power which sprang from the kingdom of Wessex and eventually became England, met headlong with the Celtic-Scoto powers who became the kingdom of Scotland. They fought out their power politics over this former Scandinavian territory, each claiming in turn that it belonged to them. When the kings went back to London and Edinburgh to concern themselves with other matters, the Border folks, split in two against their wishes, were left to fight it out, man to man, forgetting that they were brothers under the skin. On the Scottish side they still annually beat out the Marches, riding out the frontier territories as they did in the old days, ceremoniously keeping the English side at bay. There's no actual fighting, except at football matches.

Fortunately, there is a general feeling today amongst the

folks on both sides of the Border, linked as they are with a common past, that they're neither Scottish nor English but a peculiar Border race. Carlisle, which calls itself proudly the Border City, can have few citizens who don't have Scottish relations.

An outsider, once he gets over the strange and apparently differing accents, can detect common bonds between the Border folks, making them different from folks further north and south. They're not exactly the most welcoming race in these islands. Living in fear of being murdered for four centuries has certainly left its mark. Behind their outward reticence lies suspicion. Behind this, and it shows in many of their actions and words, is a convoluted cunning which defies logic.

The Cumbrian brand of suspicion towards strangers greets you as soon as you get over the county border – they start charging you to look at their Roman remains. Whatever nasty feelings the Northumbrian farmers may have towards the Wall and its visitors, I was never once asked to pay to walk over Northumbrian land, even by Councillor Woodman. But once in Cumberland, it happens twice in a few miles. Very tight, these Cumbrians.

Having said that, the first Roman relic at Gilsland to be seen is absolutely free and well worth looking at, thanks to excellent conservation work by the Department of the Environment. It's the Poltross Burn milecastle, one of the best preserved of them all.

You turn left before you get into the village proper, past Gilsland station, one of the many stations on the Carlisle-Newcastle line no longer in operation. There are some steep steps beside the railway and then a bridge across a rather pretty gorge. It was reminiscent of some of the relics back in the Newcastle suburbs to suddenly find an immaculately preserved bit of Roman life surrounded by work-a-day gardens and houses, all of them oblivious of the stranger from the past lurking in its midst.

It's a far better relic than any in the Newcastle suburbs. It covers an area seventy by sixty feet with all the wall foundations visible, including gateways, plus some of the internal barracks. Finds have shown it was occupied from Hadrian's time to the late fourth century with evidence of three periods of reconstruction. There's enough remaining of a flight of steps up to the ramparts at the north-east wall of the milecastle to indicate how high the Wall must have been in its original state – by calculating the angle of the steps. For centuries there was continuous disagreement about how high the Wall must have been. These steps were one of the vital pieces of evidence, indicating that the Wall was fifteen feet high, the height agreed by most people today. (There was of course a parapet on top, another six feet high, which protected the patrolling soldiers.)

The Department of the Environment, who looks after the milecastle so carefully, has erected a plaque, saying it's Milecastle 48, Poltross Burn, but that's all. Considering the richness of the site, its importance amongst Wall relics and that it's about the first milecastle that visitors coming from the west can have a proper look at, you'd expect some extra information. If information about this milecastle is too complicated for the layman then something about milecastles in general would be useful, about what part they played in the Wall structures.

But on the whole, throughout the central section the Department has done a good job. This is where they've concentrated their energies and they have those three fine forts, each of them very popular with the public, and many other relics which they carefully look after. From now on, they're struggling to find any scraps to uncover and conserve. From now on, relics are thin on the ground, though they're still looking.

The Department's Inspector of Ancient Monuments most closely connected with the Wall is Miss Dorothy Charlesworth. Each Inspector is assigned a different region and usually looks after a varied selection of monuments. As the Wall is our biggest Ancient Monument, she has made it her speciality.

The Inspectorate's London headquarters is in Savile Row, opposite West End Central Police Station, just along the street from the Beatles' Apple offices and Hardy Amies' couture showrooms. It couldn't be further away from Hadrian's Wall, in time or spirit. Miss Charlesworth shares a huge very stark office with another Inspector. It seemed to be completely bare except for boxes of maps and drawings.

She's small, of indeterminate age, and doesn't go in for idle chat but gets on clinically with the job. She can disappear into the background wherever she is, looking like an anonymous lady clerk in London, or yet another teacher on the Wall. She comes originally from Hexham, went to school at Cheltenham Ladies' College and then to Somerville College, Oxford. For a year she was a bibliographical assistant to Richard Wright on his edition of Collingwood's Roman Inscriptions of Britain, did research in Roman glass on a Leverhulme Studentship for two years, and worked on a catalogue of ancient glassware. She came into the Department of Ancient Monuments about fifteen years ago and has worked mainly on the Wall ever since. When she speaks, she can be very formidable, to the point, letting no one get away with slip-shod thinking.

She always goes by car, carrying her measuring rods, Pentax camera and other tackle with her. She takes her own photographs, always excluding any figures standing in the sites, though the trend is now to include human beings in archaeological photographs. Archaeologists can be creatures of fashion, like anyone else. At one time they used to dig in narrow trenches, then the fashion moved to eight foot square trenches, then to area stripping.

When I saw her in London she was about to make a quick trip up to Cumberland. The Cumberland County Council had just informed her that they were going to do some road work at Glasson, across the approximate line of the Wall. She was on the phone, ringing firstly the Department's architect in charge of the region, telling him what she would be doing and asking for labour, then she rang Carlisle Castle, where the Department has its regional headquarters, to arrange for four workmen to meet her at Glasson. 'No, no,' she was saying. 'We won't have to fill in. We'll be working just ahead of the Council men, if we're quick enough. We can leave it for them to fill in.'

In the days when wealthy amateur archaeologists were the main excavators of the Wall, such as John Clayton in the nineteenth century and even in the thirties with people like Simpson and Birley, the decision about where and when to dig was made solely for archaeological reasons. They chose a spot because they had reason to believe they'd find something. Today, such decisions are usually made by outside forces. Archaeologists, even government ones, can't afford to dig where they want, even in open countryside. They have to wait until a local council decides to build a new roundabout, widen a road, tear down some houses, and they dash in quick, have a dig amongst the entrails, make notes and take photographs, plead for anything particularly exciting to be left open or moved to safety, all the time worrying about the mechanical diggers hovering over their shoulders.

'It would be nice to select our sites one day, but I can't see it ever happening.'

All the same, she was excited about one forthcoming site thrown up by chance this year. While clearing an area north of the Tullie House Museum in Carlisle to make way for a new ring road, the local council had uncovered part of the medieval walls of the town with beneath them what could be remains of the Roman city. She was busily organising an Emergency Excavation which would start later that summer. I made a note not to miss it.

With all Department digs, they try to use student volunteers, as they do at Vindolanda, paying them a small sum to cover their living accommodation, and a certain amount of so-called professional labour. Miss Charlesworth was planning to use twelve prisoners from a local prison for her Carlisle dig, having found them successful in the past. What usually happens is that the Inspector in charge contacts the local labour exchange and takes whatever he can get. Most inspectors tell lurid tales of this sort of labour, about ending up with meths drinkers, others sleeping in the trench all day, not turning up, refusing to work if it's cold. Miss Charlesworth is strict about labour, paid and unpaid, doing a proper day's work. She works in the trenches in all weathers, and expects others to do the same.

Her biggest single problem on any Wall excavation is the weather. If your trench fills up with water, you've had it. She finds all the councils very helpful. 'The Wall is so well known that they never go ahead without telling us, which can happen in some parts of the country.' Nor has she ever had trouble with local farmers, though she can understand their worries about visitors leaving gates open.

'The Wall was there long before they were so it's hard for them to complain too much. If it suddenly bobbed up in the middle of the night in their fields, then I'd understand. But it's always been there and no doubt has always affected the price of their land.'

One of her minor problems is accommodation. Like the volunteer labour, she is on a set subsistence level. She tends to move around on a long dig, having some time in a comfortable hotel then moving into a cheaper guest house when her allowance runs out. She always finds in towns that it's difficult to get an early breakfast. Daylight is vital for digging, so she likes to be up and away early. For Housesteads she usually stays around Twice Brewed or at the pub.

Housesteads is her main working area and has been for some time. Every year she excavates there, though this year she would be doing very little because of the new Carlisle site. Her best ever find, the one that excited her most, took place at Housesteads. In a latrine she found that gold ring belonging to the fort's Commandant. 'Finding gold is always terribly exciting. It happens so rarely. This ring was in perfect condition. Gold always is, of course. It doesn't tarnish. This one contained a gem stone with a theatrical mask. It's perfection.'

She's also found many glass vessels over the years, though none which would excite the layman. Given a free hand and unlimited money she wouldn't bash on into unexcavated Cumberland but would excavate Housesteads. 'It would be unprincipled of me not to. It's always best to concentrate on one fort wherever possible. Housesteads is the nearest to completion.'

She hadn't been so far to the Vindolanda site, which I found surprising. She made a face and said she didn't want to get mixed up in any of the arguments, though she was friendly with all the Birley family. She has had enough to do on the

Wall itself. But even to *look* at what they've done, wouldn't that be interesting?

'Personally I'm not in favour of reconstructions, certainly not on the line of the Wall itself, but I've nothing against them away from the Wall, if that's what people want to do. I wouldn't want one on the Wall because we don't know necessarily that the Wall was fifteen feet high. That might be disproved one day, then what would you do? Reconstructions depend a great deal on imagination.'

I suggested that if there were any doubts they could only be marginal, at least as far as the public were concerned. An accompanying notice could always say so. Surely the public deserved to see what all the fuss was about. It was OK for the experts, they knew it all. She still wasn't convinced. The public and tourists really weren't her department. She looked upon herself as a researcher, pure and simple. She wants only to be left alone to get on with the job.

I left the Poltross Burn Milecastle, still wishing it provided more information, for the public and tourists in general, and walked into Gilsland village. I'd booked into the Romanway Guest House, purely because of its name. They sounded jolly on the phone, definitely interested in tourists.

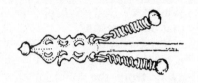

13
Gilsland:
Bide a Wee at Romanway

Ron Dawkins was in the hall of the Romanway Guest House playing a huge set of electric vibes. They blocked the whole entrance so I put my haversack down and waited till he was finished. His kids were running back and forward with cloths, helping him to dust down the vibes. He'd just dug them out of the cellar where they'd lain since he and his wife moved into Romanway the previous year. Tonight he had a big engagement on, playing in a little group at the Golden Fleece, a pub at Ruleholme near Brampton. He has a regular date there, playing four nights a week, usually on drums. Tonight he was going to delight the drinkers with a touch of class. He was trying to remember some MJQ numbers that he hadn't played for some time, pedalling like mad to keep up the echoes while the kids demanded that it was their go.

His wife arrived and made some coffee for me, ran a hot bath and took my boots and heavyweight hat to dry at her kitchen fire. After my bath, Ron took me down into the cellars to look at his hundred budgerigars. There were boxes and boxes of them, all in neat rows. Not all were budgies – some were East Indian Finches, so he said, all amazing colours and shapes. His best ones were worth £60 each. He keeps them for fun, not really for breeding, though he sold some now and again. His ambition was to win some prizes at the North of England Caged Birds Shows, but so far he'd had no luck. There were too many affluent competitors who could pay far more for a bird than he could. But it was a nice hobby. When he comes home from playing in the pub of an evening, usually around midnight, he spends an hour, feeding them. During the day, if he has a spare half hour, he comes down and talks to them.

In his two-and-a-half-acre garden, which he bought along with the house, Ron Dawkins has one of the best preserved sections of the Roman Wall in existence. His garden is in all the archaeological books – where the guest house is referred to as Gilsland Old Vicarage garden, which is what it used to be. Outside his front porch he's got two genuine Roman altars, one of them inscribed. I distinctly saw one of his guests bang his boots on them, to get the mud off, before coming into the house.

Ron is short and rather tubby and very jolly, always full of chat and laughs. 'There's not many characters around today but people tell me I'm one of them,' he said disarmingly. He and his wife come from the Newcastle area. For two years he was a representative for a protective clothing firm, travelling each day from Heddon on the Wall (that dreadful place where the Military Road begins) to Carlisle. 'I love a long drive to work. My record for the fifty miles was forty-seven minutes – and that was with the van and seven hundredweight of rags.'

His boss, who was area manager for Scotland and the North of England, was operating from Buckinghamshire, of all places. Head office said he would have to move to Cumberland so Ron, as the local rep, was given the job of finding a suitable house for his boss. He found the Romanway Guesthouse, empty for a long time and apparently run down as a guest house but ideal for a family man. He looked it over, rang his boss and said I've got the ideal place. The boss said forget it. I've had the sack.

About a year later, with another few thousand commuting miles under his belt, Ron noticed in the *Newcastle Journal* that the house was still for sale – at a reduced price. On an impulse, he and his wife decided to scrape together all they could get and make an offer. They got it for a price around £7,000, so I estimated from hints Ron gave out. It's a large, square, very handsome Victorian vicarage, in a lovely situation, the sort of house which could be worth £100,000 in London. Best of all, it has the two-and-a-half-acre garden containing a paddock and that unique chunk of the Roman Wall. He's now thinking of breeding ponies in the paddock, when he's not playing the vibes or feeding his budgies.

They didn't intend to run it as a guest house, but as a family home for his three young boys, then people kept on knocking at the door, demanding a bed, because they'd got the address from old guide books. He'd just got a table licence – to serve drinks with food – and was very chuffed with himself and was already thinking of grandiose plans for expansion. Apparently, there's a commercial on the local ITV station, Border, for McEwan's beer in which you see some Roman Britons leaning over Hadrian's Wall, knocking back pints of McEwan Ale. Ron can just see himself in the part. Mine host, bustling out on summer evenings to serve tankards of beer to terribly wealthy tourists sitting on his Wall. He can't do it legally, not at the moment, till he gets a full licence, but that's a minor obstacle. Unfortunately, McEwan's weren't impressed when he approached them for a tie-up. Instead Vaux's are going to be his suppliers. He says they couldn't have been keener – even making a new sign for him, all for free. He dragged it out over tea, a huge affair about the size of his dining room. I agreed it was discreet and tasteful, not at all flash, as befitted a guest house of archaeological fame.

Ron is very proud of his Wall, though he knew nothing about it before he chanced to come to the house. He's mugged up a lot of Roman Britain background, picked up from Department of the Environment people who look after his Wall for him. His patter with guests is very impressive, if a bit over imaginative round the edges. He's a real enthusiast for whatever he finds himself in, and was genuinely disgusted by the idea of making people pay to look at his bit of the Wall. He could easily charge. The four hundred feet of the Wall in his garden can only be seen by walking on his property. On the contrary, he encourages people to trample over his lawns, whether or not they use the Guest House.

He has had one row so far with the Department of the Environment. Traditionally, their workmen have not only kept the grass neat on both sides of the Wall but cut the lawn which leads to it. One day, they stopped cutting the lawn as part of a new economy drive. 'I rang London and told them I'd stop their workmen getting at the Wall across my land, but nothing happened. A week later I rang again, saying that my solicitor would be in touch in the morning. Three hours later, the workmen were there, cutting the lawn. I've had no trouble since.'

There were only two others staying that night at the Romanway. Both had been there for weeks – one in fact for over six months – and both worked at Spadeadam, the rocket establishment. Over breakfast next morning I said to the six monther, a manager looking figure, that it looked like rain. 'Absolutely typical,' he said, very wearily. 'It's like this all the year round here.' The other guest, a young electrician, was much more taken by the area. He said if he could get a move up here permanently he'd come. At home in Stevenage his wife spent days and days on her own without any of the neighbours speaking to her.

The Romanway had recently had some people from the Institute of Hydrology who'd booked in again for the following month when they were coming back to change the rain water meters in the surrounding hills. Apart from that, they didn't have many bookings, but were hoping for passing travellers in the better weather. Considering they're on an east-west link road, they have very few commercial travellers. 'This area used to get a lot,' explained Ron. 'But they stopped suddenly, overnight, once the M6 was built. They can get back home to Manchester instead of having to spend a night in the wilds.'

'They're strange people out here, sort of outcasts. I've found few who were born and bred here. Most of them are like us, drifted over from the North East. Even though we're so much nearer Carlisle, only sixteen miles as opposed to forty-two to Newcastle, we tend to look towards the North East. I think that's one of the reasons the house was empty for so long. It was advertised in the Newcastle papers, yet it was more suitable for someone from Carlisle who wanted to move out into the country.'

I had a very pleasant English fried breakfast, and all for a very modest charge (£1.50, B and B). Ron told me as I set off to ring him at any time and he'd come and pick me up if I got lost in the wilds. 'And don't forget, hot meals at any time, day or night! Beer on the Wall! And if you want fixed up with some lady geriatrics from the Co-op, just give us a ring . . .'

I wished him good luck, with all his ventures, and set off. I had meant to look at the Co-op place. It's the biggest most splendid house in Gilsland, built in 1865 as a grand hotel for the gentry taking the waters and now used by the Co-op as a convalescent home, but the rain had stopped and I wanted to get back to the Wall.

Firstly, I had a proper look in his garden, clambering over his kids' toys, left on the Wall from some game they'd been playing the day before. A new stretch, as long again as the bit in his garden, had been newly restored in an adjoining field so that now the Wall runs almost all the way from his house towards the Poltross Burn milecastle on the other side of the railway. It's a splendid piece, probably the best place anywhere to study the Narrow Wall on Broad foundation. (And the last place as we're almost approaching the Irthing crossing.)

On the other side of the road, finally turning my back on Romanway and the Dawkins family, the Wall is equally splendid all the way to the Willowford Bridge abutment, where the Wall, and the Roman Military Way cross the Irthing. It's a well-preserved third of a mile stretch. The path is in the Wall ditch, running clearly all the way on the right of the Wall, and contains a couple of centurial stones and two good turrets, 48A and 48B.

The path ends in a farmhouse beside which there's an official Ministry notice saying Willowford Bridge abutment, plus a chalked handwritten notice board saying admission 5p. I knocked at the farm door and asked the farmer's wife, Mrs Armstrong, if I really had to pay as I only had a £5 note. I was certainly the first, and perhaps the only, person who had come that way that day, perhaps for several weeks. I didn't *have* to pay to cross her field, she said. No one was forcing me. But if I didn't I wouldn't be allowed any further. I gave her my £5 note and she spent a long time searching round the house for the change.

'We have to pay a rent for this land, you know. We're just tenant farmers. Why should we let folks inconvenience us by wandering over our fields? Some people moan about having to pay, but they've no right to expect us to be troubled for nothing.'

What sort of trouble. I asked. She told a long story about a couple she'd argued with who hadn't wanted to pay. On the way out, she saw them let their dog run free which resulted in the death of three of her hens. No, the hens hadn't died immediately. It happened a few days later. But there was no doubt in her mind that the dog had been the cause.

She asked if I wanted to see some pictures. They turned out to be slides, which she was trying to sell, and I said no thanks. She asked where I'd stayed the night and I told her. She didn't want to be impertinent, but how much had they charged and what was it like? I gave the Romanway a rave report, saying how fantastically cheap it was, and with a big chunk of the Wall thrown in, at no extra charge. 'Huh,' she said. 'I've had reports to the contrary. I do bed and breakfasts you know. I might send them some of my overflow, *if* they're as good as you say. I have people coming back year after year.'

I tried to ask how many people came to look at the bridge in a year. But she would give nothing away. Business wasn't all that good. It was just the good weather that brought them out.

After all that, the bridge abutment was a bit of a let down, hardly worth 5p., not when you consider that the North Tyne abutment at Chollerford, which has many more visible remains, doesn't cost anything to look at. Like the North Tyne bridge, it's hard to work out how it all fitted together. You can imagine a turret or milecastle as it must have been even from a few feet of foundations, but a bridge, soaring up and across the landing on the other side, is harder to believe, when there's only a few stones to be seen lying on the ground. As at the North Tyne, evidence of a millstone and a water mill were found. But that's about all.

In one corner of the abutment turret I found an empty State Management nut brown ale bottle, left over by some disrespectful trespasser. It was already an antique in its own right. If I hadn't already got one in my own collection at home I might have put it in my rucksack. As every serious beer drinker knows, the Carlisle pubs have been nationalised since the first world war, when the government tried to stop the munition factory workers at Gretna going in for wholesale drunkenness. Now, Carlisle and district's State Management pubs have just been sold, thanks to the Tory government deciding to give them back to private enterprise, which I thought was a shame. It was just about the best beer in the country and by far the cheapest. According to the *Cumberland News*, State Management beer mats are already becoming collectors' pieces. I should have taken that bottle as a swap.

On the other side of the river there's a sheer cliff, rising about two hundred feet straight out of the water. The Irthing has moved since Roman days, leaving the bridge abutment high and dry, but nonetheless there must always have been a very steep cliff somewhere at the other side. They had to get the bridge across to the opposite bank and then build the Wall and the road up the cliff face to join milecastle 49 right on top of the cliff itself, an incredible feat of engineering.

I admired the agility of old Hutton. He not only waded across the Irthing at this point but somehow scrambled up the opposite bank, doing a long zig zag, so he says, through brambles. It must have been the autumn, after a dry summer. It was now early spring and the river I was looking at was swollen with the winter snows from the hills. I took one look at it and retreated.

I had to make a detour back to Gilsland, over the road bridge, down the road and along the other side of the river till eventually I came back to the milecastle on top of the cliff I'd been looking up at an hour previously. It was well worth it.

The view down the Irthing valley was terrific. It was even better when I walked the half mile or so further along the Wall, along one of the handsomest stretches of all, to Birdoswald fort. In this short stretch there are six inscriptions built into the Wall on its south side. I only saw a couple. It was a Department workman who told me later that I should have seen six – he'd stuck little bits of metal low down on the Wall to indicate an inscription above.

Like Willowford Bridge, Birdoswald fort has to be paid for, even though there is no museum or any special amenities or services which deserve payment. The Department of the Environment looks after the remains, but as at Great Chesters, the site is also the site of a modern farm, Birdoswald Farm. There's a severe notice directing everyone coming off the Wall from the Irthing to the far gate of the farm. This is to stop you nipping straight into the farmyard without paying to have a look at the walls and gateways of the fort. Instead, visitors are channelled down the side of the farm, on the west side, where you have to pay 5p. for the privilege of going through the farmyard. I banged at several doors and had to search the outhouses before I found the farmer's wife, a Mrs Baxter, who took my 5p but was too busy to give me much information about life on a Roman fort today, or what she thinks about tourists, except to say that the owner was Lord Henley of Scaleby Castle, but he was away in London.

Hutton got a cool reception when he arrived here from the then farmer, a Mr Bowman. He says that his ink bottles and book were taken as suspicious emblems, a sign that he was a government official, come to examine the property to put the taxes up. Perhaps Mrs Baxter thought I was a taxman, having been warned by Mrs Armstrong down the road that I was trying to prise out of her how many 5p. visitors she has in a year ...

After she'd gone in, I saw a notice saying Guidebooks for sale, price 15p., so I knocked again and bought one. I was surprised to find a guidebook. It's not a government publication, like the ones written by Eric Birley at Housesteads, Corbridge and Chesters, but a piece of private enterprise, printed in Huddersfield in 1972 and written by a Peter Howard, BA. It was very informative, if a bit technical and detailed for the layman, reading almost like an academic thesis. Birley in each of his guidebooks at least gives a simple general description of Hadrian's Wall, the story so far, before going into details of the fort in question. But the Birdoswald photographs are lavish, mostly taken by Peter Howard BA. All in all, a commendable enterprise by a knowledgeable enthusiast. Every site on the Wall of any stature should have its guidebook, however brief.

Armed with the guide, I then walked round the fort, going firstly through it to the far end of the site to look down upon the Irthing gorge. In many ways, it's the most beautiful view on the whole Wall. One Earl of Carlisle has likened it to the view from Troy. (This was the 7th Earl who recorded this impression in 1854 in a diary he kept during a tour of Greece.) It's such a different view from the wild, limitless, misty, mysterious views of the Whin Sill crags. It's a very English view, a southern English view of the sort Turner or Constable might have painted, a perfect landscape with the river bending just the right way, the tress all in line. The grassy covered plateau in the foreground, on which the fort stands, is almost perfect in its proportions.

From the Romans' point of view it was too perfect. Every time they expanded the fort, as they did many times, they ran into endless complications, having to cram everything into a confined space. They just managed to squeeze in the Vallum, tucking it in on the very edge of the plateau, before the land falls steeply to the Irthing.

The fort was superimposed on the Turf Wall, which had been built first. Being a cavalry fort, its northern third as usual stuck out over the Wall, leaving three gates with an easy exit. But when the Stone Wall replaced the Turf, they put the Wall along the North side, bringing the whole fort inside the Wall – all lovely complications for the archaeologists to try to unravel.

Out of the sixteen forts on the line of the Wall, Birdoswald is one of only four with anything really worth looking at today – the others being Corbridge, Housesteads and Chesters.

Vindolanda, of course, which will perhaps be the best of all to look at in the future, is not strictly on the Wall line. A case can be made for including Great Chesters because of its couple of gateways and ramparts, or even Carrawburgh because of the Mithraic temple, but I wouldn't put them in my top forts.

Birdoswald was an important fort, housing a cavalry regiment, the smartest unit amongst the Auxiliaries. Its main functions were to guard the Irthing bridge, to help in patrolling the western section of the Wall as a whole and to act as a central signalling station. Many watch towers have been discovered to the north of Birdoswald, linking up the outpost forts such as Bewcastle, and to the south.

There was some sort of fortification on the site before the Romans, a native stockade perhaps, and military life afterwards. It would be hard after all to ignore such a natural strategic situation. Once again, Arthurian legends are rife, this time trying to prove that Birdoswald was the site of King Arthur's last battle where he received his death wounds. The Roman name for the site was Camboglanna – meaning crooked glen, because of the twists and turns of the Irthing gorge. The name always given for Arthur's last battle is Camlann, which could have been the same place. No one knows how long the place has been called Birdoswald. In Old Hutton's book he points out an obvious derivation – that it comes from King Oswald, King of Northumbria. As we know, there's a faction which maintains Arthur was really a compilation of the deeds of several Northumbrian kings and not a Southern King from South Cadbury, Somerset, the usually accepted site for the legendary Camelot. If only the Northumbrian Tourist Board could prove a rival Northern Camelot it could be a great attraction. When Hollywood get round to doing the story once again, I'd certainly advise their location men to have a look at the fort. It would be worth their 5p. at the gate.

The fort gates at Birdoswald are some of the best to be seen anywhere, despite being in constant use today as the farm gates, with cows and tractors going through them all the time. Some of the best Roman coins ever found were dug up near the East Gate by Ministry workmen (one of their few important finds) in 1949. Several workmen had already boasted to me about this find. Inside an arm-purse were found twenty-eight silver denarii, ending with the mint fresh coins of Hadrian, vital evidence about the history of the fort and Wall. There was some publicity about the find at the time. The East Cumberland County Coroner held an inquest at the fort and Professor Richmond demonstrated how the purse had been worn and argued that it had been lost by accident, dropped in a pile of earth, perhaps by a centurion who'd been standing supervising the work. The jury agreed with him, which was important, because coins lost by accident are not classed as treasure trove and therefore don't have to go to the Crown. It went to the owner, Lord Henley, who presented the purse and coins to Tullie House museum in Carlisle, where they are still on show. (On the west side of the Wall, good finds are routed to Carlisle not Newcastle.)

There have been many other important finds at Birdoswald over the centuries. Camden in 1599 reported that there was a lot still to be seen. 'It dothe seame to have been some great towne by the great runes thereof, the inhabitants did shew me the plaice wher the church stode, the inscriptions ther are either worne out by the tract of tyme or by the clownishe and rude inhabitants defaced.'

Clownishe and rude inhabitants have a lot to answer for over the centuries. But since 1927, when Simpson started work on the site, a great deal has been excavated. Unfortunately most of the excavations have been filled in again and nothing has been done on the site since 1950. There's nothing internally to be seen, except the south wall of the granary which now serves as the retaining wall of the farmer's garden. It's obviously a very rich site. As recently as 1961 the tenant farmer himself, Mr Baxter, dug up a tombstone of a soldier from the Sixth legion, quite by accident when he was ploughing four hundred yards west of the fort. Professor Birley has dated it as late Hadrian or early Antonine.

Perhaps the most remarkable of all the finds at Birdoswald has been a series of nineteen altars found at different times in the last two hundred years or so, all from around the same area to the East of the fort. All but one of the nineteen are dedicated to I.O.M. – to Jupiter Optimus Maximus – the odd one out being dedicated to a native Cumbrian war god, Cocidius. All of them were put up by the First Cohort of Dacians (more Rumanians) who garrisoned the fort in the late third and fourth centuries. The normal Roman altar is simply an inscribed and decorated slab of stone and can be any size, from twelve inches high to six feet. Basically, they look like tombstones. These ones were all so similar, as if part of a set, but for a long time no one could explain their significance, except another chance bundle of finds, the sort thrown up by excavations.

Then a similar series turned up at Maryport, down the Cumberland coast, this time on a piece of ground already known, from other evidence, to have been the fort's *parade ground*. Immediately this offered an explanation. It's known that each year commanding officers held a ceremony in honour of the Emperor in which a new altar was set up and everyone renewed their vows of loyalty to the Roman State and the Emperor. On the same day, *every* unit of the Roman Army did this, from Birdoswald to the Euphrates. It now looks as though there was also a ceremonial burying of the previous altars in a pit beside the parade ground. Perhaps every fort along the Wall has a pit of altars waiting to be discovered, each with its inscriptions and details of the garrison and its CO. It's not the altars in themselves which are so vital – the Romanway guest house wouldn't have had two kicking around the front garden if that were always the case – but the information the good ones can provide about the army personnel and their movements.

The field suddenly came to life before my eyes as I imagined a huge church parade, the whole garrison in its number one uniform, ceremonially going through its vows, unveiling one brand new altar and burying the old one. As symbolic parades go, Trooping the Colour, which is still done every year in Horse Guards Parade, is a lot less meaningful.

The Roman attitude to religion generally, given the times and the different superstitions of its many peoples, is in the main very convincing. It's a lifetime's study in itself but worth a quick look as it was an important element in every fort and settlement along the Wall.

Religion in Roman times can be divided into three sorts – official, unofficial and native. Official religions centred round the worship of the Emperor and those gods specially associated with the city and state of Rome – Jupiter, Mars, Apollo and others. But they weren't *exclusive* religions. Once a soldier or a citizen had done his duty to the official deities, he could then go on to worship any other gods he fancied, either local gods or those from his homeland. The Romans were very tolerant. They only ever objected to a religion on political grounds, such as in the case of Christianity. By saying it was the *only* faith, Christianity was therefore anti the Imperial gods. This was one of the things they had against Druidism, the native British religion they worked very hard to eradicate when they first landed on these shores. (The other reasons were its political power and its use of human sacrifices.)

The Roman Army took the worship of the Emperor with them everywhere and it was strictly followed in all army settlements and the new towns being set up by the Romans. In coloniae, chartered towns in which everyone was a citizen, there were temples to the Emperor run by six priests. Boadicea looked upon this official religion as a symbol of Roman domination and it was one of her reasons for rebelling in AD 60.

The Romans did use Emperor worship as a way of creating loyalty amongst their various subjects and as a form of gratitude for the Pax Romana. A new recruit into an auxiliary force soon learned to know all the official religious days and their ceremonies – and looked forward to them. They were days off, time for feasting. It was the spirit of the Emperor, his being, that was being worshipped. They didn't believe he was a god himself. By swearing loyalty and obedience to him, honouring his name, they were doing little more than soldiers do today when taking an oath to the Crown, to the President, or the State or whatever.

Of the Roman State gods, Jupiter was traditionally the chief, hence Jupiter Best and Greatest. It was on 1 January each year that new altars were set up to Jupiter on parade grounds all over the empire – 3 January was the day for Emperor worship.

There's a fascinating roll of papyrus which was found in a Roman fort on the Upper Euphrates by the Yale University Expedition in 1931 which lists all the festivals to be observed throughout the years, giving exact details of the required services and the sacrifices. Each unit of the Roman Army had such a document which was brought up to date all the time as new orders were issued. (No such document made of papyrus has ever been found in Britain, alas, because of the climate. It makes those discharge documents made of bronze all the more important.) Leading deities like Jupiter, Apollo, Mars, Neptune and Hercules were celebrated with the sacrifice of a bull. Female deities were given cows, past Emperors got oxen.

The sacrificed animals were then eaten, as the event became a feast once the ceremonies had been carried out. The priests always had a look at the entrails to decide what the future was going to bring, how the next battle or campaign was going to go. Soldiers naturally fought better if they thought the gods were on their side. The whole basic principle of all Roman religious beliefs, official and unofficial, was *placating* – getting the gods, whoever they were and the more the merrier, on your side. The high philosophic ideas and concepts of Rome which have been handed down to us by classical authors were followed and believed by only a highly educated minority.

Elaborate arrangements were made by commanding officers to keep the rank and file happy by making sure the entrails were read the right way, especially if it had already been decided to go into battle.

Most of the unofficial Roman religions concerned animals or nature generally. The normal, untutored soldier was beset on all sides by fears and superstitions. It was necessary for him to come to terms with the animal spirits, or the spirits behind every pond, tree, rock and river, especially if he was far from home. There are many altars set up simply to the 'genius loci' – the spirits of the place, whatever they were, hoping none would be missed out or offended.

Before any dangerous action, a soldier solemnly swore to

the Emperor or Jupiter, plus any particular spirits he was worried about, promising that if he came through unharmed, he would erect an altar in their honour. There were spirits which protected the stables (*Epona*) or the fort's bathhouse (*Fortuna*) which would be summoned for help by the ostlers or the bathers and then gratefully thanked. An officer going out hunting would ask Silvanus to help him kill the boar – then he'd erect an altar afterwards if he was successful. This happened so frequently that there was a formula for ending such altar inscriptions – V.S.L.M., meaning votum solvit libens merito, the donor willingly fulfilled his vow which was deserved.

Apart from official and unofficial Roman deities, there were many native Celtic gods, like that one Taranis at Corbridge, the so-called Harry Lauder. Every province had its native gods and many of them travelled, especially the Eastern gods, brought by the auxiliary soldiers.

Altars in Greek have been found at Corbridge, Carlisle and elsewhere. At Carvoran the First Cohort of the Hamii (those Syrian archers) dedicated an altar to a Syrian goddess. Their commanding officer put up his own personal altar, plus an elegant little poem, in honour of his own national deity, the African goddess, Caelestis. The first temple you come to on the Wall, still in situ, the one amongst the suburban gardens at Benwell, is known to have been to a local native deity, Antenociticus, though nothing else is known about him. His temple suggests that he was more than just a local spirit but a god with his own laid-out form of worship and attendant priests. In the Roman world there were many such gods.

Of all the Eastern religions of the Empire, the one that became the best organised was Mithraism. This was above all a Roman Army religion and there are many traces of it in Britain, especially around the Wall area. Roman religions were mainly concerned with observance. You said your prayers, went through the right rituals and fulfilled your vows afterwards. But Mithras, he was after your *soul*. He wanted devotion. Following Mithras was an emotional experience, as with other religions that came from the East, such as Christianity.

Mithraism appealed to the army because of its strong sense of duty and insistence on moral conduct. It had initiation rights, a series of seven grades through which you rose, depending on passing the appropriate physical and psychological tests. It appears to have been fairly exclusive, appealing largely to the officer class, and its ceremonies took place in secret. It had its own hierarchy and temples and became very powerful.

Mithras was born in a cave under the sign of a star, so the Mithraic legend runs. He slew a wild bull and from it vegetable and then animal life sprang up. This is symbolically his act of redemption, providing good for mankind. Most Mithraic worshipping rites were symbolic, using bread, food, wine and water, light and darkness. The temples were cavelike, to represent his birthplace. There was an initiation pit, in which followers were subjected to heat and cold and then entombed in a sort of coffin from which they had to rise. Worshippers experienced mystical revelations, which were helped along by the lavish use of a heavy scent produced by burning pine cones.

Three Mithraic temples have been so far found on the Wall, at Rudchester, Housesteads and Carrawburgh, the latter being the best known and best preserved and one on which the recreated Mithraic temple at Newcastle is based. There's evidence for others at Carlisle, Castlesteads, Newcastle and Wallsend and at the three legionary fortresses of York, Chester and Caerlton. The only definite civilian Mithras temple is the one found in London at the Walbrook in 1954, now reassembled on another site nearby. Even this had a military connection, being used by legionary veterans, plus wealthy merchants originally from the East.

By comparison, most non-Eastern religions were little more than good luck rituals, elaborate touch-wood symbols to help soldiers and civilians in times of stress and war or in foreign parts. When they were encouraged officially it was as a means of commanding unity and loyalty. It's not surprising therefore that a religion like Mithraism, with its complicated symbolism and tough moral and spiritual demands, should become powerful.

The comparisons between Jesus Christ and Mithras are striking – the humble birth, the mediator between God and man, the stars, the baptism, incense, the symbolic bread and wine. On Mithraic altar stones the head of Mithras has sun beams radiating from it – this was done by cutting away at the back of the stone and inserting a lighted torch. The effect is very like a halo.

Mithras was born on 25 December, a date which was stolen by the early Christian Church, though both cults probably owe much of their ritualism to their mutual Eastern antecedents. Mithraism was known well before Christianity, even in the West, though by the third century, when Christianity had taken a hold on the Roman Empire, the Christians were blaming the Mithras followers for having copied and degraded many of their sacred rituals.

Constantine, who was proclaimed Emperor by the army in York in 306, was the first Christian Emperor. It's thought that the Carrawburgh Mithras temple was deliberately desecrated in the fourth century by a Christian commandant. Yet surprisingly, there's little evidence of Christianity from the Wall area during the Roman occupation.

Britain, being a remote province, was out of the main stream and pagan cults continued to flourish, including Mithraism, right to the end of the occupation, especially in the military areas. Only around fifty objects bearing definite Christian symbols have been found in Britain from the Roman period, compared with several hundreds for Mithras alone.

There was little sign for a long time that Christianity would rise above a local native religion. In the years before Constantine, the Romans had persecuted the Christians for purely political reasons – because they refused to conform. Many Christian martyrs were scapegoats for other things going wrong at the time – famine, unrest in the Empire, civil wars. In Britain and other outer provinces there was an *increase* in pagan practices when Rome itself became Christian – a sort of girding of the loins to meet the threat of licensed competition.

Though the evidence of Christianity in Britain is slight in Roman times, Britain was represented by three bishops at the church council at Arles in 314. But judging by evidence so far found, it was all but extinguished in England by the Saxon invaders. However, the Romans did bring Christianity to England – though like so many other things, it as good as disappeared with them.

It survived in the extremities of the old Roman province, in Scotland and Northumberland, from where it grew and developed. Northumbria later became the centre for Christianity in Anglo-Saxon England – thanks to people like Bede and St Cuthbert.

Perhaps Christianity was stronger on the Wall than anyone will be able to prove, at least towards the end of the Roman occupation, as the career of St Patrick indicates. He wasn't Irish, as is generally assumed, but grew up around the western end of the Wall area, perhaps in Carlisle. Whatever his true birthplace, he was in fact a genuine Roman Briton. His father, a Roman official, and his grandfather were both Christians.

When the young Patrick was sixteen, around the year 390, he was kidnapped on the Solway coast by pirates who carried him off to Ireland as a slave. By this time Roman Britain was suffering from sea invaders on all sides as the barbarians got braver and the Roman military establishment became weaker. Patrick was in Ireland six years and then escaped to Gaul and then to Rome where he trained as a Christian missionary. In 437 he went back to Ireland to spread the Christian message.

If the Wall can't claim Arthur for its own, it's nice to know that St Patrick was a local lad, brought up in the only Wall religion that survived.

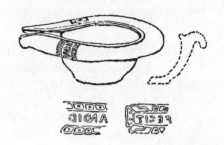

14
Naworth:
The Earl and his Problems

There are times on top of the Wall when you look out North on a fairly misty day and the whole world seems to be forest. For the last twenty miles or so, ever since the Wall country proper began, every northern horizon is so dominated by forest that you begin to feel it's coming nearer, about to take over and swallow the Wall in one huge gulp. This is not a mirage. The forest *is* moving.

Out there in that Scotch mist is the biggest man-made forest in Europe. It's commonly known as the Kielder Forest, though there are in fact about six differently named forests, with Kielder being the biggest. They're owned by the National Forestry Commission, a government-controlled body who are the nation's largest landowners. In acreage they dwarf organisations like the National Trust, the Army, Navy and Air Force put together. They own almost three million acres, five times that of any other body, and they're growing all the time. No wonder some people get worried, watching the ranks of those massed conifers creep nearer.

It all began in 1919 when the Commission was formed to establish a reserve of timber for use in war. It wasn't until 1958 that it was decided that modern armies don't need wood, the way they used to, and they announced that from now on their main object in life was conservation – keeping woodland areas alive, especially in hill areas, for the economic and social benefit of all.

In the Borders, their biggest single buy was Kielder Castle and forty-seven thousand acres from the Duke of Northumberland in 1932. (The Duke of Northumberland who built Kielder Castle in 1775 built it as a shooting box, a handy place for overnight stops in the shooting season.) In Northumberland and Cumberland the Commission now owns almost two hundred thousand acres, covering an area of three hundred square miles.

They created from nothing five villages in the depths of the Kielder and other forests, building three hundred houses and moving in about one thousand three hundred and fifty foresters and their families, plus schools, halls and shops. They live a strange, isolated, inbred life, as remote from urban life as if they were in Siberia or Alaska.

The highlights of their life include visits from Civil Service amateur dramatic societies who come up from London, no doubt on a number six tour, to entertain the foresters. The rest of the country tends to forget they're there, thinking that after Hadrian's Wall, you're straight into Scotland, not realising that in Northumberland there's hundreds of square miles in which anything can be happening.

In the last few years there's been a swing away from putting up man-made villages to go with the man-made forests. Even foresters have cars these days so they're now trying to build up existing hamlets.

It's the size of the Forestry Commission which frightens people. In the south there are critics who say their passion for conifers is ruining the landscape, not helping it, but in this poor, peat bog Border land it appears to be a powerful conservation force. It was Councillor Woodman, back at Great Chesters, who said you can't eat paper, but the Commission has not been planting on arable land. In the main, they've been reclaiming land lost to any sort of cultivation for centuries. What people forget is that this whole Border region was a forest when the Romans arrived. (Seeds preserved in the peat bogs show what the area was like.) They've been cut down over the centuries and on the poorer parts, the sheep have finished it off. Old records of those Border wars show families hiding in forests long since gone. Peace brought the cutting down of woods and the forming of huge estates. The population has always been falling, right from when the Romans left. Today there are very few villages or churches, an important clue to previous settlements. Though having said that, the churchyard at Bewcastle, where the Romans had an outpost fort, has provided the finest Anglo-Saxon sculptured cross, the Bewcastle Cross, found anywhere in Britain.

There's a second man-made element in the Gilsland area, the Spadeadam Rocket site, the site where those Romanway guests were working. This has continued the military tradition of the Border area, begun by Hadrian, continued by the Border wars, exemplified by the medieval castles and fortified churches you still find every few miles, and then brought up to date in 1957 when the Government decided to build the engine for the Blue Streak rocket on six thousand acres of Spadeadam Waste, just a couple of miles North of the Wall at Gilsland. As with the advent of the Roman soldiers, the area suddenly changed character. Millions of pounds were spent on the site, a fifty-bedroom hostel went up, nine hundred workers were taken on and the little town of Brampton became a boom town. Council houses, local schools, health services, shops had to be reschemed to plan for the sudden increase. The Romans at least stuck it for almost four hundred years. As I passed through (in April 1973) the end was announced, after only sixteen years of life. Millions of pounds had been thrown away all along, which is not unusual with modern military planning, as Blue Streak was obsolete then replaced, as Britain left its European space partners in ELDO and other tragic ups and downs. The *Cumberland News* was almost black at the edges as it reported the cancellation of the Europa rocket. I decided it was too sad to walk out to the site and hear all the redundancy stories.

It was a pleasure to return to the area's third man-made element – the Wall. It seemed so friendly and homely, almost a child of nature not a horrid man-made toy. Because stone is real you can pretend it's been there for ever, forgetting the mess the Roman ox carts and quarries must have made of the land-scape.

After Birdoswald, they must have made a substantial mess because there are *two* lines of Hadrian's Wall to follow – the Turf and the Stone Wall. They run separately for two miles, the Stone having replaced the Turf on a different line a few hundred yards to the North.

It was Simpson's clever detection work on this separate stretch of the Stone Wall in 1911 which found Hadrianic relics, thus proving that *both* Walls were Hadrianic. In Old Hutton's day, as we know, it was thought the Stone Wall was Severan.

Today the Stone Wall is under the modern road, with the line of the Turf Wall across a field to the left. I walked along the road, keeping an eye out for a handy place to jump over the Wall and have a look in the field at any likely bits of Turf Wall remains. It's a nice quiet road, without even a number, and heads for the village of Banks. All the heavy traffic heading towards Carlisle has now converged on the A69 further to the south.

Several experts, especially those who have made topographi-cal surveys have wondered why the Wall (Turf or Stone) wasn't built further to the south, taking advantage perhaps of the Irthing gorge and then the Geltsdale ridge. For once the Wall doesn't head for the highest bits of ground, the way it does on the Whin Sill, and in fact in many places the view north is definitely obscured. It's almost as if they didn't fear attacks from the north any more and were choosing vantage points with a good view to their rear. Perhaps the Brigantes inside the Wall weren't as friendly.

No one knows what the specific military problems were when the Wall was built, and doubtless we never will, but it's generally assumed that the problems were different on the western side. It seems to me that they were now intent on getting the Wall to Carlisle and the Solway as easily as possible. Why bother to mess around looking for high ground when you're now basically in an undulating plain.

A couple of fields after Birdoswald I turned down a path on

the left, signposted to Lanerton, as I could see the old Turf Wall mounds rising large and clear in the fields. It was my first proper sight of them and I hadn't expected them to be so strong and bold. I walked along the mounds, right to the bit where they join the road and the Stone Wall again. The Vallum runs right beside the Turf Wall all the way and together they make an impressive series of gigantic earth works. I came across an old piece of stone pillar at one point which I thought might be a Roman milestone as it looked like a smaller version of the one outside Vindolanda. I ran my fingers over a deep inscription and made out the word DRAIN.

Back on the road I took another turning left looking for the remnants of an old Roman quarry at a place called Comb Crag, but I couldn't find it. There is supposed to be an inscription by some Roman soldiers at work in the quarry, which proves if nothing else that soldiers were literate. But another inscription is now agreed to be a forgery, scratched by someone trying to prove that the Wall was built by Severus. The whole idea is bizarre, but no stranger than the Piltdown forgeries. Even experts can become deranged enough to create their own evidence to prove their own theories – or was it all a light-hearted joke? No one knows who perpetrated the forgery. Perhaps some dotty Victorian vicar, carried away by Wall madness when he heard Collingwood Bruce proving the Wall was Hadrian's.

At Pike Hill, just before Banks, I was pleasantly surprised to find signs of activity. One of the best known watch towers on the Wall is situated at this point. I'd expected the usual hard searching amongst the grass, convincing myself I could see it all. But there were two Department landrovers parked outside a hut, a concrete mixer and some spades. One of the landrovers was very dirty and some joker had written in the dust 'Mr Anderson, this car was late for work today'. Mr Anderson, a gentleman I had still to meet, is the foreman.

I knocked on the hut door and waited, not wanting to barge in this time. There was a movement inside, so they weren't asleep. I knocked again and went in. There were four workmen having their tea break. One was reading a cartoon magazine called *Funny Half Hour*, a publication new to me. I admired the simplicity of its title, innocent and unsensational. Two were playing dominoes and the fourth was reading the *Sun*. He stood up as soon as he saw me and offered me a cup of tea from his Thermos flask. It was my phallus friend from way back at the Chollerford Bridge abutment, the one who'd been sweeping up leaves in the autumn. He said he hadn't been sure then if I was an Inspector from London. Otherwise, he'd have been a lot more helpful. I said I couldn't possibly take his tea but he pointed to a stove and the kettle boiling away.

I told them about the new breed of farmers I'd met since crossing into Cumberland, charging 5p. to cross their land. They said it used to be sixpence, till decimalisation. Overnight, it had doubled, like so many things. 'They're real tight,' said one of the workmen. 'You don't just have to cut their lawns. With some of them you do everything but milk their cows.'

I was going through Banks when I noticed a very clean, newly whitewashed little farmhouse on the left of the road, right on the line of the Wall. A notice outside said 'LYC Museum.' On the door it said 'Welcome Friends.' So I knocked.

A Chinese face peered at me through a little window then broke into a smile and opened the door, welcoming me in. He explained that on Thursdays he was usually closed. 'So that I can do my shoppings.' I stepped inside and could see little rooms stretching ahead, all meticulously whitewashed, connected by home-made doorways. He'd banged jagged holes through the walls, linking one room to another, and had plastered them up as best he could, not bothering to put in doors or door frames. Above my head were some plastic circles suspended from the ceiling which moved like mobiles in the soft warm air from his central heating. On each of the circles was printed a phrase or word. 'One begets Two, Human Contact, The Truth of Truth is Love, Tree Healer, Warmth, Haa Hoo Hug' were some of the words I could read. That was about all there was in this first room. He said it was mobile poetry. As the circles moved, so you got an ever-changing sequence of words and phrases.

I went into other rooms with equally strange exhibitions.

There was a piece of magnetic sculpture which he switched on. He said it was by a famous Greek called Takis and was worth £2,000, but it wasn't for sale. 'No one can afford it.' There were some plastic bags which you blew up, put a pebble inside, then felt. In another room were some paintings by four- and five-year-old local children.

One large wall was empty but for a small postcard size photograph of a painting with a type-written apology beside it from a painter called Soto. 'I will show original work as soon as I can,' said the note. Mr Li Yuan-Chia, for such was the Museum owner's name, explained that Mr Soto's paintings were a long way away but he would bring them up to Banks one day. 'I can't afford money for the transport.'

I asked what made him open a museum, especially a museum like this, in the wilds of Cumberland. The locals weren't exactly known for their avant garde tastes. He said would I like some tea and to take a seat. It was real China tea, clear and sugarless and very refreshing.

His command of English was good but his accent was very strange. He pronounced museum, for example, as if it had a 'th' in the middle. As I drank my tea he explained that he'd left China at fourteen and gone to Italy where he became a painter. He then started to exhibit in London but the gallery which exhibited him closed.

In 1968 he came up to Brampton for two weeks on holiday to see a friend who came from this area. He liked the countryside so much that he decided to stay. On looking for a studio to work in he found this derelict cottage with a barn next door. 'I haven't paid for it yet, just the desposit.' As he started converting it, he moved further and further along, taking in one outhouse after another. 'I did all the work myself. If I'd paid someone else it would have taken twice as long.' To finance himself he did odd jobs, painting and decorating. He opened it as a gallery in August 1972, using his initials, LYC. The studio had somehow turned itself into a museum, so he gave up his own work to concentrate on running the museum. All the locals had been very kind and he liked Cumberland people very much. But he got a bit lonely, living in such a remote place all by himself. 'I would like someone to discuss my museum with.'

I asked if he was interested in the Roman Wall and he said he was, leading me upstairs to a little room devoted to Roman exhibits – most of them reproduction stuff of the type sold at Vindolanda museum. I bought a bronze figure of Mercury from him, a copy of one found at Corbridge and made locally by a firm at Lanercost. I hadn't room in my rucksack for any electronic sculpture.

On the way out I noticed a name I recognised, Alfred Wallis, the Cornish primitive painter. It was a small seascape with a lighthouse. It belonged, so he said, to Mrs Winifred Nicholson, first wife of Ben Nicholson, who now lives at Banks. She and her husband had discovered Wallis, and she had several of his paintings. This one was for sale at £200. It was about the only conventional painting in the museum. All the same, I couldn't see Carlisle folk rushing to buy it. I asked Mr Yuan-Chia why he didn't encourage more local artists to exhibit, such as people from the Carlisle College of Art. As provincial art colleges go, it's a very good one. John Bratby used to teach there.

'The Art College is not good enough. All my things in my museum very high standard. All very high.'

I wished him good luck then walked through the village of Banks to Hare Hill. In a field behind a farm on top there's the highest chunk of the whole Wall. 'I viewed this relic with admiration,' wrote Hutton. 'I saw no part higher.'

I scrambled around for a long time looking for it, beginning to think it had gone. I realised a boy of about ten was sitting on a fence, watching me. He never spoke or offered any help till I went over and asked him if this was Hare Hill. 'You want the Wall,' he said at once, taking my pack, helping me over a fence, through a field, along a hedge and there it was, a veritable monster bit of Wall, all of ten feet high, by far and away the highest bit of Wall to be seen today. He helped me on top and pointed out where a wren had built its nest. I tipped him lavishly when I left, all of 10p. He said he did very well in the summer, watching walkers stumbling over fences then gallantly coming to their aid.

Hare Hill is in most of the archaeological books, but they're a bit snooty about it, saying the core is genuine but that the facing stones – which contain a centurial stone brought from elsewhere – were rebuilt in Victorian days. Clayton's workmen took many liberties when restoring great stretches of the Wall now proudly shown at Housesteads, but no one objects. Hare Hill is unattended and uncared for, left for the wrens to enjoy. Perhaps they'll renovate it some day.

From Banks I headed down the road towards the River Irthing and Lanercost Priory. I'd been saving it up, knowing it was getting near, hoping for a fine evening but knowing that its situation is so beautiful and its stone work so striking that it's a delight to view in any weather. It's not as dramatic as Durham Cathedral, but then it's unfair to compare it with a cathedral, though that is one's first impulse because of its situation and size.

It's only as you enter through the gatehouse and go past the nave that you realise that the Priory is in fact a ruin. Only the nave is used today as a Church. The rest is the remains of the medieval priory. As ruins they are magnificent. They need little effort of imagination to understand, not like so many Roman ruins.

Lanercost Priory has for centuries been a highlight for everyone doing the Roman Wall. Not just because of its beauty but because it's built almost entirely of stone from the Wall – red sandstone and grey limestone which have been melded together in almost technicolor brilliance. Inside there are many Roman inscribed stones and altars, such as one to Jupiter which came from Birdoswald and another to Silvanus.

The Priory was founded in 1166 by Sir Robert de Vaux – no doubt an ancestor of the Northern brewery firm – who endowed a house of Augustinian canons with a great slice of land between the Irthing and the Wall and the incomes from many local parishes. It grew to be one of the best-known and better-off medieval monasteries, flourishing till the Dissolution of the Monasteries by Henry VIII in 1536.

For such a large building the normal complement was only fifteen canons – Augustinians were never called monks, being intellectually of a rather high class. They rarely got their hands dirty, being able to hire servants out of their lavish endowments. They devoted their time to praying, which took between seven and eight hours a day, reading and copying manuscripts, or administering their estates. In the year 1200 there were a hundred and sixty five Augustinian monasteries in England. For over three hundred years they followed a quiet, uneventful life of prayer and study.

Monastic life at Lanercost, thanks to its situation, turned out to be far from typical. Lying right in the path of the England-Scotland wars, it was robbed and overrun by friend and foe alike. A rich priory was an obvious picking. In 1296 the Scots overran almost all the line of Hadrian's Wall. Hexham Abbey suffered worse than Lanercost. They set the Hexham church on fire and locked two hundred boys into the grammar school and burned them alive. The Lanercost canons had just got most of their repairs finished when the following year the Scots arrived again, this time led by William Wallace.

Edward I, the Hammer of the Scots, stayed several times at Lanercost en route for his periodic bits of Scots-bashing. In 1306, while staying overnight on his way to Carlisle, he fell ill and had to rest at Lanercost. For over six months the Priory became the seat of the Royal Family. A party of two hundred had to be housed and fed. The records of this visit are preserved at the British Museum – down to the bills which the King ran up at the local chemist for his various drugs.

Later, it was the turn of the Scots once more. Robert the Bruce took it over in 1311. In 1346, King David II of Scotland ransacked the buildings. By the time Henry VIII got round to closing the monasteries, Lanercost's income had gone down to £80 a year and it was one of the first to go. (He closed any worth under £200 in his first attack on the Church.)

After the valuables had been confiscated and the canons turfed out, the property was turned over to Sir Thomas Dacre of Naworth Castle. He turned the monastic buildings into a private dwelling for himself and made the nave into the Parish Church of Lanercost. Members of the Dacre family lived there till 1716. After that, the old monastic part gradually fell into ruin, though still being owned by the Dacres, later the Howards, of Naworth Castle.

The Howards are still round the corner at Naworth. For centuries they have been one of the greatest families in the North, owning a large stretch of the Wall country. They handed over Lanercost Priory to the custody of the Department of the Environment several years ago.

The grounds of Naworth Castle are large and the castle is very impressive. Like Lanercost, it contains a great deal of Roman Wall stones. I went through several arches and into courtyards, all of which seemed deserted, with no signs of life anywhere. I felt I was being watched on all sides, but I couldn't see a soul. It had that sense of desertion which only affluence can bring. At last I saw a movement through an open window and ran to it, shouting up Hello. A lady, who turned out to be Lady Carlisle, told me to make for a little door in one corner of the courtyard and wait there.

As she took me along corridors and up staircases I asked if her husband was feeling well. I knew he'd just come out of hospital. He has only one leg, having lost the other in the war. His good one had been giving him pain so he'd been into hospital for treatment.

He was sitting in a chair, his good leg stretched out on a cushion in front of him. He was talking noisily and cheerfully to two people who'd been looking at some of his pictures. They were bidding farewell. His wife went to a far corner of the room to resume a conversation with a friend of hers, a lady of about the same age. They both carried on their conversation standing up. I sat down beside Lord Carlisle. He looked fit and well, much younger than his forty-nine years.

His accident happened in 1944 when he was twenty-one and serving in the Rifle Brigade as Lt Lord Morpeth. *The Times* reported the following message which he sent home to his parents: 'Had slight accident with mine. Lost my leg, left arm completely paralysed but I think I will be OK so don't worry.' It would be harder to find a more cryptic example of English understatement.

'I can hardly believe now that I sent that message,' he said, smiling rather plaintively, pouring me out a drink. 'But I suppose I must have done.' In 1945 he was awarded the Military Cross.

Since leaving the army, he has worked for his living. He became the 12th Earl of Carlisle on the death of his father in 1963. He trained as a land agent and is a partner in the Carlisle firm of J. M. Clark and Partners.

There have been many eminent Earls of Carlisle since the title was created in 1661 but perhaps the most interesting was the 9th Earl. As George Howard he was one of the leading artistic figures of the 1860s and 70s. He encouraged and collected the works of many artists and was on the committee of the National Gallery for twenty-two years. He was an established artist in his own right and a leading member of the Pre-Raphaelite school of Burne-Jones, Rosetti, William Morris, all of them close friends who used to meet at his house in Palace Green, Kensington. He did portraits and sketches of many of his contemporaries, such as Matthew Arnold, Charles Kingsley and Princess Louise (Queen Victoria's sculptress daughter). Many exhibitions of his work were held but he never sold any – for the simple reason that he didn't need the money. No one really knew, therefore, how good he was, if goodness can be measured by how much people will pay. As an artist he's been rather fogotten these last hundred years but.with the return of interest in the Pre-Raphaelites his importance is now being reassessed. (In 1973 there was an exhibition of his work at the Norham House Gallery, Cockermouth.)

The ninth Earl could devote his life to the arts because of his enormous wealth. He was one of the three largest private landowners in England with estates totalling ninety six thousand acres, almost all of it rich agricultural land. In Cumberland he had seventy thousand acres centred round Naworth, twelve thousand in Northumberland and fifteen thousand in Yorkshire including the family's most prized possession, Castle Howard. Today, the present Earl has only three thousand acres. Such an acreage would suffice for most mortals as long as they didn't have to meet the costs of a huge, rambling fourteenth-century castle out of the income. Naworth, alas, is now the Earl's millstone.

'If only the world was fair,' he sighed, 'I'd have Castle Howard. It's all very sad.'

What happened was that the 9th Earl's widow, Rosalind Countess Carlisle, a leading figure in the temperance and suffragette movements, split up the estate on her death into almost forty different pieces. There are now bits of the Howard estate all over Cumberland. As for Castle Howard and the Yorkshire estates, that belongs today to a different branch of the Howard family.

'I'm not sure whether my son will be prepared to keep Naworth,' said Lord Carlisle. He pronounced it N'arth, in just one syllable. I didn't know what he was talking about for a second. The locals pronounce it the way you'd expect, in two syllables.

'I did a lot of work when I took over to reduce the castle but it wasn't enough. The 9th Earl built a flipping great wing with thirty rooms. There were a hundred and ten steps to the top and the whole wing was a mess of dry rot. I knocked the whole thing down. I've reorganised the central part so we live in an eight-bedroom flat. We let out another five flats. We aim for widows and spinsters so there's the minimum of noise. But still the bills roll in. The roof of the Hall is leaking. Five years ago the estimate to repair it was £10,000. Goodness knows what it will be today. What does one do?

'I've looked into the possibility of giving it to the National Trust but they won't accept such buildings unless there's also an income to keep it going. I could sell, but who would buy it? Just what does one do?'

After years of thought, he'd that week decided to turn it into an official stately home. The prospect hadn't appealed to him ('I don't want to do a Duke of Bedford') but it seemed the only way. By opening his house to the public once a week the Department of the Environment would pay half the repairs provided work was done to a certain standard and with a proper architect. 'I now have the problem of installing a guide. You can't get such people round here.'

He has always been prepared, at any time, to let antiquarians look round the castle and grounds but with his natural desire for peace and quiet he's tried to protect himself from the hordes. There's a lot to see. That great hall with the dodgy roof is the biggest domestic hall in the county, measuring seventy-eight by twenty-four feet. There are many fine English and European paintings, including a large Burne-Jones of Flodden Field. Pevsner says one of the towers, the Lord William Howard tower, is the most interesting part of all because of its timbers and ceilings, unique in England. It's understandable why Lord Carlisle doesn't want to give it all up. Even those against inherited wealth have to admit that it's very often private wealth which keeps historic houses from falling into decay.

Forests can be replanted, rocket sites come and go according to the political whims, but a fourteenth-century castle can't be replaced. It will be sad if some Earl of Carlisle in the future finds he can't afford even *half* its upkeep. If the government or the National Trust don't want it, who knows what will happen. Medieval banquets?

15
The Wall:
The Foreman and his Problems

As I came down through the fields I caught sight of what looked like a large black worm, glinting and flashing in the sunlight across the valley. Spring had at last arrived and as I hurried towards it I disturbed plants and birds which had miraculously come alive. In a flooded ditch, the remains of the Wall Ditch, several wild ducks flew up in a panic, zooming off low over my head like guided missiles. I was followed by two or three plaintive curlews who circled and dived over me, warning the great black worm that I was getting near. Some grouse flew up, furious at being nearly trodden on. In a field at the bottom I was chased by some rams who thought I'd come to feed them. I shouted back at them, shooing them away, showing I wasn't scared, then I dashed for it as they came straight for me, and clambered over a gate in the valley bottom.

I paused for a few moments on a bridge, Dovecote Bridge, before making a final dash towards the black worm. I was just below the village of Walton and I could see the church's unusual pyramid-shaped tower on the horizon. It was a pretty spot, with the stream and the bridge and the church beyond, then I noticed a strange smell. A notice clearly said 'Walton Parish Council – No Tipping', but looking over the bridge I could see that the banks were covered in old mattresses, car wheels, soap packets, lawn mowers, fridges, garden rubbish and all the other debris of modern life. The Vindolanda rubbish tip is invaluable for archaeologists. Would anyone ever lovingly search through this one?

Through a gate after the bridge, just up the hill to Walton, I finally tracked down the black worm. At close quarters it looked more like a barrage balloon, tied down with pegs and ropes to stop it floating away. It was as big as it had appeared from across the valley – at least twenty yards long. It was covered with a shiny black plastic tarpaulin. Through a hole which someone had made on top I could see layers of straw. Beneath, there was Hadrian's Wall, the last bit in captivity, the last chunk which is to be seen today by anyone walking along the Wall from east to west.

I'd been told by some of the Department's workmen earlier on that they'd just produced a new bit but that I wouldn't be able to see it. I'd made a note of its whereabouts, but lost it, never thinking I'd find it. It's not on any map as yet, being so recent. Because it's in sandstone and has been covered with soil and turf and roots and bushes for so many centuries, they didn't dare leave it to its fate, not exposed all naked to a Cumberland winter. At Easter, so I gathered later, it was going to be unveiled for the season, then covered up and tucked in comfortably when winter came round again.

I felt a warm rather stale breath on the back of my neck as I was bending down, poking at the Wall beneath the straw. I feared for a moment that I'd been caught by a Department spy and I'd be accused of splitting open the worm's covering. I turned and a rather scruffy grey pony was trying to lick my head off. He was decidedly smelly, no doubt from exploring the rubbish tip. I gave him my last Polo and left him alone with the worm, smelling sweetly of mint.

All the way from Newcastle I'd been impressed by the Department of the Environment's work in preserving the Wall and its structures. I liked the idea that here at Walton, the end of their line, there was this final rather eccentrically cared for stretch. It's the Miss Charlesworths of this world, the highly-

qualified archaeologists, government and academic, who have
the fun of digging for treasures in proper archaeological sites.
They leave the more prosaic, mundane work of caring for the
curtain Wall itself to the Department's workmen and their
foreman, Mr Charles Anderson.

Charles Anderson is one of the grand old men of the Wall,
yet he never gets acknowledged in the reference books. All
students of the Wall know about the work of Simpson and
Richmond and Birley. Their contribution is in every book on
Roman Britain and will never be forgotten as long as the Wall
is studied. Yet Charles Anderson has given a lifetime to working on the Wall. More than anyone else, he can say that the
Wall we see today is his.

Richmond, Birley and Co. are the officer class, who go on to
get knighthoods, as Richmond did, for their good work. Mr
Anderson, being one of the other ranks, recently got his
reward, a BEM, so he can't complain. It's funny to think that
the British government is still giving out British Empire medals
despite the fact that the British Empire doesn't exist any
more.

Charles Anderson is foreman in charge of thirty Government
workmen – ten masons and twenty labourers – who go up and
down the Wall, repairing and preserving its fortifications. Like
the Forth Bridge (the old one), they never finish, getting to one
end and then having to start at the beginning again. Unlike the
Forth Bridge (even the new one), the Wall is growing all the
time as more of it is unearthed and has to be cared for. Working
on the Wall is a job with a future, even if it's all in the past.

Mr Anderson comes from North Yorkshire and joined the
Department of Ancient Monuments in 1927, looking after local
castles and abbeys. He was moved up to Corbridge in 1935 and
has been there ever since. He's now sixty-five and his retirement
is imminent but he'll continue to live on the Wall as he rents a
lodge on the estate of Beaufront castle not far from Corbridge.

It's the archaeologists who decide which new bit has to be
uncovered, as at Walton, then it's Mr Anderson and his men
who do it. He has several unique photograph albums dating
back to the twenties showing before and after snaps, taken by

himself, of almost every stretch of Wall and its structures. In one sepia shot you see him with Simpson or Richmond, having a bumpy empty field pointed out to him. In the next he and his men are hard at it, in their braces and mutton chop whiskers, uncovering a new bit of the Wall.

When I went to see him he took me out to where some of his men were currently working so that I could watch the preservation work in progress. It happened to be Blackcarts, that spot I'd sheltered at in the rain and hailstones all those months ago.

The same four workmen were there – the four I'd interrupted when they'd been half asleep in their hut. This time it was bright and sunny and they were hard at it. They'd taken out a huge tree, which amazingly hadn't disturbed the Wall, just grown over and through it. Since I'd been there they'd uncovered another fifty yards of the Wall and had discovered a new inscription.

Mr Anderson said he didn't know what it meant. He wasn't up on Latin inscriptions, but he was very interested in the size of the facing stones the workmen were removing, far larger than normal Wall stones. It was taking two of the workmen to lift each of them out. 'We had some back there which took all four of us to carry,' said the workman who'd been reading the ornithological book.

When uncovering a stretch of the Wall the first job is to remove the weeds and grass and earth, dig out any bushes and trees and then slice away from the sides any stones which have fallen down over the centuries. Before they'd begun, it had looked simply an embanked hedge, an overgrown mound running along the field. Now it looked an almost new piece of Wall. It was a particularly good stretch, so good that, for once, some of the lower courses didn't need to be rebuilt. This is in fact what they do – having bared the Wall, they take it to pieces then reset the stones in new mortar.

Despite the carefully chosen words of Department of the Environment officials, who always stress that all they do is consolidate and conserve and never do anything phoney like rebuilding, I would say they *are* rebuilding.

I watched the workmen as they took to pieces a large stretch of the Wall, stone by stone. Each stone was cleaned and washed, numbered with yellow chalk according to which course of the Wall it had come from, then laid out on tiers of wooden planks, exactly in the order it had come out of the Wall. When they'd created a brand new inside – a hard core of sand and cement and smallish lumps of broken stones – they then built the Wall up again, putting in the facing stones in their original order. It was like a child's game, though one which only terribly neat children would be allowed to play.

'Look at this bit,' said the ornithologist as he uncovered a fresh bit, 'three stones in a straight line.' He was pointing to three huge facing stones which had been built exactly one on top of each other, not making T junctions for better bonding which all good bricklayers, then as well as now, always do when building a wall. 'Well, what do you expect,' he said rather scathingly. 'They were just soldiers.'

Mr Anderson would have none of it. He doesn't like any criticism of the Roman builders. He pointed out that these particular stones were unusually large and heavy, strong enough to support the stones above even when simply piled one on top of each other.

'The Romans never skimped,' he said admiringly, looking back along the line of the Wall which his men had already done. 'There was no jerry building, no messing about. They laid each course properly. The archaeologists usually say the Wall took eight years to build. I think it was far longer. They had to clear the land of forests in the first place, which most people forget. Then find and dig quarries, cut and face the stones and take them up to the crags in carts.'

It's not only the Wall but the majority of the Wall structures, including almost all the turrets and the milecastles, which have been rebuilt by Mr Anderson and his men. When he began in 1935, only the three major forts – Corbridge, Chesters and Housesteads – were much as we see them today. Almost every other site, from the Benwell Vallum crossing and the Denton turret in the East to the Walton Worm in the West, is new.

The Wall's central hard core is almost everywhere new, the cement between each stone is new and almost everything has been relaid by twentieth century hands. This is not to say the Wall today is therefore phoney. It simply suggests that the Department can't afford to be too superior about those who want to rebuild bits of the Wall elsewhere, as Robin Birley is doing at Vindolanda. His Wall is as genuine as their Wall, except it's on a site two miles south.

Mr Anderson agrees that Clayton allowed his men to do lots of fiddles in the last century when reclamation of the Wall was started. Under Mr Anderson, no stone has gone back higher than it was found. Clayton's men took terrible liberties, such as building up chunks to any height they fancied, depending on how many loose bits of stone they found lying around.

'You just have to look at the barracks at Chesters fort,' he says. 'So much of it is suspiciously the same height. What they did was to build everything up to the biggest bit they found, just to make it neat. You can see from this bit here that you rarely find that the Wall has decayed neatly, in a straight line. Over the centuries, the Wall has decayed haphazardly, odd pieces falling off, that's when people didn't carry off chunks for their own use.'

Naturally, once the workmen have uncovered and cleaned the Wall they *have* to make it good. They've removed a protective clothing of grass and earth which has built up over the centuries. They can't just leave it now for the elements to finish off. However neat the Roman limestone mortar looks – and it goes a sort of dark pink over the centuries, almost like rich earth – it crumbles when exposed and certainly wouldn't last another eighteen centuries, not in an exposed state.

Mr Anderson has always hoped the Ancient Monument people would go one stage forward – having done so much rebuilding perhaps they might allow one little bit to be built up to its original height.

'I'm all for Vindolanda, but I would really have preferred to see a Wall section built on the line of the Wall itself. It would have been much more impressive up on the crags rather than down at Vindolanda. It would have looked better and you'd

have got a better view from it. For the last twenty years I've
been hoping we'd be able to do it. I used to save facing stones,
ones we found lying on the ground, just in case someone would
have the nerve to build up the Wall to its original height. I collected piles of it at Walltown Crags when we were opening up new
bits of the Wall, but in the end had to leave it for the farmers to
use. Some of it is still lying there.'

He talks about the archaeologists of old with great affection
and his conversation is full of what Mr Simpson, Mr Richmond
or Mr Birley said. There seems to have been a mutual under-
standing. He doesn't appear as enamoured by all the bureau-
cratic changes in the Department in the last few years. He says
he won't be too unhappy to retire and retreat to his garden. In
the old days, he could make his own decisions. Now everything
has its mounds of paper work and complicated chains of
command. The latest change was that he and his workmen
would be administered from Carlisle rather than York. The
Roman workmen had exactly the same problem, and probably
complained equally about the red tape When the Wall was
being built, all the orders came from York, where the Sixth
Legion had its Headquarters. When the garrisons moved up and
lived on the Wall, Carlisle became the centre.

Mr Anderson has never left his own mark on the Wall
structures, though some masons are supposed to have done. 'Mr
Simpson always used to leave a penny piece in the pivot hole in
the doorway of every milecastle he worked on.' But he's taking
a few mementos with him to remind him of his happy years on
the Wall. Unlike the Roman Britains, Mr Anderson doesn't sell
his Wall mementoes. He presented me with three tiny altars,
copies of the ones he'd helped to preserve. He made his original
models in stone, carving out the lettering with a needle, then
made a rubber mould from which he turns out plaster reproductions. He hand paints them and gives them to people as
presents. They could be mass produced very cheaply, now that
he's made the mould, and many of the hundreds of thousands
who visit the Wall every year would love to buy them. It's not
that the local shops sell a load of rubbish in the way of
souvenirs – it's just that there's so very little. The anti-tourist

farmers can't possibly say that the Wall has been over-commercialised. It's wide open. If idiots are daft enough to buy tins of London smog, they would jump at a tin of real Roman Wall, or even better, a reproduction Roman altar.

He thinks there are far more visitors every year than the official figures suggest. 'Some just sit in the car and look, others walk the Wall and don't go in the fort and others go into the fort without paying.'

Different forts get different sorts of customers. He's noticed that Corbridge has more elderly people, because you can drive right in. At Housesteads you have a fairly steep hillside walk from the road which keeps many people away. (One of the reasons they want a proper road straight to Vindolanda is because they know the car-bound public are very lazy.)

'In 1935 visitors to the Wall were rare, they were something new. Now they're everywhere and all the time there's more for them to see. Yet after all this time I'm still surprised that we haven't got one fort fully excavated.'

If it were his decision, he's not quite sure which fort he would choose. He used to think Carrawburgh was the best virgin site, till they took some random trenches a year ago and found very little. 'I was very disappointed. Perhaps Great Chesters, if I had to choose.'

Workmen in the field can often see things differently from the experts with academic books. One of the things which has always puzzled him is the Narrow Wall on the Broad foundations.

'If I'd been a Roman mason given the job of building a narrower wall on top of an existing broad foundation, then I'd naturally have used some of the existing stones. Some of the broad foundations are up to three or four feet high. Any mason would use up the existing stones first and saved getting so many new ones. I don't understand why they didn't. I used to argue with Mr Richmond about this, but I never got a good explanation. One of these days someone will come up with a new explanation of the Broad Wall and the Narrow Wall.'

Mr Anderson's query seemed a sensible one but when I thought about it later I realised that there would have been no

saving to have taken down the broad foundation first, not as far
as facing stones were concerned. Broad or Narrow, you need
the same amount. The only saving is on the internal core. So
the drag of knocking down the broad foundations and re-laying
narrow ones wouldn't have been worth it, not to save a few
yards of hard core. It would have taken a lot longer. And no
doubt one of the virtues of changing from broad to narrow was
to save time. No doubt Mr Richmond had made the same
suggestion.

Two more things have puzzled Mr Anderson during his
thirty-seven year stint on the Wall and in neither case could I
offer even a daft explanation. Firstly there's the chamfered
stones puzzle – the stones with one edge bevelled which went
on the very top of the Wall, making a sort of sloping ledge.
'I've found so many of them over the years that I now think
there might have been a *second* course of chamfered stones,
perhaps in the middle of the Wall. You'd expect top stones to
fall off the Wall first and be the first to disappear or be pinched,
wouldn't you. At the very most, they'd be the ones buried
deepest. Yet we find so many of them. Why?'

I suggested perhaps that they weren't so useful for farmers in
building barns and walls but he said not at all. They were more
useful than normal facing stones, which taper towards the
back. It all seemed a bit academic, personally, though no doubt
if Mr Anderson could prove his theory it could change the
profile of the Wall and keep the academics arguing for a long
time.

His other worry was more prosaic; in all his years neither he
nor his workmen has ever found a trowel or even a relic of a
trowel or a hammer or any remains of a mason's tool throughout the length of the Wall. 'You'd have thought when a trowel
broke a mason would just have thrown it into the mortar or
amongst the stones. That's what most masons do. Nobody saves
a broken handle. I can't understand it.'

The Roman trowels we do have, those ones lovingly displayed at the Museums on the Wall, come from the forts not
from the Wall, and were found in the remains of workshops.

Mr Anderson and his men have contributed to the store of

treasures found in forts and milecastles and temples over the years – their Roman arm purse at Birdoswald in 1949 being the best of all – yet on the line of the Wall itself little of anything has been found. 'Thousands and thousands of soldiers and labourers of all sorts must have been working on the Wall, living beside it for years as they built it, yet they left so few traces of themselves. It's a mystery to me.'

I looked suitably mystified. 'Don't get too worried,' he added smiling. 'It's not good for you. If you get too deep into the Wall they come and lock you up.'

Several academics say much the same thing, pointing out the marriage break-ups and mental break-downs amongst the Wall people. I must admit since I started on the Wall the previous year I've had a few very bad nights, lying for hours worried by the Vallum, surmising about the missing Ninth, fretting over the Foundations, not to mention new worries I'd picked up, such as 197 from John Gillam and now chamfered edges from Charles Anderson.

'I don't think the Romans were worriers. They were very happy and lived very peaceful lives for most of the time. They had all the conveniences they needed, posh houses, flush toilets, central heating.

'The extra things we've got we could do without, if you ask me, like atom bombs. The funny thing is, why did it take so long for us to rediscover the things they had? I remember just fifty years ago when I was a boy in Yorkshire watching a labourer coming round with a horse and cart to empty all the toilets. I can see him as clear as anything. Yet the Romans had water closets centuries and centuries ago. It's all very strange.

'I've noticed in all our excavations that you never come across buildings *after* the Roman period. You get many different Roman buildings, all on the same site, as they were taken down, overrun or decayed and then were built up again. But they don't seem to have been used again when the Romans left. The people must have thought the Roman buildings were spooky. They put the fear of God into people and they didn't want to use them again. It's a funny business, Roman Britain . . .'

16
Castlesteads:
The Mole Catcher and other stories

When old William Hutton arrived in Walton he had great trouble finding any refreshments. He tried a pub called the Cow and Boot but was unable to get any beer, cider or spirits. The pub only sold milk. It looks as if the temperance members of the Earl of Carlisle's family were already hard at work. There's no Cow and Boot today but a very brightly painted pub called The Centurion Inn. It had just been done up, so the bar lady told me. The new owner had changed the name from the Black Bull and was now doing beds and meals to attract tourists. People want more than milk these days. I drank my glass of beer slowly, waiting for the people to arrive, but nobody came. Walton is another of those pretty villages to the East of Carlisle which Carlisle people tend to ignore. On the wall in the bar was pinned a large notice which read: 'SPECIAL NOTICE – A MAN IS SPECIALLY ENGAGED AND KEPT IN THE BACK YARD TO DO ALL THE SHOUTING, CURSING AND SWEARING THAT IS REQUIRED IN THIS ESTABLISHMENT.'

I went into Walton Church, which was much newer than I'd expected, built in 1869, and rather boring but I bought a copy of the parish newsletter which was surprisingly jolly. The vicar, Kenneth Harper, was taking the newspapers to task for misusing the word 'charisma'. In recent weeks he'd seen it

applied to Joe Mercer, the football manager, and Tallulah
Bankhead the actress. Both of these people were said, quite
wrongly, to have charisma. 'It is of course a New Testament
word for God's gifts in our lives.' His main attack was on the
Sunday Times for using it in a motor rally report. They'd
described two drivers as having 'charisma rising like steam
from their hair'. As the author of a standard work on newspaper style, the *Sunday Times* editor would no doubt be
interested in Canon Harper's criticisms. I hoped he was on the
Walton Parish Church's mailing list.

Just outside the village of Walton I came across a row of
moles, hanging by their heads from the barbs of the wire,
skewered through the brains. I counted twenty of them. Their
fur looked quite fresh, though turning from black to grey in the
strong sunlight. Further along I came to another twenty, this
time stark naked, skinned to the bone. I could see tiny orange
maggots, lurking in the white crevices, hoping for some final
flesh. They were such clean carcasses, so carefully skinned, that
I decided the birds hadn't been at them. They'd been skinned by
human hands – yet I'd thought that fun furs had killed the
market in mole skins. Perhaps the village lads had skinned
them, for fun. But there was nobody around.

It was one of those spring days after a long winter in which
you've forgotten how hot it can ever be. It was like a Mediterranean midday, with everyone taking their siesta indoors. I
seemed to be the only stranger, the only human being around.
The tourists hadn't arrived, if they ever arrive round here. It
was all such pleasant walking, in easy rolling gentle countryside, that I was ahead of schedule. The next fort on the line is at
Castlesteads and I wasn't due there till the afternoon.

I went along the Lanercost road a mile or so to a house called
Boothby on the Roman Stanegate where I talked to an old man
in the garden, a man alone with his memories. Wilfrid Roberts
is seventy-two and at one time he was a great political figure in
Cumberland. From 1935 to 1950 he was Liberal MP for North
Cumberland and subsequently a local Socialist councillor. He
owned a local newspaper, ran various businesses, but now he
quietly looks after his house and a seven-hundred-acre hill

farm, though his wife Kate is still very active. She'd just taken over a hotel, the New Bridge, at Lanercost, where I had a very pleasant lunch.

They're both still active Socialists, which is rare in this part of rural Cumberland, even rarer for a member of the Howard family. He's a relative of the Earl of Carlisle (his mother was a daughter of the famous 9th Earl) and was born at Castle Howard. At a recent local election he was the Labour agent, fighting three opponents, all members of his own family, including his sister and the present Lord Carlisle who was standing as a Tory. (A Liberal cousin got in.)

'There's always been a branch of the Howard family which has been radical. In this area three families have been running things for decades, the Howards, the Grahams of Netherby and the Lowthers. I've tried to keep the anti-Tory tradition alive, fighting our traditional rival Tory families, the Lowthers and Grahams.'

I asked if he'd never contemplated writing his memoirs, especially his war-time political stuff, Churchill memories and all that. 'My memory is bad. It would be too boring to write and too boring to read'. He's very interested in the life of Rosalind, Countess of Carlisle, and thinks she would make a good biography for someone. She was a great woman, a strong Liberal, an early suffragette and an active campaigner for many causes. Her teetotal cause was perhaps a bit dotty. She once made Brampton completely dry for a whole week by a sequence of rousing speeches. She was a great organiser. While her husband George did his painting, she ran the estates, during and long after his life.

'She quarrelled with her eldest son. He was a Tory and she's alleged to have campaigned against him. When she died in 1922 her will was a terrible shock to everyone. She'd completely cut her son out of it. He had the title, but she'd split all the property amongst other members of the family.

'The surviving children held a meeting in this house, at the big round table in what is now the kitchen. My parents were there. Gilbert Murray was there, the professor of Greek. Like my father, he'd married a Howard daughter. Between the children, they re-hashed the will so that the Earl got enough property to manage on. No lawyers were involved. They just agreed between them that the will had been unfair so they handed over bits they'd been given. The present Earl might think he hasn't got much today, but without that meeting in our kitchen, he would have got very little indeed.'

With looking at moles and listening to memories I was about half an hour late arriving at Castlesteads. I wasn't worried. In fact I was quite pleased with myself. Only half an hour late, considering one can only estimate a time of arrival at any one stage when walking the Wall. I'd dropped a card to the owner, Major General Sir George Johnson, saying I'd be on his property about three, hoping he'd be around.

There's a long drive up to the house and I took my time walking it. I'd never seen so many daffodils. There were acres of them, all in full bloom. At first glance, the long winding driveway with its beautiful trees, shrubs and flowers, had looked absolutely wild and natural. On examining it carefully, I realised what care and planning had gone into the display.

The house was big and grand with so many big and grand bits that it took some time to decide which was the main entrance. Once again, it had the feeling of studied desertion, but this time it was real. I couldn't raise a soul. I ventured into the front hall, shouting hello, only to hear my voice echoing down corridors. I opened the door of a drawing room, being very bold, and gave another loud hello, but with no reply.

It was like so many grand country mansions I'd visited in the last few months. There were guns and boots in the hall. The furniture was ageless, terribly clean and arranged, but nicely faded so that there was no sign of ostentation, either through over-polishing the antiques or having anything so vulgar as a piece of modern furniture. In a corner of one room I noticed the required polished walnut table with that morning's *Times*, carefully folded, plus the local paper, in this case the *Cumberland News*. I'd seen so many of these tables with the papers apparently unread and apparently untouched, except perhaps by a butler who'd had the job of ironing them.

I retreated to the hall, deciding not to go any further, even if the Sleeping Princess was tied up inside and the butler asleep over his ironing board and the groom flat out on his bed and each of them waiting for me to bring them back to life. I noticed some familiar writing on a postcard propped up on a table. It was mine. In the corner of the postcard I'd sent to Sir George was a scribbled pencilled note – '3.30. Couldn't wait. Had to go out.' In another corner, I scribbled that I would come back later that day. I put the card on the table and walked back down the driveway.

I was just leaving the main gate when Sir George and his wife arrived back. I got the impression that they'd been hoping to avoid me, but they stopped and said yes, I could come back and talk to them now.

Lady Johnson was very friendly and brought tea in big white tea cups but Sir George seemed a bit suspicious. He sat four square in an armchair, large and very solid, watching me carefully. There were some very long pauses. No, neither of them was interested in the Wall, nor in the fort on the site of their house, nor in the Romans themselves. Having established that, any real point of contact had gone. I tried to talk to him about himself, but with little luck. He'd gone to Eton, Cambridge and then the Scots Guards. He'd retired from the army as head of London District.

He'd been born in the house but didn't know much about it, except that it was supposed to be Adam, or from that period. I told him how Willim Hutton had visited the house in 1801 for his book and had said that the house had recently been built for a man named Johnson who'd made a fortune in India. The price of the land had been £13,000, which seemed a lot considering he then had to build himself a mansion. In levelling the ground for the gardens in 1779, all remains of the fort had gone. Sir George listened but said he didn't know much about all that, though he had heard about some money being made in India by his ancestors.

Hutton had gone on to be rather scathing about the house, but I didn't mention that. He thought the site had been 'sacrificed to modern tastes' and that it was disgusting to have cleared away the remains of a marvellous Roman fort.

When their three children were small, said Lady Johnson, they'd been quite interested in the Romans. They'd often dug in the garden, hoping to find remains, but had found nothing. The remains that they have got are now kept in the garden in a summer house. Sir George said he didn't know much about them. But he didn't object to archaeologists or other interested people coming to see them.

From a window, Lady Johnson pointed out to what she and her husband were really interested in. It was a large rhubarb shaped plant which she said was a pedesitis, though I couldn't personally see it. Both she and her husband might not be interested in archaeology or history but they were both keen botanists. She brought out several plant books in which she'd noted down dates and places where she'd seen various speci-mens, dating back to her childhood in Brechin. She spent a long time looking for another book to show me but I said I would have to go. I thanked them for the tea then went out into the grounds to look for the summer house. Sir George told me to turn right at the big elm.

In all, Sir George has two thousand acres, half of which he farms himself. The land immediately round the house is heavily wooded and it's hard to realise what a good site the Romans chose.

Castlesteads fort is unique amongst the Wall forts in lying between the Wall and the Vallum. It's not in contact with the Wall itself. The site was chosen, presumably, to guard the valley of the Cam Beck, a strong-flowing stream which runs through the grounds of the house down to the Irthing.

It was a fairly small fort, only three and three-quarter acres, and its garrisons at various times were from Spain, Gaul and Tungria. There's nothing to be seen today, thanks to Sir George's ancestor clearing the site for the house, but all the archaeological books talk of a rich store of altars and other treasures stored in the summer house.

I got rather lost in the woods till finally I came to a large wall, about twenty feet high, with a little green door in one corner. I entered into a vegetable garden about the size of Wembley stadium, surrounded on all sides by the huge wall. There was a hidden, lost feeling. It seemed to be deserted, then I noticed a movement in a far corner. A gardener was hoeing a long line of raspberry canes. As I got nearer, I could see there wasn't just one line, but at least twenty of them, all raspberries. The gardener said he'd been growing raspberries for twenty-one years. It was only spring but already he had orders for four hundred pounds for the summer. 'You can make a start,' he said, pointing to a spade. I said I was on a walking tour, not looking for work. He feared as much. He'd waited a long time to have an assistant gardener but nobody wanted that sort of work these days. He was due to retire soon and didn't know what would happen to his raspberries. I asked him if he wasn't lonely, working for twenty-one years in such a large, isolated garden.

'I'm never lonely. There's not enough hours in the day for what I want to do. I've had enough of working with lots of people. I used to be head gardener at the Hurlingham Club, before I came here. In Putney, down in London, you must know it. I was for ever having to drive the other men on. I prefer just being in charge of me.'

He had several varieties of raspberries, including Norfolk Giant and Malling Promise, and fought a continuous battle to keep the pigeons off them. He also grew grapes and peaches. He took me across to a greenhouse against a wall and pointed out some lush looking pink peach blossom. 'I don't go in for flowers very much. Any fool can grow flowers. Raspberries, they're very hard.'

I asked about Sir George's famous summer house and he pointed to another door in the wall, saying that led into the rose garden where I'd find the summer house. 'When I was putting the roses down I came to some slabs of sandstone. That must have been the fort. It was as far as I wanted to go, so I covered them up again. I've got enough to do without digging up Roman remains.'

It was easy to see that neither Sir George nor his gardener is interested in Roman remains. One look at the summer house was enough. I'd expected it to be a proper building, perhaps an ornate sandstone folly. It turned out to be not much more than a simple wooden shed, open to the elements on one side, the sort of wooden shelter you might find in a public park. Inside, scattered any old how, were the Roman altar stones. Throughout the centuries, this collection of altars had been written up in great detail and enthused over by all Wall archaeologists. The Handbook reproduces two of them, giving more space to one of them, the altar to Jupiter, than to any other altar in the book. This particular altar was hard to find. Leaning against it were many garden tools and tin cans. On top of it was balanced a large tin labelled 'Ridento Rat Bait (Ready to use)'. I removed the tools and the rat bait and examined the lettering on the altar. The I.O.M. (to Jupiter, Best and Greatest) was clear enough but I could make out only three more lines. Being open to the elements was obviously not helping to preserve the lettering. Behind something called an Aphid Gun ('a quick knock down against greenfly') I found an altar to Discipline. Rummaging around at the back of the shed I found other altars, inscribed stones and statues. I wondered how many visitors, invited or otherwise, are tempted to pocket a few of the smaller pieces – or if anyone would ever realise if they did. At Corbridge and Chesters and Housesteads, where they have permanent guards, they have many items of far less value, yet here was a unique collection, open to the winds and chance visitors. No doubt nothing does get stolen. Only a real enthusiast would ever bother to find out that the altar stones are there, to get permission from Sir George to view them, and then track down the house and find the summer house. There is no name on the gateway to the house or any signs in the grounds to direct you to the summer house.

The Department of the Environment might be taking things rather to extremes, bothering to parcel up a twenty-yard stretch of Wall to protect it from the winter weather when they already have about ten miles of Wall which doesn't need protecting. On the other hand, it seems to be taking things to a different extreme to leave valuable inscribed altar stones in an open shed.

'Tullie House already have some of the best stones found at Castlesteads,' said Lady Johnson when I rang up later to ask why they bother to keep the stones when they don't appear to be interested in them. 'We have kept one good one, the Jupiter one I think it is. My husband wants to keep a few here because this was where they were found.'

From Castlesteads gates I walked along the road to the village of Newtown where I spotted my first Solway View. There must be dozens of houses called Solway View, in Cumberland and Dumfries, most of them like this one, many miles from the Solway. I was now in the flat, Carlisle plain, with the hills well behind me.

Further on I passed a bungalow called Roma and I wondered if the owner had seen the Eternal City with his own eyes. Two thousand years ago, the Mediterranean came to Cumberland. Now, in these days of package holidays, every Cumbrian can go to the Mediterranean.

There was no habitation here until the Romans came, cleared and conquered. Pre-historic Cumbrians lived only along the Eden valley, where shelter, water and food were more easily available, not out in the dense oak forests. The Romans were not in Cumberland for economic reasons but for a military purpose. They *imposed* their settlements on the countryside. After the Romans, the local inhabitants fell back into their own ways, retreating to the valleys. The Dark Ages were very Dark in Cumberland.

If only Hadrian's Wall had been preserved it would have helped considerably in the Middle Ages. The Border wars were made worse because there was no proper east-west cohesion. There were no roads, till General Wade resurrected the Roman Wall route, and no co-ordinated military defence. Castles and pele towers were always isolated defensive sites. You got into one, if you could, and stayed inside till you were starved out. There was no signalling down the line for the cavalry to come and help.

Having cleared the Cumberland forests, the Romans then had to bring stones for the Wall and forts from up to fifteen miles away. Unlike Northumberland, the Carlisle plain is covered in boulder clay, around twenty-five feet thick in the Carlisle area, deposited during the Great Ice Age when the glaciers were moving South from the Scottish hills. It's easy to appreciate why they originally built a Turf Wall in this area.

The weather was still perfect and the going was firm underfoot, which was fortunate. I was now cutting across fields, following the straight humps and hedges, seeing nothing of the Wall but a lot of the Ditch. The Wall line skirts the northern edge of what is now Carlisle Airport, a grandiose name for a large flat field. It's in operation and does flights to places like the Isle of Man in the summer. The local paper runs regular stories about big plans for its future, about executives commuting from London to Carlisle to do big business deals, but not much seems to happen. A little red two-engine plane droned overhead for many miles, quite prettily, more a bird of nature than a machine. I was looking up at it, trying to work out if it was following me, when I fell in a ditch and found myself face to face with an enormous rook.

It was furiously flapping one wing but failing to get off the ground. A few yards away was a rabbit, glaring at me and the rook, brave and defiant, daring us both to come at him. The rook turned and tried to get away, jumping along the ditch with its feet together as if in some sort of three-legged race. I couldn't understand why it wasn't running, one foot after the other, but perhaps that's the way rooks always use their feet, whether their wings are injured or not. It scrambled up the side of the ditch, the remains of the Roman Wall ditch, and hopped across a field. The rabbit took much longer to retreat, staring at me for several seconds, accusingly, not at all scared, then it retreated into the undergrowth and disappeared. I got out of the ditch to see where the rook had gone, whether it wanted help, but it was now another field away. I couldn't decide whether the rabbit had been attacking the rook and had injured its wing in a fight. I looked up for the red aeroplane, but it had gone.

I rested under a hedge a few fields further on at a place called Bleatarn, though there wasn't a tarn to be seen. It was so hot and there was no shade in the open flat fields. I was grateful I wasn't carrying a rucksack. Now that I was approaching my home stretch I was making Carlisle my base, staying at my mother's house. The drag of carrying everything from hotel to hotel or guest house to hostel was over. This is probably one of the reasons the Wall is so rarely walked in its entirety. Accommodation is hard to find, even in the popular sections. Doing it end to end takes some organising, even though it's not very far, unless you're sleeping under hedges.

From under my hedge I could see an old man coming across the field towards me. He was very tall with an angular face and wearing a faded suit jacket with different suit trousers. Round his knee, like a bandage, he had a thick wadge of leather. I got up and walked towards him and asked him if it was in order to walk across the fields. He said it was fine by him and where was I heading. I said Wallhead, the name of the next farmhouse along the line of the Wall. He pointed out where it was across the fields. I could see that his leather patch wasn't a bandage but some sort of protection. I asked him if he was a farmer and he said no, a mole catcher. I told him about the dead moles I'd seen on the fence at Walton. He said they must have been trapped by the village boys. It was a country tradition to hang up dead moles on barbed wire fences. The skinned ones hadn't been eaten – birds don't eat dead moles – but probably skinned by the same boys. Nobody skinned moles these days, except for fun. There was no money in mole skins any more.

'Before the war, I could get a shilling for each mole skin. You got a lot of people wearing mole skin trousers. When the price came doon to tuppence a skin, I gave up catching them. It wasn't worth it.'

Today he no longer catches moles, in fact he rarely ever sees a mole. What he does is go round poisoning them. He has a contract with local farmers to keep down moles in an area of two thousand acres from his village of Laversdale, just two miles away. He said his name was Frank Robson and that he'd been seventy last Friday. 'I'm retired now. It pays for my baccy money, that's about all.'

He went to a cluster of fresh earthen mole hills in a corner of the field and demonstrated how he poisons them. He bent

234

down on his right knee, hence the leather patch, and felt amongst the earth with his right hand, pushing the earth aside till he found a hole. 'Here, put your fingers down here. You can feel the hole.' I declined his offer. 'You won't get bitten. The mole's miles away by now. One mole can make hundreds of heaps. It's probably in yon next field by now.' I felt the little hole, quickly, just in case. He smiled. From a voluminous back pocket he took a Rowntrees cocoa tin, a vintage tin with a 1930s label, the sort you see selling in antique shops in Camden Passage. Opening it he took out a long piece of thick wire, hooked at the end. He hooked out a worm from the bottom of the tin and carefully dropped it into the hole.

'Strychnine,' he said. 'You must never touch it with your fingers or get it near your lips. You'd be a gonner if it got in your mouth.' He has to fill in a special poisons' form when buying it at the chemist, stating its purpose. New mole catchers have to be instructed in its use by Ministry of Agriculture officers. 'They come round with you for half a day to make sure you're using it properly. It's expensive stuff. It's now £4 an ounce, but a little goes a long way. I can lie enough on a sixpence to do a gill of worms. If you use too much strychnine you can ruin the worms. They go soft and the moles won't want them.'

Buying worms can be expensive. There's a worm farm in South Cumberland which breeds and packages worms, exporting them for fishermen all over the world. 'But the buggers charge half a crown a dozen. I dig up my own. It can take a lot of time. When it's ploughing time then they're easy to find. I use about eight worms an acre.

'A mole can eat well over its own weight in worms every day. They paralyse the worms by biting them behind the neck. They have teeth as sharp as needles. They leave the worm to die, carry on digging and looking for more worms, then they come back later and eat them.

'Moles are white when they're born, because they've no skin, but they soon go black when the skin grows. They're all skin, really. It's very thick. When you skin them there's nowt left.

'You get mole hills all the year round but spring is about the

time when you get most. When the ground's moist they come
nearer the surface. That's because the worms are nearer the
surface. In the winter, the worms go deeper to get the moisture
so the moles follow them. You should see their front paws.
They're enormous, almost as big as human hands. They make
the holes with their hands, pushing the earth in front of them.
When they get near the surface, they push the soil up to get rid
of it, to clear out their holes. They're so strong that they can
push the soil *through* the grass like a sieve, without breaking
the surface.'

In the days when he trapped and skinned moles, he could
skin one in seconds as he walked between the traps. 'You cut
the four feet off, then the tail and the nose, and split it up the
breast and peel off the skin. It's very easy. When you cure the
skin you stretch it on a piece of wood by nailing with five nails,
one through each shoulder, both hind legs and one at the nose.
You rub paraffin into the skin and leave it for a few days and
it'll be perfect for twenty years. You do foxes' tails the same
way.

'Poisoning is much easier. When I used to set traps you
always had to come back later and see what you'd catched.
They were dangerous for other animals. Now, I just drop the
worms down the holes and move on. I don't have to come back.
Moles are so greedy that if you drop half a dozen poisoned
worms in a field you know they'll find at least one of them. You
could use meat if you wanted to. Moles will eat meat. But it's
expensive enough getting meat for yourself these days without
wasting it on moles.'

All the same, it seemed a lot of trouble just to kill a few
moles. They don't eat crops or seeds or animals. I couldn't see
they did much harm.

'Talk to any farmer, they hate moles. Look at all the mounds
in this field. Sometimes you get them covered. It makes fields
very bumpy. They bring up stones as well as soil. They can ruin
a lawn for you, upset plants just when they're growing. No,
moles are a right pest.

'I neither hate nor love them. They give me a little job, that's
all. You couldn't live off them, but I enjoy it. I get round and

have a crack with all the farmers and sometimes have a sup of tea.'

I told him about the injured rook and the rabbit that I'd seen earlier. He asked me to describe the ditch. 'That's where the rabbits nest. I know it very well. Yon rook must have been trying to get at the young rabbits. The rabbit had probably come back just in time to save them.' Had the rook been injured by the rabbit? 'No, a rabbit wouldn't attack a rook. It's probably been shot in the wing by the farmers. They've been shooting rooks recently. It's been hard up for something to eat, being injured and not able to fly. He probably thought he'd try to eat the baby rabbits. Well, I'd better be going. I've just one more field to do.'

He dropped one final worm down a mole hole and put his tin in his back pocket. He wished me good luck with the Wall. He didn't know much about the Romans, but he was interested in anything like that.

'I'll tell you one funny thing about moles,' he said, stopping and coming back. 'I'd caught thousands before it struck me. They've got no tits. I used to think they were like rats and mice, you know, suckling their young. They don't. They feed their young by mouth, dropping worms into their mouths the way birds do. I read in a book the name for it. It's not mammals. I've forgotten. But it's in the book. I just haven't the time for books.'

17
Scaleby:
Lunch with a Lord

I arrived at Scaleby Castle, another of Cumberland's ancestral homes, to find it looking as deserted as all the rest. Once again I had difficulty in finding the main door. So many of the wings and towers and archways looked unused. But unlike Castlesteads, once inside I found it all noise and gaiety. I'd chanced upon one of the jolliest encounters I had throughout the length of the Wall.

It's the home of Lord Henley, not on the face of it a title which sounds very northern. The Barony goes back to 1799. The present Baron, Michael Eden, is yet another relation of the Earl of Carlisle. (His mother was the daughter of the 9th Earl, the artist). Lord Henley has estates in the Midlands and in Cumberland, inherited through his mother, but Scaleby Castle is a fairly recent acquisition. He bought it in 1952 to have a seat once more in Cumberland. The castle is mainly fourteenth century, built from stones from the Roman Wall. Even more important for Wall students, Lord Henley owns some of the choicest bits of Roman Cumberland. Poltross Burn milecastle is on his land, as is Willowford Bridge and Birdoswald fort. In all, he owns two miles of the Wall.

I arrived rather early for once but was invited in immediately to join a luncheon party which was already in progress.

Lord Henley said some people had come to see him about a book they were writing. I was rather alarmed but was seated at a table and given a large drink before I could ask further details about the book. Having left the popular part of the Wall country far behind, had I at last come face to face with a deadly rival? (I don't count Valerie Singleton and the Blue Peter team, lovely though they were.)

There were two young men, a middle-aged lady and Lord Henley himself, all deep in some great discussion about art. 'Conceptual before it was currency,' I distinctly heard one of the young men say. For some reason, it was a phrase I couldn't get out of my head for days. I wondered what the mole catcher would have made of it.

As the Burgundy flowed and my ears became attuned to the conversation, I gathered it was a discussion about the Pre-Raphaelites. To my relief, I discovered none of them was planning to write anything about the Wall. But alas for the two young men. They'd come face to face at Scaleby Castle, miles away from the usual London centred art world, to find they were both writing the same book about the same Pre-Raphaelite artist, Burne-Jones!

They'd both apparently written independently to Lord Henley, asking if they could come and look at his Burne-Jones paintings. They were now face to face, having made the awful discovery, yet neither seemed about to punch the other on the jaw. I was more amazed than they were. Surely, I asked them, they would now write their books a little bit differently, one perhaps concentrating more on Burne-Jones' life and the other on his paintings. No, they each said, they were both sticking to their original plan of writing a book solely about his paintings. I only hoped their respective publishers took the news as calmly. From my experience, publishers have hysterics when they hear of another book that's even vaguely similar.

One was called John Gordon Christian and was from Christ Church, Oxford. The other was Bill Waters from Cockermouth. I said I'd look out for their names in the book reviews. Mr Waters had formerly been an assistant curator at Tullie House, Carlisle, He was now working with Mrs Fisher, the lady with him, who ran a gallery in Cockermouth, the gallery which had recently mounted the exhibition of the 9th Earl's paintings. Now that they knew they were doing the same book, they were arranging to go on their next appointment together – a visit to Naworth to see Lord Carlisle's paintings.

After they'd all gone on their way, Lord Henley took me round the castle. Of all the stately home owners I'd come across on my journey, he seemed to know the most about his own home, perhaps through not having been born there and taking it all for granted. He'd made a detailed study of each bit of masonry, each tower, each window.

'Those stones are 1307. That's 1838 by Thomas Rickman. That's a Tudor window. The tower is 1465. Pevsner thinks those windows Circa 1680. The porch is 1737.'

Lord Henley's main claim to national fame is as a politician. He was Chairman of the Liberal Party for several years and is still very active in the House of Lords. ('I've had a seventy-five per cent attendance in the last ten years.') As a Conservative or Socialist peer, he would doubtless have achieved government office. His main public position today is as Chairman of the Council for the Protection of Rural England.

Like so many of the landed figures along the Wall, he went to Eton and into the Guards, but in his case he managed to pick up a few cultural interests on the way. His main interests are medieval architecture and Pre-Raphaelite paintings. 'I'm fascinated by the Romans, but they're before my period. However, it fills me with pleasure to think that I own something so important, something so fascinating as Roman remains. The very idea of the Wall is incredible. Today, the only comparable achievement is sending satellites to the Moon.

'When I think of the Romans I tend to think mainly of their lettering. It was so beautifully incised. When I'm in Carlisle, I often go to Tullie House just to see the tombstones.'

I asked him about his tenants at Willowford Bridge and Birdoswald fort, both charging innocent visitors to look at the Roman remains which happen to be on their land. As a professed lover of Roman remains, wasn't this verging on exploitation?

'Personally, I don't know why they bother. If Mrs Baxter costed her time I'm sure it wouldn't be worth the effort of taking in the money. It's so little. Perhaps she takes £100 a year. I don't know. But I agree completely with the principle of charging. Tenants have to pay a rent to use the land and it costs them money to take care of it, to build fences and such like.

'The days of the great dukes are gone, men who were rich enough not to have to squeeze the last penny out of their lands. Now it's the day of the owner-occupier who has to make the last £5 note from it.

'If landowners are being fair and making their land public, then certainly one should expect to pay to keep it so. I'm quite prepared for example, to pay to be able to walk on Dartmoor. There's currently a great row about this. It's one of the wildest, most beautiful parts of England, rare even in Europe. As a member of the public, I'm certainly willing to pay to keep it so.

'In twenty years or so I might find it's better to open all my land along the Wall to the public. The crowds are growing every year. More people want to see it. It's fairly middling farming land. Perhaps it could be supported better as a tourist area. I don't want to make it all commercial. But in future there might be so many people walking over it that it won't be viable any more as farm land.'

As the owner of an estate large enough to support him and his family, he's very lucky. 'I admit it. There's very few of us left who can live off the land. But our days are getting fewer. There are some very rich landowners left, of course. But most of the great Border magnates are slowly being snuffed out, like the Earls of Carlisle.'

Lord Henley keeps his own expenditures to the minimum so that he can still lead the life he wants to lead. He has very few staff at Scaleby, so few that he's gone ex-directory. 'There's often no one to answer the phone when I'm not here.'

I was staggering a bit when I eventually left Scaleby Castle, what with the lavish hospitality and worrying about the problems of upper-class poverty. Luckily, most people sympathise with Lord Henley and the Earl of Carlisle and such like folk, especially locally. One thing about the country which urban dwellers forget is that country people like the way things are. They like the big house, the big landowner. They like a set hierarchy where everyone knows their place, and their duties.

I continued along the line of Wall, working my way through the flat fields which surround Scaleby Castle. At Walby, I realised that it was here that Hutton too had struck lucky, getting himself invited to a rather boozy lunch. He came across a vicar sunning himself in his garden. They got into conversation and for once Hutton wasn't mistaken for a spy. He was invited to join the Reverend in his bone of lamb, which he enjoyed heartily.

As I came down a lane, I heard a lot of noise coming from a farmyard. Two little boys were shouting encouragement at two farm labourers chasing half a dozen cows round the yard, trying to trap one of them in a pen. In one corner a tall grey-haired man was carefully putting on a shiny green coat, the sort that surgeons wear, with an opening down the back. They got the cow into the pen at last, to the cheers of the boys.

The man in green was a vet, about to do a pregnancy test. The farmer was selling the cow and to prove it was in calf he needed a certificate from the vet. The vet pulled on his gloves and his hands disappeared up the rear end of the cow, shouting jokes all the time at the two farmers. The vet, who was broad Scots, was poking fun at their strong Cumberland accent. One of them had shouted at his sheep dog 'gan yam', meaning go home, and the vet was saying what kind of foreign language was that.

There was a young bull amongst the cows, a Charollais. Though it was only fifteen months old, it had cost them £1,000. It had a ring through its nose and this was really the main attraction for the kids. After he'd finished with the pregnant cow, the vet was going to give the rest of the cattle, including the bull, a blood test for brucellosis. The cows were fairly easy to catch. They offered no fight as their tails were lifted and the needle stuck in. The farmers shouted out the number of each cow, reading it from their ears, while the vet wrote it down. I waited for the bull to be done, but it was getting late so I moved on.

There were easy paths for the next mile or so across the fields then I was brought up short by a great roaring in the distance. Could the bull have turned on the vet and the farmers? It was a mechanical roar. I'd hit the motorway, the M6, the first road of any size I'd seen since leaving Newcastle. This stretch of the M6 was finished in 1972 connecting Carlisle to London with three hundred miles of continuous motorways. The noise was incredible after the silence of the flat fields. I wondered if the Roman carriages made much noise as they sped into Carlisle. I wondered if I'd had too much to drink at Scaleby.

Over the bridge, I had another strange encounter. On the left of the road is a seventeenth-century building called Drawdikes Castle. It was once a pele tower and is now a farmhouse, though a rather ornate and unusual one with busts along the roof. A Roman tombstone, brought from Stanwix, is supposed to be built into the south wall of the house.

It was the front garden of the house which amazed me. It was covered in millstones. They were everywhere, on the flower beds and the lawns and paths, along with other bits and pieces of stone work, half-pillars, stone troughs, parts of arches and carved cornices. Some of the troughs were filled with flowers but most were empty. I couldn't decide whether the garden was a dump or a part of a strange collection.

As I stood there a man came rushing out of the door and raced towards a blue car parked in the drive way. 'Excuse me,' I said. 'Are these your troughs?'

'I'm in a hurry,' he said. 'Can't stop.'

I followed him to his car and talked to him through his car window.

'But what do you do with them?' I asked.

'I collect them,' he replied. 'I've got eight hundred troughs and about forty millstones. Before the war I could get a stone trough for threepence each. Now they cost £20 to £30 a time.'

'Do you sell them?'

'I told you. I just collect them. I'm a crank.'

With that, he wound up his window and drove off, leaving me little wiser.

I went to the back of his house and eventually found the Roman tombstone, built into the Wall as the Richmond handbook says. '*Dis Manibus*', a phrase I'd come to know very well, was exceptionally clear.

Opposite the farm house, on the other side of the road, is a disused army camp, Hadrian's Camp. During the last war and until the 1960s it was one of the best known army camps in the country. Thousands of National Servicemen passed through – so must thousands of Hadrian's Army. This was the site of Milecastle 64, though no foundations have ever been found.

I was now approaching the outer suburbs of Carlisle, my home stretch and one I knew very well. Most travellers follow the busy Brampton road into the centre of the town at this spot, now that a built-up area is looming ahead, but the Wall line keeps to the right and still has a farm and several fields to go through.

I cut behind a pub called The Near Boot. I used to drink half pints of beer there when I was sixteen, pretending I was eighteen. Then I headed down Tarraby Lane which was overgrown with high hedges, far denser than I remember from my schooldays when I plodded along it on cross-countries from the Grammar School. This time I was delighted by the bumps and mounds in many of the fields and I picked out what I was sure was the site of milecastle 65.

In the heart of the lane, I met two young surveyors, measuring up the fields. I stopped one and chatted, asking if he realised we were standing on the site of the Wall. He was Scottish and said I shouldn't bother about Hadrian's Wall. Go up to his home town of Falkirk and explore a real Wall, the Antonine Wall.

Emerging from Tarraby Lane was like emerging from a rural tunnel – out of the darkness of the overgrown hedgerows into the glaring light of the suburban semis of Stanwix. The Wall line treads daintily through the semis and enters the grounds of a large house called Home Acres, now the site of Carlisle's

College of Art, a thriving foundation these days, even though my Chinese friend back at Banks didn't think much of it. When I was a boy in Carlisle it had a reputation for producing strange looking people with long hair and arty clothes. Now that every shop assistant, junior clerk and apprentice has long hair and wears arty clothes, how on earth do art students manage to look like art students?

Stanwix – pronounced with a silent 'w' – is what is known in Carlisle as a desirable suburb, not as posh as living out in the country in a beautiful village like Wetheral or Burgh, but as far as town life goes, very smart. It's full of prim little post-war semis on the outskirts and in the centre some Victorian terrace houses. It lies on a plateau above the River Eden and commands a handsome view of the city, a strategic view, guarding the main road from Scotland which crosses the Eden at Stanwix Bank.

The Romans built their third and final major bridge to carry the Wall at this point. Their Eden Bridge was probably bigger than either the North Tyne or Irthing bridges, judging by the size of the river which had to be crossed, but very few details of it have been found, except for a few stones dug up when the river was dredged in 1951. The Roman bridge is thought to have been about forty yards downstream from the present bridge.

Stanwix must have been a magnificent sight in Roman times, what with a cavalry fort on the hill, the large military bridge carrying the Wall and probably another one carrying the Stanegate road, and then over the river the town of Carlisle, the largest town in the whole region of the Wall. I never dreamed of such magnificences when I was at primary school at Stanwix, back in the 1940s. My only military memory is knitting woollen squares to be made into blankets for soldiers to help them beat Hitler.

The Roman fort at Stanwix covered 9.3 acres, making it easily the largest and most important fort on the Wall. Its garrison was the double strength ala Petriana, the thousand-strong cavalry regiment, the only cavalry unit of its size in

Britain. This was the regiment, formerly at Corstopitum, which was moved up to the Wall during the second plan.

The senior commander of the whole Wall garrison lived at Stanwix, which would indicate that in Hadrian's time the biggest threat must have been around this area. Perhaps northern tribes were raiding across the estuary from the Scottish side of the Solway, or English tribes were hiding in the Lake District, or perhaps there had been a disaster in this area from an unknown source which needed an extra large garrison. Perhaps it was simple strategy – this section of the Carlisle Plain has always been a vital meeting point for many routes and doubtless needed special protection.

Today, there are no Roman remains to be seen in Stanwix. For all its pride of position in Roman days, it has been for centuries a dead loss as far as archaeologists are concerned. Stanwix makes fewer appearances in the antiquarian books than almost any other fort. Camden didn't manage one word about it. Hutton had a few non-Roman experiences here, but only managed to see one Roman relic, an eighteen-inch high figure in a niche in a stable block. 'I wonder the boys had not belted him out of the world.' He enquired about the figure, but was told it had been there for as long as anyone could remember and that it was a 'Roman Chief'.

I could find no trace of it, nor any other evidence of Stanwix's famous past. The sole memento is a plaque on a house at the beginning of Church Terrace, which says that beneath this spot lies the foundations of Hadrian's Wall, built AD 126. I wonder where they got that date from?

In the 1930s, excavations traced the outlines of the fort, but found little else. The last date on which any work was done on the site of the fort was in 1940. While digging an air-raid shelter, they came across bits of the Wall. I do remember a lot of building activity in the playground when I was at Stanwix Primary school but I always thought it was for the temporary prefab classrooms. They're still there, so I noticed as I walked round.

St Michael's church is also on the site of the fort. It's a nineteenth-century church, all red sandstone, with no trace of

246

Roman stone. A cavalry man's tombstone was found in the wall of the previous church on the site in 1790. In the past, grave-diggers used to protest about the number of stone slabs they hit when working in the churchyard.

You can still see today what a good site Stanwix was. From the churchyard there's a fine view down to the river. In 1934 they discovered a treasure chest of brooches, uniforms, har-nesses, mountings hidden in fifteen feet of river silt, washed down at some time from a workshop on the slopes of the fort. For a huge fort, the vicus development outside the fort walls must have been equally extensive.

I walked slowly down to the river as it was a beautiful early summer evening, vaguely hoping I might see something in the river silt. There seemed to be a lot of fishermen around, all moaning, and all, surprisingly, with Lancashire accents. Car-lisle is a rather isolated, closed city. People leave but these days they seldom arrive.

I walked round the river to the suspension bridge and watched the sun setting across the city, picking out the Castle and the Cathedral, a skyline now dominated by the new Civic Centre. As I stood on the bridge I saw a straggle of fishermen coming towards me in the dusk, slowly and deliberately, weighed down by baggage. All of them seemed to be carrying marquees on their backs. Others joined them from the banks of the river, till they formed a long line, hunched under their loads like the Seven dwarfs. They tramped in single file over the bridge, silently, deep in their own thoughts. I followed them, fascinated by so many identical fishermen.

At the end of St Aidan's Road a coach was parked, the driver asleep on the front seat. He jumped up when he heard them and opened the boot for them to stow their tackle. I caught the last one as he climbed aboard. He told me they were a fishing club from Failsworth, Manchester, up on a day's fishing. It had been a disappointing day – not what they were used to on such a plentiful fishing river. The best catch had been a fifteen-pound chub which meant a prize of £7 for the catcher. The day's fishing cost them £2 each, for the bus and for the prize money. He said it wasn't a long trip by any means, not with the new

M6 motorway. The Eden was a favourite fishing river for clubs all over Lancashire. It was usually very good. Perhaps the next day out would be better. They were off to Oxford.

I walked into Carlisle. It had been a rather mixed-up, full of little events, anti-climactic day. Stanwix had been the climax of the Wall for the Romans. It's a shame there's now nothing to be seen and so few memories or records to relate.

I was thankful that I was going to spend the night at my mother's house in Carlisle and didn't have to look locally for somewhere to stay. Old Hutton spent the night in Stanwix itself, saving another day for walking across the river into Carlisle. And what trouble he had finding a bed for the night. He was turned away from one place after another.

'Do *you* think I will turn away one of my constant customers for you,' said a very haughty lady at one Stanwix house.

At a third place he has a rather interesting exchange with a well-dressed lady who comes to the door. Hutton describes her rather cattily as 'a fine figure, once a beauty yet showing as much of that valuable commodity as could be expected from forty-five.'

He asks her for a bed for the night, saying he will pay anything. She says she does have a spare bed, but it doesn't suit her to let him have it.

'Do not suffer me to lie in the street,' implores Hutton.

'You are a stranger to me,' she replies.

'So I am to every one else. If I must not sleep till I am known I must walk one hundred and fifty miles for a bed.'

'What! Are you on foot?'

'Yes, but if I am, I have not the appearance of a common traveller. Pray, Madam, favour me.'

'I am a single woman; and to take in a stranger may give rise to reflection.'

'Did you ever hear of a woman losing her character by a man seventy eight!'

'I do not keep a public house.'

Hutton gets the door closed in his face – but a week later he discovers some interesting information.

'When dining at a public table in Carlisle, I mentioned this singular adventure. The whole company in a moment recognised the person I alluded to and told me "She had long been connected with the Duke of − − − ; had issue by him and that whenever he came into those parts, he chose to see her." '

So much for Stanwix's posh face.

18
Carlisle:
Fifty Years Digging

Carlisle was a thriving Roman community long before Hadrian and his Wall. It's thought the first fort might have been set up by the Governor Cerialis around AD 71. Certainly Agricola in AD 80 had a strong wood and turf fort on the site. Carlisle was always a natural base for any moves North into Scotland.

The first known excavations of the Roman remains of Carlisle were made in 1892 (during the building of extensions to Tullie House) and the foundations of the Agricolan ditches were uncovered. In the process, a great timber platform about forty feet was traced and was thought to have been a base for the Roman catapults.

The Romans called Carlisle Luguvalium, after a sun god called Lugos or Lug. Not much is known about this god whether he was local or imported, but it's thought the French city of Lyons has a similar derivation.

Around 122, when Roman Carlisle had been going for a good forty years, Hadrian moved the army a mile over the river to Stanwix. The shifting of the soldiers gave Carlisle a chance to develop as a real town, but it must still have been very much a military town, living off the Stanwix garrison, the highest buying unit of the entire Northern area, outside York. No wonder the Roman town of Carlisle grew to seventy acres, twice the size of Corbridge. We know from inscriptions and other remains that Carlisle had a thriving cosmopolitan population, bringing in Eastern merchants attracted by the trading possibilities, plus the usual shop keepers, tavern owners, money lenders and the rest.

Carlisle as a walled Roman town possibly had the status of civitas with a great deal of self-governing rights. St Patrick's father was thought to have been a magistrate in Carlisle. But because of the lack of knowledge of town walls or buildings, unlike Corbridge, no one yet knows for sure the exact size or status of Carlisle.

It might even at one time have been a legionary head-quarters, albeit a temporary one. If only Carlisle could tell its story we might know what happened to the Ninth Legion, the legion which disappeared.

The last record of the Ninth in Britain is at York in 108. Later, around 122, its place at York was taken by the Sixth Legion who arrived either with or around the time that Hadrian arrived. The usual explanation is that the Sixth took the place of the Ninth.

There's been a widely-held theory for a long time that the Ninth Legion was destroyed in the Carlisle area, having been sent over from York to cope with local difficulties. Because of the loss of the Ninth, Hadrian ordered the Wall to be built. It's a neat theory. Such a shame that today's archaeologists point out the lack of proof. The Wall is so magnificent in every way, a monument to the might of the Roman army, that it's nice to think that it took something like the loss of a legion to have brought about such a colossal reaction. To think it was just another frontier line, another order passed down through the Roman civil service, would be very disappointing.

There's another theory, put forward by C. E. Stevens, that the Ninth was sent to Carlisle to help build the Wall. As the Carlisle side was originally built of turf, this explains the lack of stone inscriptions which the other legions left on the Stone Wall sections. It was *during* the building work that the Ninth was destroyed – a theory which also helps to explain the sudden and drastic changes in the plans for the Wall.

Whatever the exact role of the Ninth in the creation of the Wall, most experts believe its last days in Britain are somehow connected with Carlisle. There are tile and pottery kilns in the area which show the Ninth or part of it was stationed here for some time.

The Ninth's disappearance from Britain is still a mystery, but the latest theory (1973), is that it was finally destroyed in the East, perhaps in Armenia in AD 161. This is what Professor Birley thinks, but he's open to suggestions – and possibly better verse than these lines he scribbled during an academic seminar in 1971:

> The fate of the Ninth still engages
> The minds of both nitwits and sages,
> But that problem one fears
> Will be with us for years
> And for ages and ages and ages.

Carlisle prospered as a Roman town till the end of the Roman period. At the end of the fourth century there was a new province in the north west called Valentia, as the Romans subdivided the country, partly for defensive reasons. It's thought that Carlisle became the provincial capital. This is something else which excavations in Carlisle might one day show.

After the Romans, the Dark Ages in Carlisle were as dark as anywhere else in the north and for two hundred years no one knows what happened. It's now thought that perhaps the Roman fortifications remained intact and helped to repel the invaders. Yet again there are Arthurian legends about Carlisle being the site of a great victory against the Saxons.

In 685 the Roman Walls of Carlisle were well known and well established enough to be a tourist attraction. It was in that year, as Bede records, that St Cuthbert came to Carlisle to visit an English queen who was staying in a Carlisle nunnery. (Being fit enough for a queen shows something of Carlisle's status.) Bede describes how St Cuthbert was led by the citizens to see 'the walls of the town and the remarkable fountain, formerly built by the Romans.' This remarkable fountain is yet another undiscovered site.

It was during the post-Roman period, before the Saxons took

over, that the town's name changed to Caerluel, the castle of Luel, a British attempt to translate the Roman name Luguvalium. It's one of the few place names in England which has retained its native British origins. The Saxons changed almost everything else into English. Carlisle, despite its present spelling, still betrays its Celtic background – the same Celtic 'Caer' which comes in so many Welsh place names.

Carlisle Castle, which stands on a slight promontory just a hundred yards North of Tullie House, was curiously enough not part of the Roman fort. At first sight it would seem the ideal situation for a fort but the Romans, presumably feeling secure, decided to spread out on the plain. Later of course, they had the vast military protection of the Stanwix fort and the Wall to keep them safe. The Castle is Norman and has a stirring history as a Border stronghold during the English-Scottish wars. For almost five hundred years it was on the front line of all the battles. For most of the eleventh century it was part of Scotland. The castle housed Mary Queen of Scots and later fell, or at least gave in, to Bonnie Prince Charlie.

Today the castle is looked after by the Department of the Environment and houses its area offices. It also houses the county archivist, Bruce Jones. His is rather a new profession, one which grew up after the war. Now every borough and county of any size has its own archives department. He started Carlisle's archives almost from scratch in 1962 and now has a staff of eleven in two centres, Carlisle and Kendal. They gather and arrange material of all kinds and ages, medieval church documents, diocesan records, factory records, family letters, right up to presentday council meeting minutes. 'You can't say that any documents are more valuable than any other. They're all pieces in a jigsaw, all of them unique. You can find as many pictures of the past as there are people willing to ask questions.'

Recent questions have come from students of the history of architecture, looking at the plans which the Adam brothers had turned down for Lowther Castle, to nineteenth-century social historians who are suddenly taking a new interest in Carlisle.

Newcastle, today's first city on the Wall, is still very much a big industrial Victorian town, despite all the brand new buildings. Carlisle somehow seems folksy, a by-water which has picked up bits of every age yet retained few strong feelings of any. Even its handful of old factories and back-to-back houses seems cuddly, a stage attempt at grime and industrialisation. I was surprised to hear from Mr Jones that Carlisle had its industrial revolution before Lancashire, an industrial boom based on water power which brought thousands of workers flooding into the area. When steam came and power looms took over, Carlisle's mills couldn't compete with Manchester and Liverpool. Carlisle's industrial revolution was all over by the 1840s.

In the textbooks, Carlisle is never mentioned, but it's now being realised that there were not just factories but social agitation long before Manchester. Mr Jones says records of early groups of Chartists have been discovered in Carlisle which pre-date the Lancashire and Midland ones. Even more surprising, it looks as if the Co-operative movement might have had very early beginnings in Carlisle. As every schoolboy knows, the Co-op movement is said to have been begun in 1844 by the Rochdale Pioneers. 'New records show that there was a Co-op movement, just like the Rochdale one, in Upperby in Carlisle long before 1844.'

As an outsider, Mr Jones is pleased to be in Carlisle. 'People in the north are more interested in the past than those in the south.' He lives in the village of Burgh, right on the line of the Wall. But after twelve years he still feels an outsider. 'Cumbrians are welcoming, but you still feel you're looking at them through a window. They have such close links with each other that you always feel a stranger. I've worked in other parts of the country before I came here and never felt it so strongly.

'I make a point of giving lectures to local WI meetings to encourage interest in local records. If I take with me a sixteenth-century document about their village I always find that the WI ladies will know almost every name. They'll say "That's so-and-so's family, they're still living there," or "they married so-and-so in the next village". These kinds of groups are very strong. Everyone is akin to someone else and these extended kin groups matter. It's a very Celtic characteristic, one I haven't come across since I lived in Wales.'

Mr Jones was rather attracted by this enclosed, cut-off feeling when he first came to Carlisle in 1962. He felt it in the streets when he walked up from the station, in the untouched market place, the old Town Hall, the medieval shop fronts in Fisher Street and Abbey Street, all rather humble and small scale, but still direct links with Carlisle's past.

What he obviously didn't realise was that Carlisle was simply behind the times in desolating its city centre. Ten years after every other town in the country, Carlisle is now in a paroxysm of self-destruction, knocking down the unique and old to make way for grandiose but ridiculous ringroads and roundabouts and civic centres.

When the motor car is obsolete, perhaps they'll regret all the medieval streets, the Georgian houses and the historic buildings that were knocked down to make way for it. Historically and architecturally, there are not many reasons why people should come and look at Carlisle today. Perhaps if they find some of Carlisle's greatest days, its Roman past, the charabancs will start rolling in.

In the meantime, Carlisle's Roman past is centred on Tullie House. This is a fine Jacobean house, perhaps the finest house left in Carlisle, which houses the library and the museum, with its priceless collection of Roman relics from the western sector of the Wall. Beside it is the cathedral, where Sir Walter Scott was married. It contains many Roman stones, used by the Normans in building the cathedral around 1130. Tullie House, like the cathedral, is on the site of Carlisle's Roman fort.

The smell of Tullie House was so familiar, a warm vintage polish smell which hadn't changed in twenty-five years. I used to step with awe into Tullie House, keeping my voice down and my head down as I crept into the children's library and went for the secret shelf where my friends had hidden the latest Biggles or Just William. The assistants seemed so frightening, spinster ladies with grey hair who could silence you with one look if you dared to giggle. Moving into the Big Library, like going into long trousers or flying up from the Cubs, consisted of desperately trying to be the part, staggering out with real novels by W. Somerset Maugham.

In the entrance hall to the library the bust of Robert Burns was still there, though a felt pen moustache was a recent addition. Through the window of the reference library I could see the old dossers asleep round the sides and the students in the middle, just as it was in my day, when I made a pretence of studying in the Ref. during the vacations. This time the old men looked clean and neat while the students were the ones who looked scruffy and smelly. There were even some black students. In my day, Carlisle was racially intact. The only foreigners were Scottish.

Further down the entrance hall there was a display of State Management memorabilia – the state-run chain of local pubs, currently being sold off to private enterprise. Three old men were noisily pointing out the old photographs, the bottles, the beer mats, capping each others' memories of long forgotten booze-ups and barmaids.

I went outside and round to the museum entrance, passing the sunken Roman shrine in the flower garden, the only Roman structure, alas, which can be seen in Carlisle. No Roman buildings have been uncovered, so far.

Robert Hogg is curator of the museum. Once any archaeologist ventures west of Birdoswald they're in Hogg country. For decades, the Richmonds and Birleys have recorded in their books the help he's given. Mr Hogg hasn't written any books. He's very conscious in fact of not being a normal academic archaeologist. It just happens to have been his job for almost fifty years.

I'd never spoken to him before though I'd often caught sight of him in the past, a tall stern looking figure in a white coat, more like a surgeon than a curator. His office was a surprise. It was quite spartan with bare floorboards, highly sanded and highly polished, the minimum of furniture and bare white walls. There were no signs of the sort of lifetime's junk I'd expected. His accent was even more surprising, so broad and local that I wondered how Oxbridge archaeologists, coming up from the south, make him out on their first meeting.

His surname, he explained, was nothing to do with pigs. It came from the Border term for a yearling sheep, a hogget. All those Border families called Hogg, including the present Lord Chancellor, had originally been shepherds. James Hogg, the Scottish poet, was always known as the Ettrick shepherd.

Mr Hogg left the Creighton Secondary School in Carlisle at sixteen and was very fortunate to get a job. It was 1926, the year of the General Strike. He joined Tullie House as a junior assistant on twenty-six shillings a week, where he followed his main interests, natural history and geology.

In 1930 they got word at Tullie House that the great Roman archaeologist, F. G. Simpson, was coming to live in Carlisle. He'd rented a house in Brampton Road and was going to start excavations at Stanwix. No one on the staff was an archaeologist or had any interest in Roman affairs. The curator at that time was also the librarian and that was his main concern.

'As the most junior member I was detailed to help Simpson. I said I didn't want to. It wasn't my interest. The curator, Mr Gray, said in that case I was saying I didn't want to do my job. I had no alternative. So at nineteen, I set off with Simpson to walk up Stanwix Bank to look for the fort. It was very strange. I was going to an area I knew very well, yet to look for something I didn't know anything about. I didn't even know the Romans had been there. It took us six blessed years to find that fort.'

It was a very difficult fort to trace. In helping to dig through the layers of different periods he realised that an archaeologist had to be aware of many sciences – geology, botany, architecture. His school education had been minimal but he decided to take a correspondence degree from London University in natural sciences. For six years he worked at it, studying in the evening after a hard day's work, losing so much weight that he went down to nine stone. 'I got my degree at last, just as the blessed war broke out. Life came to a standstill for everyone.'

There was a knock on his door as he was talking and in came a local doctor, an old friend who'd helped him in the 1930s with his practical biology work for his degree. He'd brought with him a silver comb, an old family heirloom which he'd

decided to give to Tullie House, if they wanted it. 'It's Victorian,' said Mr Hogg looking at it. 'But it's not my period. But
leave it with me and one of my assistants will date it.'

After the doctor had gone, he said he didn't expect it would
be of much interest for the Museum, but it was hard to refuse
gifts. People became very upset if their kindness was spurned. It
was often worse when things were accepted and put on show
because the donors fussed about their gifts not getting enough
prominence.

After the war, he came back to the museum and eventually
became curator. He has a staff of four, specialising in different
things – a biologist, a natural historian, an art expert, Mr Hogg
himself on archaeology and a museum technician. Their budget
for the year, including all salaries and purchases, is £12,000. It
can be seen how low salaries are in the museum world, even for
someone who has become eminent in his own field. His own
salary is little more than that of an unskilled worker in a
Midlands car factory.

'I don't mind my salary being small. What could be nicer –
to work in a lovely place, at a fascinating job in my own home
town. All the things I care about are round about me. But it's
bad for the museum to have such little money. All small town
museums have the same trouble. You become used to nothing
and you work for nothing. The time will come when the public
will regret it.'

We went on a tour of the museum, going first into the cellars
to look at the store rooms. They were a revelation, so vast and
jam packed with treasures which the public never see. There
were two rooms devoted to biological specimens, drawers of
water beetles, cases of red shanks showing every possible
plumage change, all beautifully arranged and tabulated.
'Amateurs spend a lifetime collecting then leave their collections to us and we have to classify and store them. For the
general public we arrange displays of all our familiar common
animals in the exhibition galleries but those store boxes and
cabinets with their extensive ranges of insects, flowers, bird-
skins and eggs are for the use of the research student.'

In another cellar were the Roman Britain remains, row upon

row of large metal boxes, all labelled, dating from a 1911 box with pottery and inscribed stones found at the Poltross Burn milecastle, all the bits marked in Simpson's hand, to a box marked '1966 Brougham' which contained fragments found during part of the M6 excavations.

'For the general public a museum is a holiday experience. They don't come here in their working life. But on holiday, if the weather's bad and they can't swim or have a picnic, or they can't watch football or don't want a pint, they might come to the museum. And when they've seen us once, that's it for most of them. They've had the experience. Our aim is very simply *to be here*. You can't see these Roman relics anywhere else in Carlisle. Just here. As far as the general public are concerned, the collections are presented for them in a clear and attractive manner for their enjoyment and instruction, whenever they feel the desire to visit them. It is their heritage and sometime in their life they will wish to see it.'

But couldn't more people be made aware that Tullie House is there, lurking in the middle of the city, filled with treasures? Couldn't he do more – shout, knock more people over the heads?

'I've been round every village in the county. I never stop lecturing. Every time we have an exhibition, I beat the big drum. What more can five people do? We've got the collections to look after.'

His assistants were currently working on two exhibitions, both of paintings, and a major conservation project connected with some local woods. All round the year there is the problem of cataloguing. They get an average of a hundred and thirty additions a year, from paintings to glass bottles. The Department of the Environment sent them fifty packing cases of Roman pottery from the M6 work.

Upstairs on the top floor is stored one of Carlisle's most valuable yet strangest collections. Roman relics are to be expected, but once again, Pre-Raphaelite paintings turn out to be a local speciality. This time they're not the work of the Ninth Earl of Carlisle but are from an amazing stroke of good fortune which came Tullie House's way.

As one would expect, Tullie House can't afford to buy many paintings out of its minuscule budget. Even today, its annual allowance is only £450. To try and spend it as wisely as possible, they have a London representative to advise them. Today's adviser is Roger de Gray, who must have a very difficult job. Even unknowns charge £450 for just one painting. But in the 1930s they had Sir William Rothenstein as their London man.

It was through friends of friends that Rothenstein agreed to help Carlisle in 1933. He was then a distinguished figure, Principal of the Royal College of Art, and getting on in years. He was allowed a yearly sum of £100 to buy works of art of little known men. 'With this modest sum,' so he wrote later in his memoirs, 'I was able to get together the nucleus of a good collection at no great cost to the City of Carlisle.'

Apart from young unknowns of the day, he also managed to buy at a reasonable price many examples of the work of leading artists he'd known since his own student days or who had studied under him. In ten years, during which time his allowance went up to £200 a year, he bought over one hundred paintings for Carlisle. Many of them are of great value today and include works by Burne-Jones, Legros, Millet, Pisarro, Whistler, Augustus John, William Orpen, Wyndham Lewis, Paul Nash, Stanley Spencer and Ruskin Spear. When he resigned his honorary post in 1944, shortly before he died, Rothenstein presented Carlisle with a gift from his own collection, a large drawing by Burne-Jones called 'The Three Graces'. 'In memory of my very pleasant relations with Carlisle since I was entrusted with the task of adding to its public collection.'

In any books of the Pre-Raphaelites you find Tullie House, Carlisle, amongst the picture credits. Once having acquired a speciality, they attracted other similar paintings, notably the Bottomly Bequest. This collection, from a Dr Gordon Bottomly, contains over a hundred paintings, many of them Pre-Raphaelites.

I couldn't see any of the Pre-Raphaelites on show, not even the Burne-Jones. They were all stacked in a store room. The public painting rooms were full at that time with local works and abstracts.

I'd been fascinated by all the store rooms, thanks no doubt to being personally conducted round them by Mr Hogg, but I began to have the suspicion that the most boring parts of a museum are its public rooms. There did seem an inordinate amount of store rooms at Tullie House, all crammed with unseen treasures.

He defended the private rooms by saying they were necessary to house all their specialist collections. You couldn't have two hundred school parties, which is what they get every year, traipsing round the store rooms. And as for what they showed and didn't show, experience proved that the public wanted well known objects and animals, not rare specimens.

As curator, he is responsible for the paintings and for the natural history specimens, but his main professional concern is still Roman Britain. Whenever national or international dignitaries come north, he is dug out to take them for an hour or two on the Wall. 'The Town Clerk rings me up. I don't mind. Americans are so appreciative. "It's your actual Roman Wall? No kidding!" They run up and touch it, pose beside it with their three cameras round their waists and two guide books in their hands. They come from Minnesota and have no roots in Minnesota but they've been told that long ago their relations once came from the north of England.'

He has done nothing at the Stanwix fort since the thirties but he's been involved in many excavations in other parts of Cumberland. The most important Carlisle work was the section he took in 1954-56 which revealed the shrine now in the Tullie House garden, the first piece of Roman Carlisle to be seen. 'I've called it a shrine by a process of elimination. It's not a well. It's not a grave – graves weren't allowed inside fort walls. In twenty years, no one has yet come up with a more logical interpretation. If someone did I'd abandon the shrine idea.'

It was he who did the work on the River Eden, getting in quick when they were dredging to rescue a few stones from the Roman bridge. He's written many papers over the decades for the archaeological journals, but so far no books. He gave me an offprint of a 1973 article he did for the transactions of the Cumberland and Westmorland Antiquarian and Archaeological Society. It was entitled 'Factors which have affected the Spread of Early settlement in the Lake District.' It was only thirty-five pages long. 'I hope you enjoy it. It represents my last thirty years' work.' I felt suitably humble.

It might or might not remain the summit of his lifetime's study. That day when I saw him, in the early summer of 1973, he was looking forward to something which could set Carlisle on the Roman archaeological map once and for all. During the present road-widening work nearby he'd found to his delight what he thought might be the long lost original walls of the Roman fort at Carlisle, though so far nothing was definite. But having spent fifty years digging around Roman Carlisle without actually finding anything in the city, apart from that little shrine, his own excitement was obvious.

Encouraged by all the excited noises, the Department of the Environment's Miss Dorothy Charlesworth had recently come hotfoot from London to have a look. Bad news for Carlisle – and for Mr Hogg. Her first opinion was that the remains weren't Roman but medieval.

'I hadn't said they were definitely Roman,' said Mr Hogg. 'I thought it *might* be. It still can be. The medieval town walls might have used the same stones as the Romans used, making it impossible to tell the difference.'

However, Miss Charlesworth was interested enough to arrange for a full-scale emergency excavation for later in the summer. This was the one she was planning when I met her earlier. Mr Hogg, and everyone else, had meanwhile to wait.

I rang Professor Birley with the sad news that so far Miss Charlesworth was sceptical, asking if he was coming over to see the summer dig. 'I back Robert Hogg,' he said. 'Without seeing the stones. I'm sure he's right.'

I set off to finish the final stretch of the walk to Bowness, almost impatient to get it done and come back to Carlisle to see what the summer dig would find.

19
Bowness:
End of the Wall, End of the World

Getting out of Newcastle had seemed to take for ever but in
many ways it had been easy. The road west is dead straight and
follows exactly the line of the Wall. Getting out of Carlisle
doesn't take very long, as it's a city only a quarter of the size,
but the complications are endless. The Wall bends round the
back of the city, through a mass of sewage works, railway
depots and the power station, before at last it hits fresh air once
again on the banks of the River Eden. Not just fresh air – you
enter an area of strange, hanging, dateless air. This last stretch
of the Wall has always been one of the forgotten parts of
England and in many ways still is.

Throughout my jaunt so far I'd managed to line up places or
people of interest on every stretch. One look at the map and
you can see a castle or a stately home worth visiting, apart
from all the Roman remains. Not only does this final western
stretch have no Roman remains, it seems to have nothing at all
to attract the absolute outsider, unlike the east.

Between Carlisle and Brampton, a distance of only ten miles,
the area is stiff with titles and grand houses. I visited four
(Naworth, Castlesteads, Scaleby and Boothby) and talked to
their occupants, but could have seen more. But between Carlisle and Bowness, a distance of some fourteen miles, there's not

one in sight. *Tatler*, should it ever penetrate this far, must seem a foreign magazine. Where have all the squirearchy gone?

I set off, after leaving the Carlisle boundary, by following the River Eden as it meanders slowly to the Solway and the sea. The Wall takes the same route until the hamlet of Grinsdale, where it heads straight for the next village of Beaumont. But the Vallum, just to confuse the issue, leaves both the river and the Wall to its meanderings and picks a straight course all the way to Bowness.

This final zigzag course of the Wall has confounded archaeologists throughout the centuries. On the exceedingly high and rocky crags, up on the Whin Sill, the Romans stuck to straight lines almost everywhere, despite the difficult terrain. Yet here they are, down at sea level, and they're wandering all over the place. Had they given up all thoughts of a simple geographical line of defence? Military experts have often picked holes in the line the Wall now takes, criticising the need for thirty four changes of direction in a stretch only fourteen miles long, whereas in the seventeen-mile stretch on the other side of Carlisle to Gilsland there are just nineteen changes.

It seemed to me that the answer lies in the Solway. It's impossible to know now, almost two thousand years later, what course the River Eden took as it joined the Solway. The Wall perhaps zigzagged in and out of the high water marks, possibly to little knolls long since gone which were safe from flood water. The fact that they were dodging in and out, looking for vantage points to guard any possible crossings of the Solway, indicates to me that there *was* a plan and that the plan was defensive. Otherwise, they would have just gone inland all the way, straight to Bowness.

I noticed a lot of activity in the fields beside the Eden as the farmers spread their fertilisers. I said hello, grand day, to all of them, but not one replied. In the village of Beaumont, pronounced Beemont, I had my first conversation of the day with an old man outside a cottage beside the church. He said he wasn't a local. He came from Moorhouse, all of two miles away. He'd retired to Beaumont for the peace and quiet. I asked him what had happened to the church at Kirkandrews on Eden, the previous village on the line of the Wall. With a name like that, I'd confidently expected a church. 'Tummledoon,' said the old man. 'They put it up a few times and it tummledoon.' I asked if this catastrophe was recent. 'About a hundred years ago, so the locals telt me.'

I went into the church at Beaumont which is on a strange little knoll, a perfect vantage point over the surrounding countryside. It was obvious why the Romans had a milecastle on the site. Foundations of Hadrian's Wall were found during excavations in the Churchyard in 1928. The church itself is twelfth century, small and sturdy and very attractive, typical of Cumberland's small fortified medieval churches, a place of refuge as much as worship. There's a piece of a Roman font, or so it looks, built into the wall round the churchyard and nearby at the crossroads an inscribed Roman stone built into the field wall. The Vicar of Beaumont, so I discovered on the notice-board, has his rectory back along the road at Kirkandrews. I pressed on instead to Burgh-by-Sands, the biggest village between Carlisle and Bowness and the first Wall fort since Stanwix.

Since leaving Carlisle I'd been in a trancelike state as I'd zigzagged for two hours or so across identical rectangular fields, making my way, ignored by almost every local, from one deserted looking hamlet to another, tracing the line of the Wall. I'd begun to feel a displaced person in a displaced land. Arriving at Burgh was like stumbling into suburbia.

Burgh, pronounced Bruff, has always been a smart little village, a haven for Carlisle's middle-class executives who commute to the city. Some of the older houses have been tarted up, a rare sight in Cumberland, and there are many new detached highly desirable modern residences. About twenty years ago I once cycled out to Burgh to have tea with a girl whose dad was the manager of Binns, Carlisle's answer to Harrods. (They are now connected since the House of Fraser bought both.) I think I stayed the night at her house, or perhaps I made that up later, being carried away with such a social catch. I definitely remember they had a TV set.

Today the local commuter gentry include the regional

manager of Laings the builders, the county archivist and a sprinkling of doctors, all of them of course terrible foreigners. They mix well, but you've got to have served your time for two centuries at least before you're a genuine local.

Burgh was a fairly big Roman fort, almost five acres in size, and had at one time a garrison of Moors. The bath house for the fort has been located in what is now the vicarage. The church itself is built almost entirely of Roman stones and is on the site of the fort. I stood around, looking for a likely local to talk to.

It was midday and the village looked deserted, then I saw two herds of cows being shooed along the main street from different directions. This was a lengthy operation as Burgh is a very long village. I rested by the roadside in the shade as they passed, hoping for a word with the farmers, but no luck. When they'd gone I saw a cleric coming towards me down the road, taking his dog for a walk. I said are you the Vicar of Burgh and he said yes, come and have a cup of coffee. It was as if it had all been arranged, as if I could now claim my £5 for having spotted him. I blurted out my project, what I was doing sitting by the roadside in Burgh on a sunny summer day, and he took it all for granted. He led me into his vast and rather worn down vicarage and brought coffee and a large straw basket covered with a tea towel, the sort of basket farmers' wives take to market. I expected home-made scones, perhaps a pot of Cumberland rum butter or a bit of Kendal Mint cake. Out of it he took an almost perfect Roman burial urn, several pieces of Samian ware, the remains of two darker Coarse pots and several other bits and pieces. I picked up one of the Samian fragments, its rich redness glinting as if it had been made only yesterday, turned it over and there was the potter's mark, clear and bright. I was very excited. After a year looking at Roman exhibits, big and small, public and private, I could tell it was a fine piece. I copied down the potter's stamp, telling the vicar I'd send the details on a postcard to John Gillam at Corbridge, the Roman pottery expert. How on earth had he come by so many pieces?

'Perfectly simple,' said the Vicar, the Rev. Jack Strong. 'I was digging in my potato patch and out they came. My eleven-year-old son, Jonathan found some of them. He had come home from school one day fired with enthusiasm because he'd just been told that our vicarage was on the site of the fort. The first place he dug he found some pottery. I've told Miss Charlesworth. She says all the fields round here were part of the vicus and she hopes one day to excavate.'

Mr Strong comes from Manchester, which makes him very much a foreigner. He met his wife, who is a local doctor working for the Council, while at Manchester University. He's been at Burgh seven years and still finds it rather strange. He'd previously been in the heart of industrial Lancashire in Oldham, a tough job in a tough area which hadn't helped his health. In a parish only a mile square he'd had nine thousand parishioners. At Burgh he has under nine hundred parishioners in an area of twelve square miles.

Burgh has usually been a well-off village. In medieval days it paid more taxes than any other village in Cumberland. In the early nineteenth century there was a dye works, a candlewick factory and many looms, all of them long since disappeared. He'd found out these things, he said, so that he could answer questions from strangers like me who stopped him in the village. On the subject of the locals he wasn't so fluent, choosing his words carefully.

'It's just the *feeling* of the place. Bishop Bloomer (the Bishop of Carlisle who appointed him) said I'd find Burgh a lay-by. It's more than that. You have a lay-by for people passing through. People don't pass through this area. We've been by-passed for centuries.

'They're conservative with a small 'c', untouched and unchanged in their general outlook. They have a deep rooted sense that nothing will change because things have always been the same. The area somehow draws in people who feel that way already. There's talk for example of a Solway Barrage – a dam across the Solway to build a huge freshwater lake. I think it's an exciting idea, though I know that's all it is so far. The locals don't just take it with a pinch of salt – but with the whole potful. They know it won't happen because nothing ever happens round here.

'The way the farms operate is very strange. I haven't come across any of what I'd call homogeneous farms. They don't seem to have two fields together but one field here, one there, another a mile away. That's why they walk their cows about all day. I haven't seen a farm since I lived in Cheshire. Even the wealthier farmers, and there are several, have their fields all split up. It's very important to know whose ditch is whose, which hedge belongs to which person. They certainly believe in that phrase from Deuteronomy, "Cursed be he who removeth his neighbour's landmark".

'I'm sure it's all to do with history. They have had such insecurity for century after century that they've built up this carefulness, this independence, never putting all their eggs in one basket.'

Mr Strong's researches have found no trace of any squire-archy, though there was a manor house in Burgh at some stage, but no one knows when. The only big landowner the area has ever known is the Earl of Lonsdale, but he's always been an absentee, living further south near Penrith. He owned most of the Marsh at one time and many farms but no one seems to know what he owns now.

'It's always been a troublesome area with raids constantly back and forward across the Solway. The gentry moved out very quickly to the security of the Eden valley or into the fells. The locals were left to get on with it and look after themselves as best they could.'

Pevsner in his volume on the buildings of Cumberland and Westmorland makes the point that it's the Military Architec-ture of the area which is of most interest. As with the Romans, security not display was the medieval watchword. He counted in all fifty-eight castles, big and small, still to be seen in Cumberland today, a vast amount for a relatively small and underpopulated county. But on this corner of Cumberland the poor locals were left to fend for themselves, having been deserted by the squirearchy. They couldn't manage anything so grand as a castle to hide in. They had to make do with the village church. As fortified churches go, St Michael's, Burgh-by-Sands, is an excellent specimen.

We entered through the vestry, down a sparkling white corridor, up a staircase and into a small room where he unlocked the church's treasures, notably a set of baptismal books which run from 1653 to 1791. There are several Roman-looking carved stones set in the walls inside the church, though no one has been able to identify them. To the left of the altar is a carved face with a long moustache with what looks like a huge wasp crawling over it. 'Mr Hogg has looked at this. He says if he could find another one like it he might be able to date it.' It looked Moorish to me – after all, there was a Moorish garrison here in Roman times.

The church is primarily twelfth century but the tower, its most notable feature, is thought to be fourteenth century. You get into the tower from inside the church – there are no doorways from the outside – through a huge iron gate known by its Cumberland dialect name, the yett. (Naworth Castle also has a yett.) It's strange to see such a large prison-like gate right in the body of a church. Once through the yett and into the tower, the locals were safe. The ground floor of the tower has another Roman-Moorish looking carving, this time on the lintel in the doorway. 'It looks like an elephant to me,' said Mr Strong, running his fingers over it. 'Perhaps with a hippopotamus beside it. You wouldn't have found many of those creatures in Burgh nineteen hundred years ago. It's a marvellous piece of work.

'I find all the Roman connections fascinating, but one has to be careful. People can find themselves worshipping history instead of God.'

It was in this church on 7 July 1307 that the body of Edward I, the Hammer of the Scots, lay in state. He died a mile outside the village on Burgh Marshes where he'd been encamped, waiting for an opportunity to cross the Solway. It was strange to have caught up with Edward I once again, having thought about him first at Lanercost Priory where he'd held court all those months. He must have travelled a great deal along the Wall line on his forays against the Scots.

I thanked the vicar for the coffee and conversation, deciding to head for the Marsh to look for the monument to Edward I which was first put up in 1685. He hurried back to his vicarage which he hadn't locked. At one time he'd been rather scornful of the locals and their passion for security, locking things up and forever counting their hedges and ditches. The previous week he'd had his newly bought £300 colour TV stolen. He hadn't insured it either. The policy was on his desk, waiting to be posted. The locals were right. Border raids still go on.

I stopped for a few moments in the village pub, the Greyhound. I asked a man at the bar if the Earl of Lonsdale still owned the Monument and the Marsh and he said he did, though no one ever saw the present Earl round these parts today. Now in the old days, each new Earl always held races on Burgh marsh, the Burgh Barony Races, when the whole village had a fete day. The old Yellow Earl, he really knew how to enjoy himself and made sure others did the same. The man was very loquacious, for a local, but he was finishing his drink and was soon gone. I got nothing out of the publican himself. He was a stranger from Longtown (five miles the other side of Carlisle) and had only been here twelve years. 'They're very clannish round here. You can never get to know half the people.'

When I got out onto the Marsh to look at the Monument I found a sudden cool wind and a vast emptiness. The sudden suburb of Burgh had disappeared almost at once. The Monument isn't much to look at – the interest is that it's there, stuck in the middle of nowhere. It's about twenty feet high with a cross on top. The inscription is about the Earl of Lonsdale's good work in restoring it in 1876 as much as about King Edward I himself.

The Earls of Lonsdale have been prominent in these parts for centuries. As the last big landowner along the line of the Wall, the biggest of them all in fact, I decided he was worth a visit, even though his home is twenty miles down the M6 near Penrith. Nobody in Cumberland can be unaware of his family's influence. I used to walk to school every day down a street named after his family, Lowther Street, and on Saturday mornings I watched the children's matinees at the Lonsdale Cinema. (It has a new name now, totally lacking in any inspiration – the ABC.)

As far as the general public is concerned, the family's main claim to national fame is the Lonsdale belts for boxing, bequeathed by the famous Yellow Earl. He is still remembered with affection by many Cumbrians – though the present member of the family must regret his dafter eccentricities. Hugh Lowther, the fifth Earl of Lonsdale, held the title from 1880 till his death in 1944. He inherited one of the largest fortunes and largest estates in England and spent all the income without any re-investment. He painted all of his carriages yellow, and later his motor cars, and always had his servants in yellow livery. He was the first President of the Automobile Association – whose colour today is still yellow. In Cumberland the Tory party's colour is still yellow, as can be seen at every local election, despite the fact that nationally the Tories are always true blues.

The Lowthers have lived at Lowther near Penrith for almost one thousand years, probably from the times of the Danish settlements. Their first title deed, still in existence, dates back to 1060. The Lowther who first got together the family millions, to add to the titles and land they'd already acquired, was Sir James Lowther, who became first Earl of Lonsdale in 1802. He brought the industrial revolution to West Cumberland, expanding the town of Whitehaven, which after London and Bristol was the largest port in Britain.

His engineers in the West Cumberland coal fields were the first to use steam power to pump water out of the coal mines and make deep mining possible. He was the first to realise the potentialities of natural gas – now the biggest thing to have hit the other coast of Britain for centuries. Natural gas was seeping into the deep under-sea mines and was proving a danger, until he led it to the surface. As early as 1870 the street lamps of Whitehaven were running on natural gas.

Sir James Lowther also enlarged his huge agricultural estates and on one of them he employed Wordsworth and his father. (There's a particularly bad poem by Wordsworth praising

Lowther Castle and its 'majestic Pile and stern mien' which luckily doesn't appear in most anthologies.)

It was this Lowther who extended his possessions to include almost all of the English side of the Solway Firth – and therefore the last fourteen miles or so of the Wall. He bought seven manorial estates on the Solway, including the Barony of Burgh. The previous owners had long been absentees and their manors long since gone. What Sir James wanted was their land, though he didn't object to a few more ancient titles. He built up the family ownership to one hundred and two Lordships of the Manor in Cumberland and Westmorland. Even more important, he controlled nine rotten boroughs, parliamentary constituencies which he filled with his placemen. To this day, the Lowther family have had more members in the House of Commons than any other family. At the last count the total was one hundred and seven MPs. Most of them, of course, date back to the pre-1832 years.

By the time the Yellow Earl took over in 1880, determined to devote his life to sport in all forms, the industrial millions were well and truly pouring in. In 1910 he was personally spending at a rate of £180,000 a year, most of it coming from his coal and iron ore royalties. Alas for the family, the Yellow Earl wasn't interested in commerce or industry or in taking precautions against the 1930s Depression. West Cumberland was badly hit. By 1935 his disposable income had fallen dramatically to £6,000 a year. On his death in 1944, £1.7 million had to be paid in tax.

The present Earl, yet another James Lowther, is the Seventh Earl, great nephew of the Yellow Earl. As a bright young businessman he was brought over from Newcastle in 1949 where he'd been working, to take over the management of the family estates, even though he didn't inherit them till the death of his grandfather in 1953. In eight years, by massive rationalisation, he discharged unpaid liabilities of £2.1 million. In 1953 when he became Earl the turnover of the estate was £100,000 a year and it employed seventy people. Today, the turnover is £2½ million and the employees number three hundred. It's a remarkable success story.

It could be argued that he has had many advantages, such as Eton and an earldom and all those thousands of acres, but he's been the first head of the family firm for a century to have put these advantages to good use. Not just for the Lowther family. By rationalising and diversifying the estates, developing a Wildlife Park, opening a caravan site, he's brought increased employment and prosperity to part of the Northern Development Area.

He's been pretty clever with his trees. Every century or so the Lowthers have maintained 5,000 acres of trees, mainly oaks. It's only grand families that can afford to be so far sighted. In the Napoleonic wars they sold the oaks for shipbuilding. This market disappeared when iron ships came in. His Victorian ancestors found a new market – oak for railway wagons. A hundred years later, when it was his turn, British Rail switched to steel wagons. By careful research, he found a new market – oak for fencing the motorways. So far he's cleared 1,500 acres of oaks for the Motorways and produced £750,000. His latest fences are on the M4 motorway to Bristol. He opened his own sawmill for the oak which has now become a thriving business in its own right.

The Earl lives with his beautiful American wife at Askham Hall, Penrith, on his Lowther Estates. Lowther Castle, which fell into disrepair during the Yellow Earl's money troubles, has been cleaned up and looks very grand, but it's in fact a romantic ruin, an unlived-in shell, though a great attraction for tourists.

Despite the Yellow Earl's shortsightedness, the family still owns the freehold of twenty-seven thousand acres in Cumberland and Westmorland, plus another forty-five thousand acres over which he has manorial rights. 'We have eleven miles of the Solway coast which comes into that category,' he said. 'We sold the actual farms round Burgh some years ago.'

He was very excited, the day I met him, about yet another project – Horse Driving Trials. He was providing facilities for the first trials of this type in the north. Several important people were coming up for two days to take part – staying at

Askham as his private guest. Naturally, the problem of Burgh Marsh wasn't exactly foremost in his mind that day. But he said yes, he was quite interested in Roman remains. When he lived in Newcastle he often took friends to look at the Wall. He used to have a few Roman objects in one of the walls of the Lowther Castle, a damp wall which he was going to pull down.

'Tullie House would have liked them but I sold them instead at Sotherby's for £8,000. I was short of capital and needed the money for a new cow shed and other improvements.'

When he took over the title he didn't feel like reviving the Burgh races. 'It would have meant me paying for it out of my own pocket.' And though the Edward i monument on Burgh Marsh was rebuilt by a former Earl of Lonsdale, he refuses to spend any money on it. 'Because one of my forerunners was stupid enough to put it up it doesn't mean to say that it's my responsibility. There was rather a stink about it a few years ago. An eleven-year-old girl thought it was in such a bad state that she wrote to the Queen about it, saying it was a wicked shame to let it fall down. Buckingham Palace got on to the County Council. There was quite a fuss so I agreed to contribute £100 towards repairing it – but it was only a *contribution*. I wasn't admitting ownership.'

But surely he must own it, as lord of the manor of Burgh? 'Neither the Council nor the Department of the Environment feel able to be guardian of it either.'

'I'm denying it,' he said, smiling defiantly.

Naturally, when you're building up a run-down estate you have to look to the pennies and the pounds. But the present Earl can't really be said to be grasping. He could no doubt make a fortune out of the mineral rights he owns over thousands of the Lakeland fells. He maintains that they could be exploited at a profit, then the land replaced afterwards without the environment being desecrated, but the slightest move could upset the environmentalists. He knows also that he could develop his eleven miles of the Solway coast, but the Solway is one of the most important wild life preserves in the country and the wild life people would also raise a national outcry, though he himself is a supporter of many local naturalist bodies.

'Both areas are highly sensitive so I've decided to avoid any decisions. I've just leased fifteen thousand acres of the Lake Districts fells and one thousand five hundred acres of Solway land to the National Trust. They're having Burgh Marsh for one shilling a year. The locals can of course still graze their sheep on it, but between now and the year 2000 the National Trust is responsible for looking after it. In the year 2000 my successors can then decide what to do.'

Back on Burgh Marsh, it was nice to realise that it was all safe, at least for the time being. The tide was coming in fast up the Solway from the Irish Sea and I could see far out a little line of haaf net fishermen, standing in the water up to their thighs. From time to time the one at the end of the line, in the deepest water, moved his position and came down the line to stand in the shallower water. I went to the mud flats, took off my boots, and paddled out, the dark grey mud oozing between my toes, hoping to get a closer look. I seemed to walk for ages without getting any nearer. The Solway tides are very dramatic. When the tide is out, the sand and mud banks stretch for literally miles, so that you can't believe the sea can ever come in and actually cover the Marsh, cover it so deeply that you can stand on the grassy banks and actually dive into the sea.

There was a sudden glint and I saw one of the fishermen take a salmon out of his haaf net and pop it into a bag on his back. Or rather *her* back. To my surprise the fisherman who'd just bagged the salmon was a woman. I got out my camera and took a shot of her, feeling a real rubber-necking hick but unable to resist the sight of a woman doing what I'd always thought was a man's job. You have to be pretty strong to handle a haaf net. I've often tried to pick one up on the shore but been unable to manage it. Haaf netting is one of the most ancient forms of fishing and is peculiar to this part of the Solway. Its name suggests further evidence of the old Norse settlers. Each haaf net is about twelve feet long, four feet wide and supported by a framework of three stout posts. In appearance they look like football goal posts which have been cut horizontally in half.

Haaf net fishermen can work on their own but they tend to

work in groups of about three to six, standing in a line so that they can span a channel about fifty foot across. They wait there, hoping for the salmon or sea trout to swim into their line of nets. As the water gets too deep for them, they move into shallower water, one by one. There is a great art in manoeuvring the heavy nets as they change places, letting the tide do the work.

I waited and watched for a long time, hoping they would come in, but they'd obviously just started and were now catching the best of the tide.

The Romans adored fish. Every rubbish pit in every vicus across the line of the Wall is littered with their fish bones. They particularly liked shell fish and must have imported them by the thousand. You don't find oysters up in the Whin Sill. They're bound to have fished in the Solway, for shrimps if not for salmon.

At Drumburgh, where I rejoined the road, I found several lines of haaf nets drying in the sun. Each of them was securely locked with a padlock. They would be no use to a stranger, even if a stranger managed to manhandle one of them, and surely a fisherman wouldn't expect another fisherman to pinch his net. But it does happen, which makes Cumbrians very canny, whether they're Earls or humble fishermen.

Drumburgh has a Castle, which would appear to disprove my generalisation about the lack of castles in this area, but it's only a castle in name. It was built as a fortified manor house by Thomas Lord Dacre in the sixteenth century, using stones from the Roman Wall. Today it's a simple farmhouse with at one end the crumbling remains of a turret. I noticed on the doorstep of the blocked up turret entrance a small Roman altar, painted rather crudely bright grey. I knocked at the door then went round the back but could find no one at home.

There was a Wall fort at Drumburgh, but a fairly small one. The Romans were no doubt taking advantage of this first hump of higher land after four very flat marshy miles since leaving Burgh fort. It must have been a good vantage point for watching the Solway salt flats. Today the view is still good but as a hamlet it has little character.

Old Hutton, being a bit forward, walked straight into Drumburgh Castle, looking for someone to talk to, and found the only person present was a woman at the fire 'in dishabille'. He doesn't elaborate on whether she was undressed or just half-dressed, but she naturally didn't reply when he spoke to her and rushed out of his sight. He was very perplexed and was about to leave, realising he was unwelcome. 'But in two or three minutes she returned in a better dress, loosely put on, with a large tumbler of brandy and water.' These old men of seventy-eight have all the luck.

I came across two council workmen at the next village, Glasson, putting up a wooden fence beside a new stretch of the road. Behind the fence was a line of hawthorn seedlings. I asked them why they were putting up a fence *and* a hedge. 'The fence is temporary, just for five years or so till the hawthorns get hold. The cows coming up and down the road all day would destroy the hawthorn if it wasn't protected.' They were struggling with each post, trying to sink it into the ground. 'I can feel the sandstone slabs underneath,' said one workman, hammering away. 'It's a right booger.'

In a land of deep clay for miles around, sandstone slabs could only mean one thing. 'Yes,' said the man. 'Miss Charlesworth has found five yards of the Wall's foundation course, but we had to cover it up again.' I was the second person that day to enquire about the Roman Wall. Two Swedish girls had asked them about it only an hour ago. I hurried on.

As I approached Port Carlisle, the next village and the last one before Bowness, I could see nothing of the Wall line but once again I could see the tracks of the old railway and of the canal. They'd been my companions all the way from Carlisle. Each used the route of the Roman Wall. It was probably their construction in the first half of the nineteenth century which finally destroyed any remaining bits and pieces of the Roman fortifications. The Roman remains, such as they were, had lasted 1,700 years. The canal which took its place lasted only thirty years. The railway, in its turn, lasted barely a hundred years.

The canal from Carlisle to Port Carlisle was opened amidst enormous excitement on 12 March 1823. It was the peak of canal fever and local industrialists in every part of the country were agog at the prospect of cheap transport. In Carlisle, civic pride was at stake because they wanted to bring the sea right to the doors of Carlisle's new factories and keep the upstarts like Whitehaven in their place. The canal cost £90,000, and was eleven miles long with eight locks. A couple of isolated fishermen's cottages at a place called Fisher's Cross were glorified almost overnight with a grandiose new name, Port Carlisle. A brand new harbour was specially built there by that ubiquitous industrialist, the Earl of Lonsdale. Port Carlisle was to be laid out with long boulevards and handsome houses with Tuscan porches.

Along this canal in 1829 travelled Stephenson's Rocket, in a barge bound for Liverpool. This is its only claim to fame today. The canal was abandoned in 1853, never having paid its way. The railway age, which came early to Cumberland, thanks to its proximity to Newcastle and the home of steam engines, killed the canals.

As early as 1835 the Newcastle-Carlisle railway was being built, the first railway to cross England. Soon afterwards there were lines all over the Solway coast and West Cumberland. Railway fever was the new madness. George Stephenson himself came over from Newcastle to be engineer of one of the new railway companies. There were many rival railway companies, each needing an Act of Parliament before they could start operating. The Maryport and Carlisle Railway Act of 1837 had a clause which said that if the engines frightened the horses on the turnpike roads then the company had to build a screen between the railway and the road.

Each of the rival railway companies had its own station in Carlisle and there was fierce competition between them. During one row the Lancaster and Carlisle Railway Company actually seized the station in Crown Street belonging to the Maryport and Carlisle.

Now that steam engines have gone for ever, though their

romance lingers on and grows more romantic all the time, it's a wonder nobody's done a film about the coming of the steam age. Irish labour was brought across the Irish Sea in boat loads to do, as ever, all the dirty work. Cumberland couldn't have seen such activity since the Romans brought their cart loads of men and materials for their equally grandiose enterprise.

Perhaps the most amazing part of the local railway madness was the fact that in the 1850s they actually built a railway viaduct *across* the Solway below Bowness, linking England with Scotland. The expense of this must have been colossal. It ran for about two miles across the sea, from one deserted bit of Cumberland to an equally deserted bit of Dumfriesshire, all in the hope that West Cumberland merchants would want to send their goods directly into Scotland rather than go round by Carlisle. This of course finally killed any hope that Port Carlisle had of being a port – the viaduct cut it off at once from all sea-going ships.

Port Carlisle today is a lovely place. The harbour is a marvellous folly. It sticks out at high tide as a strange sandstone island covered in gorse and wild birds. At low tide you can walk across the mud flats and scramble up the massive sandstone harbour steps. It's like a secret island from an Arthur Ransome story. My children love it.

The railway station is also still there, and you can walk along the overgrown platforms. The locals talk fondly of the last train to use that end of the line, a horse-drawn train called the Dandy, a very popular Sunday pleasure trip for Carlisle people before the last war.

Even the canal can still be seen, a soggy ditch just as you come into the village. The main street is, alas, the only street, though it does a contain a few handsome houses, one with five bays and a Tuscan porch. They never got round to the grand streets that were meant to go off at right angles. There are openings off the main street, one of them proudly called Scotch Street, but it only has a couple of houses in it.

There is just one remnant of Port Carlisle's Roman glory to be seen. At the end of the village to the left there's a little altar built into the wall above the front door of a house called Hesket House. This was formerly the Steam Packet Hotel, a name which conjures up lovely Mississippi images, probably the same sort of images which the Earl of Lonsdale's engineers had when they thought they were creating another New Orleans.

The altar looked as if it had been painted the same grey colour as the door, making it very difficult to find. I had my Richmond Handbook in my hand, where a drawing of it is reproduced, otherwise I might have missed it. I knocked on the door to ask why it had been painted over.

'Not another one,' said the young wife who opened the door. 'I've had antiquarians complaining to me for over a year now. They keep saying I'm committing sacrilege. I don't give a damn about it personally, but my husband did give it a scrub the other day with a brush to try and get some of the paint off. I won't paint it again, I promise. Now, does that please you? I don't know why anyone bothers to look at it, I don't really. It's the same with our view of the Solway. People are always saying what a lovely view, but I don't see it. I'm that used to it that it never interests me.'

They made some interesting pre-historic discoveries during the digging of the canal at Port Carlisle. Near the edge of the sea they found an almost complete forest of oak trees, lying embedded eight feet deep in muddy clay, each fallen tree pointing out to the Solway. The trees were in such good condition that many were used for the jetties in the building of the Port Carlisle harbour. (The President's chair of the Society of Antiquaries of Newcastle is made from a piece of oak from this same glacial forest.) Had the advancing ice age destroyed them all in one fell swoop? Was it a colossal storm perhaps some time later? Excavations on the Wall over the years round Glasson and Port Carlisle have shown that the Romans laid their foundations on piles three feet above the prostrate glacial trees.

The next village is Bowness on Solway, the final point on my trek from Wallsend. It has a completely different atmosphere from Port Carlisle, even though it's just over a mile away. There's an enclosed feeling, as if the village has turned its back on the world, unlike Port Carlisle which was opened up for its moments of canal and railway glory and has retained a welcoming air. In Bowness, the main street is narrow like a Sicilian village. You feel people are watching from upstairs windows and not approving. I met a gaggle of wild-looking kids with straw in their hair who giggled and turned away when I asked them if they knew where the Roman inscription was. They went into a huddle then shyly took me to a barn wall near the bus stop where I could see Bowness' only Roman relic, a chipped and weary looking inscribed stone.

Old Hutton in 1801 saw five hundred yards of Wall outside Bowness. According to Collingwood Bruce, there was a chunk of it seven feet high when he first visited here in 1831. They were using gunpowder to remove it.

The Romans built a large fort at Bowness, all of seven acres, the second largest on the Wall, and had a Tribune in charge of the garrison. They chose Bowness as the end of their Wall because this is the last point on the Solway where the sea is fordable, though you'd hardly believe it when you see the sea at high tide. Camden in 1599, like many visitors before and after, thought at first it was a pointless place to have built such a large fort. 'I marvailed at first why they built here so great fortifications considering that for eight miles or thereabout there lieth opposite a very great frith and arme of the sea; but now I understand that at every ebbe the water is so low that the borderers and beast stealers may easily wade over.'

Bowness gets its name from being on a bow-shaped corner of a ness, or peninsula. The coast bends south after Bowness and you're at last on the open sea. John Wesley, dashing round the country on his conversions, crossed the Solway here on foot in 1766. He must have had a good guide. Though it's still possible today, you have to know the channels and quicksands to avoid. Many locals have done it, but it's a long journey. You'd be lucky to get back again before the tide turned. Scotland is still rather a distant place. The locals have no reason to go there. In the days before the last war, when Bowness's crazy Railway Viaduct was still open, many Scotsmen used to walk across it on Sunday, purely for the drink. Scottish pubs were always closed on Sundays.

There's still a hundred yards or so of the viaduct to be seen at the other side of Bowness village, a strange overgrown arm which points out to sea, then dramatically drops short.

Though Bowness was where the Romans chose to end their Wall, recent excavations have shown that a string of small forts and towers, without any sort of linking wall, stretched for forty miles further down the Cumberland coast. While the Wall kept out raiders from what is now Scotland, the West Cumberland forts were a protection against the Irish raiders who increasingly came by boat across the Irish Sea.

My last visit was to the church at Bowness. As at Burgh, it is on the site of the Roman fort. It's a Norman church and is built mainly of Roman stones from the Wall. In the church porch there are two enormous church bells stolen by the villagers in the seventeenth century from two villages across the Solway in Scotland. It was a reprisal against a gang of Scotsmen who'd pinched the Bowness church bell and had been careless enough to lose it, dropping it into a deep pool in the Solway when they were being chased by the men of Bowness.

I went round to the vicarage to try my luck, to see if this vicar had found anything in his potato patch. He was rather suspicious, asking continually if I had a card, why hadn't I written to him first. I said I was just passing through. I thought he might know something about the local history. He said he was a newcomer. He'd come from a parish near Cockermouth only nine months previously. He didn't know a great deal about Bowness yet, except that Pope Pius II as a young man had once come there on a visit. I was very surprised, so he went to search for some papers in which he'd copied down the information, but couldn't find them.

We weren't making much progress. I was leaving when I happened to admire the lettering on the front cover of his parish magazine. He immediately brightened up, asking eagerly if I knew anything about typography. A little, I said. He led me through to a back room, where with great excitement he pointed to a massive printing press, a hundred years old, called an Arab.

From one of several rows of metal he chose some Eric Gill

Perpetua and made up a page of type which he fitted into his machine. He climbed onto it and started pedalling hard. The huge wheels and cogs started turning and from one end came a newly printed page of lettering. I was suitably impressed. The Arab had been blue when he'd bought it, so he said, still pedalling away, but he'd painted it himself, British Racing Green. Since leaving Wallsend almost a year previously, I'd gone off at enough tangents. Victorian typography was an interesting subject but I couldn't see how I could tie it in with the Roman Wall. I made an excuse, saying I'd have to leave for London.

'It's a strange area round here,' he said. 'It's an isolated community, End of the Wall, end of the world.'

20

End:
Counting the Cost

Before trying to think about what it all meant, if anything, I decided to make a second visit to two places. I wanted to see what Housesteads was like in the height of the season and what progress had been made in Carlisle.

It was standing room only at Housesteads but once we started walking, either east or west, it was possible to get away from the crowds. I took two of my children, aged eight and six, and we stayed the night at the Twice Brewed Youth Hostel. I couldn't believe it was the same place I'd visited back in January. It was absolutely full and the noise from fifty-six school kids was overwhelming. I had to keep my hands over my ears. I don't know how the warden and his wife keep sane. My kids loved it.

I'd planned a long walk from the hostel, along Crag Lough, down Milking Gap to Vindolanda and back. I was very worried about the steep steps at Steel Rigg, the steps I'd slithered down in the snow. They went up without stopping, running all the way, while I kept pausing for breath, puffing heavily, trying to make them admire the view and give me a rest. They'd disappeared over the horizon by the time I got to the top, rushing into the gulleys then belting up the crags on the other side.

I'd made the mistake of showing them on the map where we

would have our picnic lunch, overlooking Crag Lough, and then tea at Vindolanda. We made such speed that we had lunch at eleven and tea at one thirty. Next day, when we did Housesteads and Sewingshields, we had lunch at ten and tea at twelve. If we'd done a third day, we would have had lunch for breakfast.

They hated the flat bits, coming down into the valley to go to Vindolanda, moaning all the time it was boring. It was the scale of the top of the Wall they loved, seeing yet another chunk stretching ahead, climbing up then rushing down again. Neither were they all that captivated by the Forts, even though we met Professor Birley by chance at Vindolanda, taking round two of his grandchildren. They liked meeting him, not because of his knowledge but because he took them behind ropes where the public weren't meant to go and they could see the excavations close-up.

Perhaps if I'd been introduced to the switch back of the Wall in the first place when I was a child, not taken to a mausoleum-like fort to see a few foundations, I might have been captivated from the very beginning.

I went back to Carlisle to see how Miss Dorothy Charlesworth's emergency excavation was getting on. She'd seemed so dour in her London office but now she was terribly excited, if a bit stunned. A mass of Roman leather work had been found: some first century pottery and a platform heeled sandal which to everyone's amusement looked just like a presentday fashion clog. But the big excitement was being caused by some massive wooden platforms. She wasn't sure what they were, but said they were definitely military – which she'd never expected. It had been assumed, thanks to Mr Hogg's work, that the dig was *outside* the limits of Carlisle's first century fort. "The evidence is rather disconcerting," said Mr Hogg, "but it's not my dig and I'm not involved. I've had my throw at the coconuts. The site should have been sterile so what she's found is fascinating."

Professor Barri Jones from Manchester came up and thought perhaps the barracks of a legionary headquarters had been found. Could this at last be the site of the missing Ninth? Miss Charlesworth wouldn't commit herself. It would take at least another year's digging to know what it was, that's if she was given the time before the builders arrived to cover the site.

While in Carlisle I went to the local offices of John Laing, the international building contractors. When passing through previously I'd suggested a project which the area manager, Nigel Redfern, said he'd get his staff to work on, if they had time.

For the first edition of his book on the Roman Wall, Collingwood Bruce approached a contractor friend of his, Sir Robert Rawlinson, who was to be responsible for building work in the Crimean War, to estimate the cost of the Roman Wall at 1850 prices. His results were fascinating. He worked out that the Vallum would cost £23,271, the Ditch £34,906 and the Wall itself £1,021,269.

The relationship between the high price of the Wall and the low cost of the Vallum is particularly interesting – showing it to be fifty times more expensive. It lends support to those who think the digging of the Vallum was to keep troops and labour occupied as much as anything else.

Rawlinson worked on a labour force of ten thousand, which was the amount Bruce thought the Romans probably had available. On this reckoning, Rawlinson said it would take two years at the very least to complete the job.

It seemed apt that Laings, a building firm which began its life in the Wall country at Carlisle, should try a modern estimate. I returned to find acres of beautiful designs. They'd had draughtsmen all over the place working on it, bringing in reinforcements from Manchester. They'd entered into the spirit to the extent of Latinising their own names on the drawings – Septimus Robertus was one of their main artists.

Mr Redfern's men had decided that the best idea would be a series of travelling shutters, running on tracks on either side of the Wall, into which the concrete would be poured. This is basically how they build motorways today. (Mr Redfern was the quantity surveyor on the first stretch of the M1 back in 1958.) You pour in raw materials at one end, and out comes the motorway at the other.

I'd allowed them in their drawings to build the Roman Wall in concrete, as long as they stuck exactly to the Roman measurements. They could have done it in dressed stone, which was what Rawlinson worked on in 1850, but the cost would have been even more ridiculous than doing it in concrete. The 1850 cost of facing stones similar to the Romans' was twelve shillings a cubic yard. Today, the price is £10 a yard.

They offered two estimates for building the Wall at 1974 prices. They'd devised one method whereby the Wall would be at the original Roman height but much narrower, built on the cantilever principle, with the platform sticking out like a concrete arm. It would be just as high and just as strong as the Roman Wall, so they said. They could offer it at a modest £55 million.

To build the Wall completely to the Roman plan, to the same width and height and design, all in reinforced concrete, would cost £80 million. This enormous figure shows how much building costs have risen since 1850, if such a comparison were necessary. More important, by considering the value of £80 million in relation to present-day government spending, it gives another clue to the scale of the project in Roman times. It must have been a tremendous burden on the finances of the Roman Army.

The Wall was meant to last, that is very clear. Whether it was put up for prestige, for defence, for offence, to keep the barbarians out, to keep the Brigantes in, or simply to give the soldiers something to do, it was put up to stay up.

It was still going strong in 410 AD, the date normally given for the end of Roman rule, having been overrun only three times in almost three hundred years. The details of these invasions are currently the source of many arguments amongst the archaeologists, but on each occasion there was a mitigating circumstance, such as the army being occupied with civil war elsewhere, helping the British Governor of the day to be the next Emperor.

There's now a body of opinion which thinks that Hadrian's Wall was in fact never finally conquered, perhaps lingering on for a further two hundred years after the Romans had gone, being manned by the local militia when necessary, till eventually it was abandoned. While the rest of the great Roman Empire fell relatively quickly to a series of barbarian attacks from all sides, the British province, especially in the north, carried on much as before for a considerable time.

The Romans gave us a lot, apart from the Wall. They brought law and order, peace, trade, education, factories, water mills, new cereals, vegetables, baths, canals, fine buildings, Christianity. They introduced many things which disappeared with them. They knew the secret of making glass, which wasn't rediscovered till the thirteenth century. They had light-houses, which didn't come back till the nineteenth century, lavatories and central heating which became commonplace only this century. British roads were never as straight again until the motorways.

Hadrian's Wall, its forts and military stations, were the outward signs that the Romans were here, busily civilising the population. Other signs of civilisation were much softer and subtler. They were noted by Tacitus in a nicely cynical passage describing what effects Agricola and the Romans had had on the Britons. 'A distaste for the Latin tongue gave place to an aspiration to speak it with eloquence, our national dress became acceptable and the toga was commonly seen. Gradually they were drawn towards the blandishments of vice, of colonnades, baths and elegant banquets, but what was regarded as the refinements of civilisation were in effect their chains of enslavement.'

Perhaps this is why the most obvious sign of the Roman presence, the Latin language, never lasted. However idealised the civilising might have been, it was still basically being imposed from outside. Once they'd gone, there was a reversion. Darkness and destruction returned, which is so often the case when the old masters move out. Portugal and Spain moved out of South America a hundred and fifty years ago, yet chaos is still evident. The British have left Africa, but not to peace and unity. It could be argued that great Empires, like the Roman and the British, don't actually do any good, except to themselves. In the long run, people, like nations, have got to work it out for themselves. The invaders who eventually followed the Romans, the Norsemen, the Angles and the Saxons, were of an inferior civilisation, but they were here to stay, for good or for bad. This became their country, not their colony, and we became England, not Britannia, speaking English not a Latin tongue.

In walking the Wall I found myself thinking as much about the recent present as the ancient past. If the walk has shown anything it's shown how the most brilliant of modern inventions has a limited life span. Coal, steam, ships, canals, railways have in their turn destroyed the old and the natural in their panic towards progress. In crude commercial terms, they have helped to destroy an economic growth field that could outlive any of them – tourism.

St Cuthbert in 685 was the first known Wall tourist when he came to Carlisle and looked round the Roman Walls. Since then, interest in Hadrian's defences has waxed and waned but never disappeared. The most reassuring development is that there is more of the Wall to be seen today than at any time in the last fifty years. It's growing every year. As a tourist attraction, it's hardly begun, despite what some local farmers might do and say to stop its expansion.

Telling farmers that it's a vital chunk of history is difficult, outside of a school classroom, and so is explaining that all knowledge is an end in itself and shouldn't need to be defended. The thing about the Wall which I never realised when I lived there is that it's not a study of a load of old stone. It's a study of a people who once lived there. In learning about other people we learn about ourselves.

Our friend, William Hutton, thought no one after him would walk the Wall in its entirety again, considering his own exploit rather foolhardy. He arrived home in Birmingham on 7 August 1801, after a loss by perspiration of one stone, an expenditure of forty guineas, a lapse of thirty five days and a total round walk of six hundred and one miles.

I lost no weight but I did spend at least ten times as much

money. I took a year over the journey to experience all the seasons, doing a stretch at a time, spinning out the pleasures as much as possible. In all, I probably walked no more than two hundred miles. I wish it had been longer.

Appendix 1

Recommended Bibliography

Twenty-two books, for wider or more specialised study, which should amuse and inform the discerning reader. Most pre-war publications need not be heeded, though several still appear on standard reading lists, most notably the work by Collingwood and Myrer. Where available, paperback editions have been listed. Finally, a modest selection of booklets, guides and learned journals.

GENERAL BOOKS ON ROMAN BRITAIN

Britannia by Sheppard Frere, 1967, new edition 1978, Routledge and Kegan Paul
  Today's Big Book on the subject, academic but straightforward, giving all the latest developments, by Professor of Roman Archaeology at Oxford.
Life in Roman Britain by Anthony Birley, 1964, Batsford
  Easiest book for absolute beginner, lots of good illustrations, well written, full of human interest.
The Roman Army in Britain by P. Holder, Batsford, 1982
Roman Britain by I. A. Richmond, Penguin edition, 1963
  Formerly the definitive general book by the late Sir Ian Richmond, still very much up to date. Excellently arranged in sections rather than in one continuous historical narrative.
Roman Britain: Life in an Imperial Province by K. Brannigan, Reader's Digest/Hodder, 1980
Roman Britain from the Air by S. S. Frere and J. K. S. St Joseph, Cambridge, 1983
Roman Britain and Early England (55 BC–871 AD) by Peter Hunter-Blair, Sphere edition, 1969
  Well written run through nine difficult centuries. Puts the Romans in perspective.

GENERAL GUIDES

A Guide to the Roman Remains in Britain by R. J. A. Wilson, Constable, 1980

The Northern Frontiers of Roman Britain by D. J. Breeze, Batsford, 1982

Hadrian's Wall by Breeze and Dobson, Penguin, 1978

THE ROMAN ARMY

The Roman Imperial Army by Graham Webster, 1969, Black
Not just the best, the only general book on the subject in English. Early political history of army heavy going, but excellent on army composition and organisation.

Roman Britain and the Roman Army by Eric Birley, 1953.Titus Wilson, Kendal
Not alas a general book, despite the title. Professor Birley is the foremost expert on the Roman Army (Webster's book is dedicated to him) but he has not yet written a general book for the layman. These are collected papers, first published by learned archaeological journals over the last forty years. Academic, but fascinating examples of archaeological detection.

HADRIAN'S WALL

Handbook to the Roman Wall by J. Collingwood Bruce, 13th edition, revised 1978, Hindson, Newcastle
First published 1863 and still going strong with not a rival in sight. A blow by blow archaeological account of every site on the Wall in order from Wallsend to Bowness.

The North West Frontier of Rome by David Divine, 1969, Macdonald
A military study of the Wall's purpose and use by an eminent defence journalist. Stimulating assault on some traditional academic attitudes, but rather complicated for absolute beginners.

Research on Hadrian's Wall by Eric Birley, 1961, Titus Wilson, Kendal
A history of the history. Professor Birley's comprehensive account of the work done by archaeologists and antiquarians on all Wall sites from Camden onwards. Academic.

The Frontier Peoples of Roman Britain by P. Salway, 1965, Cambridge

First general look at a hitherto largely ignored subject – the civilian settlements of Northern Britain. Academic, but of interest to all serious Wall students.

ANTIQUARIAN BOOKS

The History of the Roman Wall by William Hutton, 1801, John Nichols, London
An idiosyncratic account by a 78-year-old Birmingham shopkeeper of his 600-mile walk to and from the Wall. Some good contemporary social insights and great fun to read. A first edition of Hutton cost £12.50 in 1973 from Steedman, 5 Grey Street, Newcastle.
The Roman Wall by J. Collingwood Bruce, 1851, Russell Smith, London
The first of the modern studies of the Wall. Immensely detailed and still valuable. (It was after this mighty work that Bruce produced his shorter Handbook.)
The Border Antiquities by Sir Walter Scott, 1817, 2 vols, Longman, London
A history of the castles, churches and other buildings on both sides of the Border, in fact and in legend, from Roman times onwards. Highly romantic and extremely beautiful. Over 100 engravings of buildings around the Wall country as they looked in 1817, each a work of art.

GENERAL BOOKS ON THE WALL

The Steel Bonnets by George MacDonald Fraser, 1971, Barrie and Jenkins
Highly readable account of those endless Border wars, its heroes and families, by the author of the Flashman novels.
The Story of Carlisle by Joyce and Brian Blake, 1958, City of Carlisle
Lively, straightforward account of the city's history, published to celebrate its octo-centenary.
Portrait of Northumberland by Nancy Ridley, 1965, Robert Hale
Border Guide edited by John Walton, 1958, HMSO*
Produced mainly as a guide to parks run by the National Forestry Commission. Contains good sections on Border geology, vegetation, animal life.

*NOTE: all HMSO publications available direct from HMSO, 49 High Holborn, London, WC1.

ARCHITECTURE

Northumberland by Pevsner, 1957, Penguin
Cumberland and Westmorland by Pevsner, 1967, Penguin
   The two relevant volumes in Sir Nikolaus Pevsner's monumental
   series, The Buildings of England. Northumberland (being an
   early volume in the series) has Roman notes by Richmond.
   Roman Cumberland is dealt with by Barry Cunliffe. Both books
   invaluable for Wall travellers.

BOOKLETS

Hadrian's Wall by A. R. Birley, 1963, HMSO
   Best of the many general guides, expert yet lively, 52 pages, well
   illustrated.
The Army of Hadrian's Wall by Brian Dobson and David Breeze,
   1972, Frank Graham, Newcastle
   Best military booklet, detailed and scholarly but brief, 48 pages,
   illustrated.
Hadrian's Wall, Central Sector by Robin Birley, 1972, Frank
   Graham, Newcastle
   Brightly written guide to the best known archaeological sites,
   from Corbridge to Birdoswald, 64 pages.

FORT GUIDEBOOKS

Corbridge, official D. of E. guide by Professor Eric Birley, 3rd
   edition, 1954, HMSO
   First published 1935. Contains good potted history of Romans in
   the north, plus detailed history of the site and museum. Needs
   updating. Illustrated, 32 pages.
Chesters, official D. of E. guide by Professor Birley, 1st edition 1960.
   More up to date on potted history. Details of fort, bridge and
   museum plus excellent guide to the Bath house. Illustrated, 36
   pages.
Housesteads, official D. of E. guide by Professor Birley, amended
   1971. HMSO
   First published 1936, now up to date. General history plus details
   of fort, milecastle, vicus and museum. Illustrated, plus excellent
   pull-out plan of fort, 28 pages.
Vindolanda publishes its own guidebook which is regularly updated; it also publishes a children's guide.
Frank Graham, Publisher, Newcastle has done a whole series of

guidebooks which cover the most important sections of the Wall.

LEARNED JOURNALS

Archaeologia Aeliana, annual journal of the Society of Antiquaries of Newcastle upon Tyne.
Selected papers by experts, mainly academics, covering all periods of N. E. history, including current Roman-Britain work. Annual subscription £3. Membership enquiries to Charles Daniels, Department of Archaeology, University of Newcastle.

Transactions of the Cumberland and Westmorland Antiquarian and Archaeological Society
Annual collection of papers, including latest Roman-Britain work in the N. W. Annual subscription £3. Membership enquiries to W. Rollinson, Institute of External Studies, University of Liverpool.

Appendix 2

Visitor's Guide

Some personal suggestions for the discerning visitor who intends to inspect Hadrian's Wall in the flesh and is desirous of seeing the best sites, acquiring the most suitable accommodation and savouring the more pleasing walks.

MAJOR ARCHAEOLOGICAL SITES

1. *Housesteads* On the Military Road (B 6318), 8 miles west of Chollerford. Car park on road, then ½ mile up-hill walk to fort remains and Wall. Still the best archaeological site – it really *feels* like a fort – set in the nicest countryside. Hard going for the elderly. Small museum.
New information centre opened by the National Trust in the Housesteads car park area. Small display area giving information about Housesteads and Hadrian's Wall. Toilets. Normal D. of E. opening hours.*
2. *Vindolanda* Two miles South-west of Housesteads, take left turning ½ mile after Housesteads car park. Car park beside site. The up and coming site, full of activity and excitement. The only *living* site where excavations in progress can be seen almost all the year round.
Sections of the fort walls and some internal fort buildings excavated, but main interest is in the vicus (village) site. Not on the line of the Wall but contains a reproduction section, twenty feet high, the only place where the Wall can be seen as it was. Large country house museum described as superb and housing

*March–October; Weekdays 9.20–7pm; Sundays 1.50–7 pm. November–February; Weekdays 9.20–4.30; Sundays 1.50–4.30.

296

the remarkable finds from this excavation. Seasonal café facilities. Open all year, except Christmas.

3. *Chesters* Half mile west of Chollerford on B 6318. Car park. Fort remains scattered and disappointing, but excellent Bath house (through the fort, down by the river), best anywhere in the north. Remains of Roman bridge on the other side of the river. Look for the phallus. Very good museum beside the fort. Normal D. of E. opening hours.

4. *Corbridge* Half mile north-west of town. Car park right on site, so excellent for elderly or lazy. Large remarkable site with large remarkable remains but a mausoleum piece. New museum housing some of the best finds from the excavation site. Normal D. of E. opening hours.

5. *Roman Army Museum* On the Military Road (B 6318) nine miles west of Housesteads. A large new museum devoted to the Roman soldier and his way of life and standing next to the Walltown Crags section of Hadrian's Wall. Life-sized reconstructions of Roman soldiers in Uniform Displays. Café. Open March to October.

MINOR SITES: (without museums or staff)

1. *Birdoswald* One and a half miles west of Gilsland. Once a fort, now a farm. Only a few chunks of Wall and gates to be seen but worth it for magnificent views of the Irthing valley. Pay farmer's wife 20p. for admission.

2. *Best milecastles:* Harrow's Scar (M 49) beside Birdoswald; Poltross Burn Milecastle (MC 48) at Gilsland; Winshields Milecastle (MC 40), north-west of Twice Brewed; Housesteads Milecastle (MC 37), $\frac{1}{2}$ mile west of fort.

3. *Best turret* Brunton Turret (T26B) near Chollerford.

BEST PARTS OF THE WALL

Of the original $73\frac{1}{2}$ miles of Wall, there are approximately 10 miles left standing today, none at the original height of 15 feet. It does reach ten feet now and again, as at Walltown Crags, but most of the existing stretches are around five to six feet high.

There are isolated chunks of the Wall standing at the roadside between the Newcastle suburb of Denton and Chollerford and on the west between Gilsland and Walton, but the so-called Wall Country is confined to a central 15-mile stretch, all of it open and unspoiled, which stretches from Sewingshields Crags, six miles west of Chollerford, to Walltown Crags, one mile north-east of Greenhead. There is a clear path along the Wall all the way and for up to a mile at a time it is possible to walk on top of the Wall itself. The highest, most spectacular stretches are at Housesteads, Crag Lough, Winshields Crags and Walltown Crags.

MUSEUMS

The museums at the five major sites on the Wall mentioned above deal mainly with local finds. There are also two major Roman Britain museums in the cities at either end. (The British Museum, London, has the nation's biggest collection of Roman Britain antiquities, many taken from the Wall.)

1. *Newcastle* The Museum of Antiquities, the Dapartment of Archaeology, University of Newcastle, Keeper Dr D. J. Smith, phone Newcastle 328511. Right in the heart of the main University building. Contains most of the best finds from the eastern side of the Wall. Recreation of a Temple of Mithras, complete with lights and music and commentary. Not to be missed.

2. *Carlisle* Tullie House Museum, Castle Street, Carlisle, phone Carlisle 34781. Part of Carlisle's Public Library and Art Gallery building. The best finds from the western end of the Wall. Very well displayed. Tape recorded guide available.

ACCOMMODATION

Luxury Living
Sharrow Bay Hotel, Ullswater, Penrith, Cumberland: Pooley Bridge (08536) 301; dinner, b. and b. from £49*.
An hour's drive from the Wall, so not strictly a Wall hotel, but perfect for doing the Lake and the Wall. Nicest hotel in the north of England. Meals, rooms, setting, all works of art. Impeccably English. Absolutely necessary to book.
Gosforth Park Hotel, Newcastle 3 (0632) 364111. B and b. £51.
Five miles north-west of Newcastle, near airport. The N.E.'s answer to international jet setting, dripping with every modern convenience. V. expensive.

* All prices quoted are for 1984.

Hotels: Bed and breakfast from £10–25.
The Hadrian, Wall, Northumberland; Hunshaugh 232.
   Traditionally English. V. comfortable, quiet.
The George, Chollerford, Northumberland; Humshaugh 205.
The Royal, Hexham; Hexham 602270
Beaumont, Hexham; Hexham 602331
New Bridge, Lanercost; Brampton 2224.
Angel, Corbridge; Corbridge 2119.
Crown and Mitre, Carlisle; Carlisle 25491.
Royal Station, Newcastle; Newcastle 320781.
Swallow Hotel, Newcastle; Newcastle 325025.
County Hotel, Hexham; Hexham 602030.
Manor House, Haltwhistle; Haltwhistle 20210.
Riverside Hotel, Corbridge; Corbridge 2942.
Lion of Corbridge; Corbridge 2504.
Vallum Lodge, Once Brewed; Bardon Mill 248.

Guest Houses, Farmhouse and Bed and Breakfast Accommodation
List available from the Hexham Tourist Information Centre,
Northumberland. Tel (0434) 605225.

Youth Hostels
Once Brewed, Bardon Mill 360; bed £2.15–£3.25.
Accomb, Hexham 602864; bed £1.35–£2.15.
Etterby, Carlisle 23934; bed £1.90–2.90.
Greenhead, Carlisle; Gilsland 401; bed £1.90–£2.90.
Adult Membership £5. YHA, St Albans, Herts; St Albans 55215.

TRANSPORT

By Air: London Heathrow to Newcastle Gosforth, 1 hour.
By train: London to Newcastle, 3 hours. Phone: 01–278–2477.
   London to Carlisle, 4 hours. Phone: 01–387–7070.
   Newcastle to Carlisle, 1½ hours, stopping train. Phone Newcastle
   326262, Hexham 602862, Carlisle 44711.
Local taxis: Mr Batey, Hexham 602500; Armstrong's, Hexham,
604551; Davison's, Hexham, 602992; Dodd, Hexham 603362;
Duncan, Hexham 604146.
Taxis also available from Bardon Mill and Haltwhistle.
Tynedale Tourist Office run a tourist bus service which links the
main Wall sites during the peak season (high summer) only. They
issue a leaflet about the service.

MAPS

Archaeological Map of Hadrian's Wall produced by the Ordnance
Survey, two inches to the mile, 2nd edition 1972, £2.10.
Available either folded to put in the pocket or flat for sticking on
a wall. First produced 1964 but so many new discoveries since
then have necessitated a new edition. Covers entire Wall and
shows every archaeological site either in black (meaning
extant) or in red (it was there but you can't see it). Also modern
roads and buildings. Essential for all Wall walkers.

Ordnance Survey, One inch to the mile, Sheet 87, Hexham, £2.40.

Ordnance Survey, One inch to the mile, Sheet 86, Carlisle, £2.40.

The two ordinary tourist maps which cover the central and most
popular sections of the Wall. Puts situation of the Wall in
perspective. Useful for planning journeys to the Wall – using the
archaeological map when you get there.

WALL WALKS

Organising a round trip takes careful planning, unless you've
somehow got a car to pick you up at the other end. Never try
walking back along the Military Road. it could ruin your day. But
the Central Section of the Wall is so beautiful and rich that a walk
along the Wall and back is always interesting.

Day Trippers The easiest and most popular walks start from
Housesteads, walking along the Wall in either direction, returning
when you have had enough:—
1. Housesteads East to Sewingshields Crags, 1 hour. Gentle stroll.
2. Housesteads West over Crag Lough to Steel Rigg, 2 hours. More
   arduous.
3. Round trip from Housesteads to Steel Rigg, south to Twice
   Brewed, east to Vindolanda and back to Housesteads, 4 hours. A
   perfect day—taking in two forts, the best of the Wall, plus a pub
   in the middle at Twice Brewed.

Three-day Trippers 1st Day: Taking it easy, mainly by car. Start
Corbridge, walk round the town, visit fort and museum. Drive
north to Military Road to lunch at Hadrian Hotel, Wall, or The
George, Chollerford. Visit Chesters fort, Museum, bath house,
bridge abutment, Brunton turret. Drive to Hexham, visit Abbey,
dinner at the Royal County or the Beaumont.

2nd day: Walking but leisurely. Park at Housesteads, inspect fort
then take the round walk to Steel Rigg, Vindolanda and back.

3rd day: Walking but harder. Start Steel Rigg (car park available). Walk over Winshields Crags, the highest part of the Wall, then over Cawfields Crags to Walltown Crags, visiting Roman Army Museum. Four and a half hours. Bus back along Military Road, or train from Haltwhistle to Bardon Mill—or walk back, another glorious four hours.

We are most grateful to the Northumbria Tourist Board, 9 Osborne Terrace, Jesmond, Newcastle upon Tyne (0632–817744) and the Cumbria Tourist Board, Ashleigh, Windermere (096–62–4444) for helping to bring the tourist information sections up to date; potential visitors will find the staff there very helpful.

Index

Note: *Italic* page references refer to the appendices.